The Harmless People

Warrior Herdsmen

Reindeer Moon

The Animal Wife

The Hidden Life of Dogs

The Tribe of Tiger:
Cats and Their Culture

Certain Poor Shepherds:
A Christmas Tale

The Social Life of Dogs:
The Grace of Canine Company

The Old Way

The Old Way

A Story of the First People

. . . .

Elizabeth Marshall Thomas

Sarah Crichton Books

FARRAR STRAUS GIROUX

New York

Sarah Crichton Books
Farrar, Straus and Giroux
19 Union Square West, New York 10003

Library of Congress Cataloging-in-Publication Data
Thomas, Elizabeth Marshall, 1931–
    The old way : a story of the first people / by Elizabeth Marshall
Thomas.— 1st ed.
        p.   cm.
    "Sarah Crichton books."
    Includes bibliographical references and index.
    ISBN-13: 978-0-374-22552-0 (cloth : alk. paper)
    ISBN-10: 0-374-22552-4 (cloth : alk. paper)
    1. San (African people)—History. 2. San (African people)—Social
life and customs. 3. Hunting and gathering societies—Namibia—History.
4. Hunting and gathering societies—Botswana—History.   I. Title.

DT1558.S38T46 2006
305.896'1—dc22

                                                    2006002668

Designed by Dorothy Schmiderer Baker

www.fsgbooks.com

1   3   5   7   9   10   8   6   4   2

In loving memory of my parents,

Laurence and Lorna Marshall,

and of my brother, John.

Contents

....

Contents

PART TWO

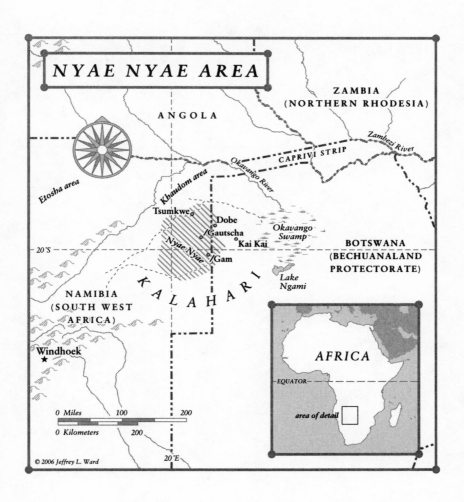

NYAE NYAE AREA

ANGOLA

ZAMBIA
(NORTHERN RHODESIA)

Zambezi River

Okavango River

CAPRIVI STRIP

Etosha area

Khaudom area

Tsumkwe

Dobe
/Gautscha
Kai Kai

Okavango
Swamp

20°S

Nyae Nyae

/Gam

BOTSWANA
(BECHUANALAND
PROTECTORATE)

K A L A H A R I

Lake
Ngami

NAMIBIA
(SOUTH WEST
AFRICA)

Windhoek

AFRICA

EQUATOR

area of detail

0 Miles   100   200

0 Kilometers   200

20°E

© 2006 Jeffrey L. Ward

About Words and Names

The five groups of San or Bushmen are called the First People. Most call themselves Bushmen when referring to themselves collectively. I respect this and use the term Bushman rather than San in the text. Two groups appear in this book, the Ju/wasi (the singular is Ju/wa) and the /Gwi. Although today some of these people read and write, they had no say in the spelling of their language, which has been chosen by others. The *Ju* part of Ju/wa might better be spelled *Zhu*, following the International Phonetic Alphabet, but it isn't, because when Lorna Marshall, my mother, wrote the first important ethnography of these people, she rendered the *j* of *ju* as the French *j* of *je* or *jolie*. Others have followed her example. Today, her *j* rendition seems to be standard.

Meanwhile, the /wa part of Ju/wa is also spelled /'hoan, also /hoan, as was eventually suggested by linguists in an attempt to reproduce the phonic subtleties. My spelling is therefore somewhat archaic, as most academic publications now favor *Ju/'hoan* (also *Ju'/'hoan* and *Ju/hoan*). But to the average reader, the word would appear to be pronounced "Jew-ho-an" or "Jew-hone"—never mind the slash mark and the apostrophe. Missionaries with linguistic inclinations determined the spelling of the Fijian language with similar

results. For instance, an important Fijian beverage made from kava and pronounced "yang-gona" is spelled *yaqona*. Many of us would take that for "yak-kwona."

The same fate seems to await the Bushman languages. If only the linguists would settle for approximate, layman-type spellings such as are used for other African languages. That way, although not every nuance is represented on paper, the word looks something like it sounds. All else quickly gets confusing.

And it's only the Western world that cares about our spelling. I used to work for the Embassy of the State of Kuwait and will always remember asking an important Saudi personage how, in preparing correspondence for his signature, I should spell his name. He said, "Spell it any way you like."

Today, *Ju/'hoan* and *Ju/hoan* are pretty much in the literature, but they look so very much like "Jew-hone," while to the layman's ear the actual word sounds so much more like "Ju/wa," that for the sake of the readers this book uses the latter version.

The language of the Ju/wasi belongs to a language group called !Kung, (the *u* as in *pull*) and the Ju/wasi are also sometimes known as the !Kung. This language, like all Bushman languages, uses clicks. The dental click (/) resembles the sound we represent as *tsk*, as in *tsk tsk*. The alveolar click (≠) is somewhat the same but farther back in the mouth, where *t* and *d* come from. The alveol-palatal click (!) has no corresponding sound on our part and is made by pressing the tongue against the top of the mouth and popping it down. And the lateral click (//), made in the cheek, resembles the click one makes to urge a horse.

Interestingly, the Ju/wasi had relatively few personal names in use because their lifestyle fostered small, partially isolated populations in which people were inevitably named for relatives. The approximately 550 people in the areas we studied had forty-one personal names for women and forty-eight for men. We knew twenty-three men named Gao and eighteen women named /Khoa, for instance, which meant that in any group there could be several people with the same name. We even knew two brothers who had the same name, having been named for two different men who also had the same name. People did not have surnames, but certain people had distinguishing nicknames—some honorary, such as Male ≠Toma, others descriptive, such as Lame ≠Gao, Short /Kwi, and Crooked /Kwi; some calling attention to a special physical feature such as Gao Beard, Bau Shortface, Gao Feet, and ≠Toma Longface; some to commemorate an event, such as Tsamko Bone Arrow; and some mildly pejorative, such as Lazy /Kwi. These and others appear in the manuscript.

Today, most of the Ju/wasi have surnames, usually the father's name. The eldest son of Male ≠Toma was named Tsamko, for example, and now is Tsamko ≠Toma. His eldest son, named for his grandfather, is ≠Toma Tsamko.

PART ONE

....

PART ONE

I

Fifteen Hundred Centuries

If you look at a map of Africa made in the 1940s, you will see in the southwest portion of the continent a sparsely inhabited bushland about the size of Spain. Within this is the Kalahari Desert, an area of about 120,000 square miles, much of it as seemingly empty as the Antarctic. In the interior, the map shows 20° south latitude crossing 20° east longitude, which formed part of the border between South West Africa and the Bechuanaland Protectorate, now Namibia and Botswana. But there, the map is otherwise blank, without place names or topographical features, because the mapmakers did not know of them. When in 1950 my father, Laurence Marshall, was looking at such a map in Windhoek, then a frontier town with unpaved roads, a government official told him that the place he was viewing was the end of the earth. No white person, he thought, had ever been there, and no Bantu person, either.

Yet that was where my father planned to go. He wanted to visit the hunter-gatherers who were believed to live there and was considering the map because he was preparing to take my mother, Lorna, my brother, John, then eighteen, and myself, then nineteen, into that country. But how to get there, where we might find water, how much

. . . .

3

of the interior was dry bushland and therefore habitable, and how much was true desert and therefore not habitable, was just a guess.

How we would find the hunter-gatherers was also just a guess. Much later, we were to learn that perhaps ten thousand people known as Bushmen lived there by hunting and gathering, and that perhaps one hundred thousand square miles were more or less habitable, at least for part of the year, which meant that the population density, if you can call it density, was one person for every ten square miles. Obviously, we would not find these people easily.

But find them we did. We found people who called themselves Ju/wasi and were living the lifestyle of our ancestors, a lifestyle of the African savannah that began before we were human beings, changing in form but not in essence as time passed and the climate fluctuated, and lasting until the last third of the twentieth century. That any of us are here at all is due entirely to the long-term culture that these hunter-gatherers, with their courage, skills, and knowledge, continued to uphold.

To me, the experience of visiting this place and these people was profoundly important, as if I had voyaged into the deep past through a time machine. I feel that I saw the Old Way, the way of life that shaped us, a way of life that now is gone. I also feel that I saw the most successful culture that our kind has ever known, if a lifestyle can be called a culture and if stability and longevity are measures, a culture governed by sun and rain, heat and cold, wind and wildfires, plant and animal populations. Any human culture is a work in progress, modifying as its members adjust to new conditions, but no matter what conditions your environment offers, no matter what you use for language or what gods you worship or whether your decisions are made by group consensus or by a hereditary leader or just by someone bigger than the rest of you, for those who live in the Old Way certain elements never vary. Your group size is set by the food supply, your territory must include water, the animals you hunt will always be afraid of you, and the plant foods will always be seasonal, so you had better remember where they grow and be there when they're fruiting.

Today, we find this hard to picture. If Europe had known a similar stability, the continent would still be covered with forests and steppes, the fauna would include Irish elk and lions, and little bands of people along the Dordogne River would still be painting the walls of their caves. Yet while much of the world was changing, the Ju/wasi and their ancestors maintained at least the material aspects of their culture. Archaeologists were eventually to find objects like those used by modern Ju/wasi in sites that dated back to the Upper Paleolithic but were perhaps much older—at one site that went back thirty-five thousand years, the excavation was discontinued, and the extent of its antiquity was not determined.[1] Sites from other parts of Africa demonstrate that gracile, light-bodied hunter-gatherers who made objects like those of the modern Bushmen once lived all over the continent, in all kinds of environments. Ancient pan graves containing such objects were found in Egypt.

Aspects of this culture were known to the very first members of our lineage, whose bones were found near Port Elizabeth, South Africa, in the Klasies River Mouth Caves, where they had rested for 150,000 years, some of the earliest remains of *Homo sapiens* yet discovered. This original lineage was to branch and branch again as its people traveled to all corners of the world, changing themselves, adapting to different climates, perhaps even finding mates among a different kind of hominid, until they became the many varied phenotypes that today enhance our planet. But some descendants of the original people didn't experience much change. Small and light bodied, deft and graceful, these very successful people stayed in the places that had shaped our species, living in the Old Way, with aspects of the culture such as group size, ways of gathering foods, and territorial requirements very similar to those of many other creatures, all shaped by necessity in a manner that most of us today cannot imagine. Yet this was the situation in the 1950s. To go there was indeed time travel, and for the rest of my life I saw everything through the lens of the Kalahari. But back then, I didn't understand what I was seeing.

For one thing, not much was known about our human origins. The Taung australopithecine, *Australopithecus africanus,* had been discovered by Raymond Dart in 1924. But the importance of the fossil and its recognition as a human ancestor were not acknowledged for more than twenty years because Dart (as he himself once told me) had two strikes against him when he found it. He was merely a graduate student at the time, and a South African at that, and therefore in the eyes of the higher-ups of the archaeological community, he wasn't important enough to discover the earliest hominid. So the implications of the fossil were not acknowledged until about the time we were starting our work.

Today, our beginnings are better understood. Our creator was an ice age, which began when most of Africa was covered by rain forest. As the world became colder, the growing glaciers captured much of the world's water, and not enough rain fell to support the great reaches of the world's forests, which became prairies, grasslands, and steppes. In Africa, most of the land that once had been rain forest slowly changed to open woodlands, and later to open savannah.

Our ancestors were there when all this was happening. The evolutionary biologist Richard Dawkins presents a compelling image: You are standing beside your mother, holding her hand. She is holding her mother's hand, who is holding her mother's hand. On and on goes your lineage, each of you holding the hand of your mother, until your line is three hundred miles long and goes back in time five million years, deep into the African rain forest, where the clasping hand is that of a chimpanzee.[2]

As our ancestors lost the rain forest and began to adjust to the new conditions, they had several things with them in addition to their DNA. If we look across the aeons to our next of kin who stayed in what was left of the rain forest—the great apes, most especially the chimpanzees—we can guess what some of those things might be. A good candidate might be the half-dome shelter of grass and branches used by savannah hunter-gatherers, a structure sometimes called a *tshu*, that shares important characteristics with the nests of great apes and thus, by inference, the probable nests of our rain forest ancestors. Whether in the rain forests or on the savannah, when those of our lineage find a new place to stay, the individuals fan out from the group and each one quickly whips together a little structure by weaving flexible branches into a curved, basketlike frame that then is stuffed with leafy twigs (in the rain forests) or handfuls of grass (on the savannah). The structures are used for resting or sleeping as long as the group stays put, and are abandoned when the group moves away. At the next stopping place, the individuals make new structures. If the group later returns to the old place, the individuals do not reoccupy the old structures but instead make fresh ones.

Many creatures, such as nesting birds and denning wolves, make shelters, but these differ quite profoundly from the nests of the primates in that bird nests and wolf dens are the products of lengthy group effort, some (as with birds' nests) with materials gathered far away, and often are designed for permanence, sometimes to be used for generations.

Large primates have a different strategy. They make a little structure in a few minutes, using materials directly at hand. They use the structures for a short time, abandon them when they move on, and make new structures at the next destination.[3]

The people we knew in the 1950s used such structures wherever they camped. A woman would break branches from a bush, set these in the ground, weave the tops together into a basketlike frame, a half dome, and cover it with handfuls of grass. If the group moved, she would make another. If the group returned to the former area, she would make another and not reoccupy the first, which would probably no longer be standing.

Could such a custom continue for so long? That question would never be asked about our rain forest relatives, but only about us, not only because most of us understand other creatures so poorly and assume that all their habits are permanently hardwired, but also because by now we have become so accustomed to rapid, perpetual change that we cannot imagine life without it. And indeed, our species has made many changes since that long-ago time. But for as long as the Old Way lasted for our species, our living arrangements were not necessarily among those changes, or at least, not all of them, and not for all of us.

Thus the little nestlike structures continued to be made, probably because of their temporary nature and the ease with which they are assembled. If our ancestors made new structures every few days, making nests in the trees while big trees were available, making similar nests among bushes as the big trees vanished and the savannah began to spread out around us, adapting the structures in minor ways to changing conditions, parents teaching children for as long as we lived in the Old Way on the savannah, we had no chance to drop the habit. Neither did our primate relatives who stayed in the forests. All the great apes make nests, and all make them in trees—except adult gorillas, who over time became too big for the average tree and solved the problem as our ancestors seem to have solved it, by making nests on the ground.

Although our bodies changed as we became human beings, and although we changed many of the things we thought and did, we didn't change anything unless we had to, because change for its own sake is undesirable, experiments are risky, and life is tenuous enough without departing from what is known to be helpful and safe. Repetition is a form of permanence. Whenever we could, all else being equal, we stayed with the tried and true.

One of the functions of a nest is to partially protect its occupant from all but the most determined predators, so the difference between a nest in a rain forest tree and a half-dome shelter on a treeless bushland is not as great as it might seem. The nest in the tree offers protection from predators below, while the shelter on the ground offers at least a measure of protection from predators from behind—a popular approach of the cat family. Fire is often credited as our main help against predators, but we did not control fire until later, and fire is not as helpful as many of us might suppose (more will be said about this later). This makes the savannah shelter a nest without a tree, and means that the structures have changed less than their makers.

Another good candidate for extreme antiquity is the straight stick about three feet long and an inch or so in diameter—a humble item, surely, but very important. Today, these are known as digging sticks. While we still had the rain forest, our environment consisted largely of sticks, of course, and surely we broke them off trees for many purposes, just as chimpanzees now use sticks for dipping ants and poking into beehives, say, or hurling at those who displease them. The Peabody Museum of Harvard has a collection of tools used by chimpanzees, including several such sticks, one of which a large male chimpanzee was seen using to beat a female. (The rare event, reported during a lecture at Harvard, outraged a group of politically correct female graduate students, underexposed to life and overexposed to academia, who vehemently attacked the female lecturer for reporting the event as science without censuring the male aggressor. This scene, too, was older than our species, wherein a group of primates mobs a conspecific who has temporarily fallen in status.)

In the dim, dense rain forest, most of our food had come from plants that struggled to get enough sunlight. Throughout the year they put out a profusion of moist leaves and tender buds, meanwhile providing a welcome supply of fruits and berries. The plants didn't mind if we ate a few leaves, and they wanted us to eat the fruits and berries because we would pack the seeds in dung and drop them at a distance, just as the plant intended.

On the savannah, though, the plants had more serious difficulties. The problem faced by most savannah plants is not lack of sunlight, but too much of it, and the drying that it causes. Thus some plants were grasses and others were covered with thorns to conserve water, while still others spent most of the year hidden deep in the earth in root form as bulbs, corms, tubers, and rhizomes, with nothing aboveground to show their presence. Of course they needed sunlight, but they would wait until the rains began before sending up a stalk or vine and some leaves. The root would shrivel in the process, but with the rain and with the energy it was getting from its leaves, it would fill out again and be ready to send up another vine a year later. Until then, though, the vine and leaves were a liability, leaching moisture from the root and also betraying its location. So the root would stop feeding them. They'd dry and drop off. A wildfire might come by and burn them, or the wind might blow them away. This was what the root intended. Secure in the earth, with nothing aboveground to show its presence, it would wait out the dry season where animals could not find it. Naked mole rats sometimes eat these roots, but these little conservationists eat only part of a root without doing too much damage. Eventually the root repairs itself and the mole rats can tunnel up to it and eat more later.

As for us, with the loss of the rain forest we were reduced to eating dry berries, the shallow bulbs of little onions, ground-growing nuts, and the edible ends of grass blades, as well as grubs, large ants, baby birds, snails, and caterpillars. Many other creatures were also eating these foods, especially other primates such as ancestral baboons. These were about the size of macaques in those days, weighing perhaps 15 to 30 pounds, so they were smaller than us with our larger bodies, perhaps 60 to 140 pounds.[4] But if modern baboons are any indication, their groups were bigger than ours. A large group of small animals is more efficient at foraging than a small group of large animals, because a large group can cover a wider area, with each individual needing less food. If the baboons found a food-producing place before we did, they picked it clean and deprived us. We needed more food, but where to find it?

Like the baboons, we would have been pulling up the little wild onions that grow on the savannah, and like the baboons, we would have noticed the shriveled stalks discarded by the deeper roots, suggesting something farther down. But the hands of a primate are not made for serious digging, as anyone who has tried to dig a hole two or three feet deep in hard earth without a tool will quickly testify, and the baboons couldn't do it. Neither could we, with bare hands.

Enter the digging stick, perhaps a branch with a slanting point where it broke off the tree, or perhaps a stick found at the edge of a burned area where fire had removed the outer layers and hardened the point. But sharpening a stick would not be difficult, especially for primates who were already using sticks for various purposes and knew about altering them slightly, as chimpanzees still do today, chewing the end of a stick, say, to make a little brush for gathering ants. Making a point on a stick is not much of a leap. Perhaps we took a sharp stone to it. With sticks, we chopped away the earth around the shriveled stalks, followed them down, and found the roots. We have been eating roots ever since.

Archaeological evidence suggests that some of our ancestors may also have used the horns and bones of antelopes for digging, although evidence is scanty on the subject because a stick is less likely to appear in archaeological remains. But surely horns and bones came later, after we already knew about deep digging. And, unlike the sticks, they didn't remain in use. Nobody uses them now, probably because to get them you must first get a carcass, while a suitable stick can be found on almost any tree. The people who are called the First People still use sticks to this day, and probably will for years to come, as many prefer them to shovels. A digging stick weighs less, is easier to carry, and costs nothing. It also has more uses than a shovel: it can balance a load, extend your reach, or be a cane, a lever, a boomerang to knock nuts from a tree, or a weapon to smite an attacker. Over the millennia, many a predator has been discouraged by a sharp whack on the snout. For digging roots, a stick is better than a shovel, because if you stand up and dig with a shovel (for which you really should wear shoes), you can't feel what you're doing. Any judgments about the hole and its contents are made visually. But if you sit on your heels and chop the earth with the point of a digging stick, each blow says something to your hands and arms, and as you get near the root, perhaps feeling its hairs when scraping away the loose dirt with your fingers, you can modify your digging to expose the root unsmashed. And you can do this in about the same amount of time you would need if using a shovel, but you would spend less energy, because a digging stick weighs less than a shovel, because the downward blow is easier to make than the up-and-out movement of a shovel, and because it's easier to scoop or brush the loosened dirt out of the hole with your hand than to hoist it and heave it on a shovel.

A digging stick is humble, yes. The very name of this item in the English language shows how seriously we underrate it—we assign specific nouns, not vaguely descriptive phrases, to objects that we consider important. Our long stick with a blade at the end is called a spear, for instance, not a stabbing stick. (!Kung speakers have named the digging stick, of course—the word is *!ai*.) But even if a pointed stick seems insignificant to us in our innocence, as an invention of consequences it ranks with the discovery of the deep roots themselves and has made more difference to our species than virtually all the other inventions that we celebrate with more enthusiasm. And a modern digging stick is not very different from the rain forest sticks we used millions of years earlier except that we sharpen one end and take off the bark.

Then, too, there is the ostrich egg. This useful item is first a meal and then a water bottle. To use these eggs, we had to do only two things—steal a fresh egg without being kicked by the ostrich, and open a hole in the shell. Unless the egg is opened carefully, the contents will spill, so the best way to eat the egg without wasting the contents is to pick up a rock, tap open a small hole in the shell, and stir the contents with a stick. After sucking out the egg, we had an empty eggshell, with obvious implications. An ostrich egg holds from five to five and a half cups of water, more than a day's supply. No further refinement was needed except a wad of grass for a stopper.

A man sits in front of a grass shelter, or tshu.
Visible in the background are a spear, a digging stick,
and an ostrich eggshell used for storing water.

On the dry savannah, the need for water limited our foraging. One ostrich eggshell filled with water could expand the foraging range of its owner by fifty to one hundred square miles.[5] Some people still use ostrich eggshells to this very day, for this very reason. The Ju/wa Bushmen used them in preference to many other possible water containers, such as leather bags and animal stomachs. The leather items leak and spill and require considerable preparation, while an empty ostrich eggshell can be used immediately. An ostrich eggshell is thick and strong, and is even simpler than a digging stick. In terms of what it has done for our lineage, it might be equally important. We could not have carried ostrich eggshells until we became proficient hind-leg walkers, but we could have been using them ever since then, and they cannot have changed one iota.

Today there are 233 species of primates, but only baboons, red guenons, and people live outside the forests. And only one kind of primate—our kind—found a way to reach the deeply buried foods, carry small amounts of water, and modify tree nests into ground nests so that we could sleep anywhere and didn't need to stay near cliffs or rocky hilltops or big trees—the places where baboons and red guenons take refuge. We moved ourselves beyond our competition. This has been true for millions of years and was true in the rolling bushland of the Kalahari in the 1950s, where water was scarce and there were very few large trees and no cliffs or rocky hilltops. Out there, the people were the only primates.

Our human version of the Old Way was born in the rain forests but developed on the savannah. For fifteen hundred centuries, we kept the Old Rules, then broke them all and erased the Old Way from our lives. Among the last to lose it were the Ju/wa Bushmen in the Kalahari interior, who in the 1950s were still living entirely from the savannah, as people had done since people began, eating the wild plants and the wild animals they caught and killed, making their clothes from animal skins and their tools from stone, wood, bone, and plant fiber. They had no agriculture, no domestic animals (not even dogs), no fabric, no manufactured items, and no metal except for a few lengths of wire and a few bits of tin or steel that, beginning in the 1920s or '30s, they obtained in a usurious trade at the few scattered settlements of the Bantu pastoralists at the edges of the Kalahari. If a Bushman wishing to trade journeyed to one of the Bantu settlements, the pastoralists might give him a piece of wire about ten inches long in exchange for five or six jackal skins.

The bits of metal replaced some of the Bushmen's former materials of bone, stone, and wood—by the 1950s most arrowheads were made of cold-hammered wire rather than bone, but arrowheads made of bone and even one or two made of wood were still in use. Because the size, shape, and purpose of the arrow were unchanging, this minor use of metal did not alter the technology.

The hunter-gatherer life of the savannah, which began when our ancestors lost the shelter of the trees, survived until the 1970s or '80s, by which time the First People had been forced to change profoundly. And although today a few individuals may remember the Old Way and keep some of its skills, no human population lives by it any longer. Even so, it clings to us still, in our preferences, in our thoughts and dreams, and even in some of our behavior. All over the world, many men who hunt are following the Old Way whether they know it or not, even the Americans with gun racks in their trucks. Hunting offers too many variables to be learned from books or videos, so many a successful hunter learned the skills from an older man, often his father, who also learned from another man, probably his father, in a lengthy chain that reaches to the men who hunted Irish elk and bison at the edges of the European glaciers, and beyond that to the African savannah.

2

Our Lineage

We often imagine our lineage vaguely. Millions of years ago there were Australopithecines—Lucy and the rest. They vanished, time passed, and suddenly there was *Homo habilis*. Nothing much happened for a while, and then *Homo erectus* appeared. As for ourselves, the *Homo sapiens*, we enter the picture as cavemen.

This vision is like taking four far-apart frames from a full length film and trying to guess what the film is about. We might all agree that the few fragments don't give us much to go on, but the sporadic image still clings. Better to think of Richard Dawkins's hand-holding chain of daughters and mothers. Better to think of the animals in the rain forests who were our mothers, because we were like them when we began our journey toward our human state.

Five million years ago, we were three to five feet tall if we reared up, hands off the ground, to take a look around. Our males were much bigger than our females. Surely we were partly covered with hair—not with fur, implying an undercoat, but with hair resembling that of chimpanzees, gorillas, bonobos, and orangutans. The hair was probably more or less straight but not long or heavy. Under the hair our skin was probably pinkish white, as is the skin of most animals. Perhaps our bare faces, fingers, and toes were pigmented as

. . . .

1 7

protection from the sun, but perhaps these exposed areas were pink when we were children, like the faces of young chimpanzees.

Because our males if not our females were bigger than most other primates, and because all of us were too big to run along the smaller branches of the trees as did the monkeys, we might have traveled along the ground with the help of our knuckles, but our lineage was arboreal and had been since the Miocene, perhaps even since the days of the dinosaurs, so we had traditionally climbed and lived in trees, and while still in the rain forests we spent much time in the trees because most of our food was in them. We looked for seeds and budding leaves, also for slugs and caterpillars, and we listened for birds, perhaps hornbills, who called to one another when they found fruit. We would know why they were calling and, following the sound, we would spread out to find the tree where they were feeding. Whoever saw the fruit first might also cry out, as the hornbills had done and as a chimpanzee might do, giving a food call that the rest of us would hear, and we'd hurry over. We would climb up to the fruiting branches and throw things at the hornbills until they flew noisily into the sky. If the fruit was on branches too slender to support us, we might shake them to make the fruit fall.

We would stay near that tree as long as the fruit lasted, making nests in nearby branches so that we could sleep out of reach of predators, and when the fruit was finished we would move on together to another place. We would know most of the fruiting trees in our section of the rain forest, and even without the aid of hornbills, we would visit them regularly.

Then the climate began to change. The world became colder and the glaciers developed. It is at this time that we find the mother whose hand our lineage is holding. Along some of the larger rivers, strips of rain forest remained, and our relatives who occupied those particular riverside forests were able to live life as before. Environmentally speaking, not much was happening as far as they were concerned, so their bodies and their lifestyle changed very little. They became the modern chimpanzees.

As for us, however, we were not fortunate enough to live along the rivers with their permanent, sheltering forests. In the forests we occupied, the environment deteriorated, the trees withered out from under us, and we were forced to adapt. So we did the best we could from day to day, moving about in small groups, shape-changing slowly as the streams ran dry and the heavy rain forests became open woodlands, which in turn shrank away until nothing was left but a few little trees and endless stretches of grass and thornbush.

Out on the open savannah with the sun burning down, not many creatures moved about by day, but we did, teaching our children the things our parents had taught us, but having to make some adjustments. When we traveled, for instance, we could no longer spread out as we had done in the rain forest because big trees were not at hand to climb in case of trouble. Instead, like soldiers in combat, we began to travel in single file behind a leader who was watchful for danger. Most other savannah animals did the same. If we stopped to rest, we sat together in a circle, doing as other animals did because the circle as an antipredator device is as effective as it is important. Cows or sheep in a field lie down close together but face in different directions, birds on a telephone wire face both ways unless they are facing a storm, and even the dog who sleeps on your bed normally faces away from you so that together, as the dog sees it, you can cover all sides of the room. Even if he nuzzles up to you at first, he'll probably change position later. Remembering in our hearts our experiences with predators, all of us feel vulnerable to attack from behind, and to this day we favor circles.

What determined the size of our groups? Water was the single most important factor—water and the food supply around it. In the rain forest, we had been free to travel wherever there was food, as water had been everywhere—in the morning mist, in streams and rivers, in every fruit and berry, in the breath of every leaf. There, we could have lived in groups of forty or fifty, perhaps coming together at night and spreading out to forage by day in smaller parties. But as the glaciers formed elsewhere and the rainfall lessened, many rivers ran dry, and the sources of water became scarce. Streams and rivers became uncommon, some merely the conduits of water from elsewhere passing through without influencing the surroundings. The Okavango River, for instance, cuts a track through miles of semi-desert with little else than grass and low thornbush on either bank. No people and few animals lived in these stretches. We could not have lived on the banks of such rivers.

So we probably lived on the shores of seasonal lakes. The Paleolithic camps of the Kalahari, many of which were still in use in the 1950s, are on the shores of seasonal lakes. After the rains that fill these lakes, water remains around the edges in waterholes, but even these were few. Yet the need for water limited our foraging. We would have been obliged to stay within a half day's walk of a source, at least during the dry season.

Perhaps for short periods, some groups of our ancestors could have lived without water, as did some groups of Bushmen during the 1950s, if their groups numbered no more than ten or twelve individuals. These people would get moisture from little green melons called *tsama* melons, from certain watery roots, and from the rumens* of the antelopes they killed. But as a way of life this was only for those who could not do better, because it put the foragers so close to the edge. People under such conditions survived the hottest weather by digging the watery roots, squeezing the pulp, drinking the juice, digging gravelike pits, lining the pits with the squeezed pulp, urinating on the pulp, lying down on it, covering themselves with earth, and waiting there for the day to cool, thus conserving the water in their bodies. But this was done by only a few, and only in extremis. We did not become a species that thrived in this manner. Our development as a species depended on our being able to live near a source of water.

During a gathering trip, we could spread out over five or six miles (about as far as anyone can go in a day, do the necessary work of gathering, and get back to water and to the safety of the group in its encampment by dark). This would be roughly fifty square miles, if we lived by the shore of a large lake, or twice that if our source was a spring or waterhole. Thus the size of our group would depend upon the amount of food that the area could produce. This calculation was not firmly fixed, as in the past we were surely not very different from the modern hunter-gatherers, who sometimes made foraging trips that lasted three to five days, carrying water with them in ostrich eggshells. Also, leftover rainwater was sometimes available in hollow trees, and certain roots and melons held substantial

*The rumen is the "first stomach" of the even-toed ungulates. The rumen contains the cud, the vegetation that the ruminant quickly gulps down to regurgitate and chew at leisure.

An ostrich egg is a useful item: it is first a meal, and then a water bottle.
An empty ostrich egg holds from 5 to 5½ cups of water,
more than enough for a day's supply. No further refinement is
needed except a wad of grass for a stopper.

liquid. Even so, in the long run, it was the source of water and the gathering opportunities around it that limited our range.

In the six thousand square miles known as Nyae Nyae, there were only seven waterholes that the Ju/wasi considered to be permanent and had not failed in living memory, even during drought. Eight more were considered to be semipermanent; they might go dry during years of drought. Some were at the edges of pans, tucked away under rock ledges. One was at the edge of a fault, where a block of stone had sunk away from its neighbor, leaving a three-foot cliff. And one was a natural sinkhole in the middle of a pan called Nama. The sinkhole itself was very deep, with the water far below the surface, but several groups of people used it until two or three spotted hyenas tried to drink, fell in, couldn't get out, and drowned. Their bodies floated face-down with their ears and hairy backs showing above the waterline. Of course the water was polluted for years thereafter. The people went elsewhere. Thus the problem of drowned animals shows, I think, why the people did not dig deep wells, although possibly they could have done so. Better to use a natural waterhole where the water is near the surface.

Here are four passages from my notes and journal that suggest what it might have been like for our species in Paleolithic times, out on the dry savannah. The people in the passages, besides myself, are /Gwi or Ju/wa Bushmen, but what the place was like, and what the people were doing, was not new. The first passage is about distance.

> *I am alone an hour's walk from camp, sitting in the long grass at the edge of an arm of the pan, listening to the wind moving the grass and to something going* huff, huff, *miles away—a lion—and looking at the hazy gray sky. It will be dark soon, and I'm looking at the miles and miles of yellow, silver grass and black bushes in the grass, and thinking how the wind may have blown for thousands of miles before it touched a person, and perhaps it blows over a Bushman camp tucked away somewhere, one point in the enormous, vast veld that goes hun-*

dreds of miles in every direction and it is all like this, just grass and grass and grass, and a few bushes and a few thorn trees and a few antelope in small herds and a few groups of lions and a few groups of Ju/wasi, as far apart from each other as the stars—all living in this country but so small and few that they are hardly aware of each other. The wind stops. The air seems very still. The sun is moving down and the sky in the west is yellow. A cold night is coming. I hope I can remember how I came here so I can find our camp before the night sets in. In all that space, you could miss it by the slightest turn or step, and walk right by.

The second passage is about cold weather.

It was almost morning, and very cold, below freezing. Water in a gourd had frozen to solid ice. The winter sky was leaden black with dull moonlight and stars. The wind lifted and blew very cold, and some little dark birds that were hunched freezing in the thorn trees gave out a few shrill cries. The shadows cast by the last of the moonlight were almost gone. Daylight was coming and a mouse that lived nearby was throwing up footfulls of sand to plug in his burrow for the day. At their camp, the people were also freezing cold because they were almost out of firewood. They were sitting in a half circle around what had been their fire, all packed close together with the children between them and the infant held close between his mother's belly and her leg—all maybe getting a little warmth from each other and from the still-warm ashes. The wind was exceptionally strong, blowing the sand from around the roots of the grass tussocks, blowing soft ashes away from the little hearth so that everyone was sprinkled with white. The people were wrapped in their leather capes but their skins were almost gray with cold.

The third passage is about shallow roots.

We are in an open forest. The trees seem large and old, with fine, intricate branches and light gray bark. Fine, tall yellow

grass grows all around. The sky is bright. Flies are buzzing—
little, fast-moving, high-buzzing wild flies. The ground is
pocked with little dents. People have been digging here for tiny
onions. All the women sit down and begin to scrape, picking up
the chivelike bulbs and peeling and eating them. It is rather hot.
We are all down in the yellow grass—chunk chunk sounds of
the digging sticks, an irregular rhythm—the faint fresh dust
rising—people crunching the onions and talking like mad with
their mouths full. The three children who are too big to be car-
ried sit together in the shade and play.

The fourth passage is about water. The people mentioned here
lived where there was no water.

When I got there, the mother gemsbok and her calf were dead
and the leopard had run away. The mother's sides were raked
by the claws of the leopard. Her calf was soft furred and tawny
brown with a white belly. The leopard had removed its intes-
tines and had eaten its face up to the eyes. The mother had milk
in her udder, which had four teats like goats' teats, all covered
with hair, two large teats in front and two small teats behind.
The two men milked her, stroking the milk veins in the bag,
milking a squirt into their palm and licking it off. The gems-
bok, lying on her side with one hind leg slightly raised, was so
big that both men could squat below the leg to milk her. I tasted
some milk, which was strong and gamey, also harsh and salty,
very different from the mild, sweet milk of cows. Then the two
men rolled her on her back, skinned and opened her belly, then
opened the rumen. Inside was her cud, a big, dark green,
crunched-up mass of small leaves? grass? which she had eaten.
It looked wet and spongy. Two big white worms rose up from
the rumen, not knowing what was happening, but the men paid
no attention to them. Instead, they took handfuls of rumen and
squeezed the juice into their mouths. I tasted a little of this too.
It was watery, but tasted something like oak leaves, slightly bit-
ter. The men then dug a bowl-shaped pit beside the gemsbok,
lined the pit with a flap of her skin, and squeezed out about a
gallon of water.

3

Meat and Fire

On the savannah, the seasons begin and end with rain. Big cumulus clouds with lightning flashing inside them build on the horizon, advancing, then retreating, casting their shadows on the parching veld, until at last they sail slowly overhead and release their rain—fat, soft, far-apart drops that the Ju/wasi call female rain, or small, hard, fast-falling drops of male rain. Within days of the start of the rains, the entire savannah is in bloom, flowers everywhere, with gleaming, shallow lakes where once there were clay flats. Migrating birds from Europe join the African birds. For those who lived in the Old Way, this was a season of life and activity.

During and after the rainy season, our savannah ancestors would have gathered many kinds of foods. Roots that had been dormant during the dry season would put out their vines of melons or ground-growing nuts, the thornbushes would cover themselves with berries, and the trees would put out nuts, fruits, and pods of peas and beans. Animals also took advantage of the rains to multiply, so that our ancestors found edible caterpillars, baby birds, and swarms of large ants that tasted of honey. Soon enough there was plenty of food, and our ancestors could go wherever they pleased to gather their food because rainwater would collect in many places—in shallow lakes and pools, in temporary waterholes, and even in hollow trees. During this season, the savannah was, in its way, almost as good as the rain forest. Our savannah ancestors could scatter over the veld in small groups and live almost anywhere, as did the Ju/wasi in the 1950s.

However, in time the rains would stop. The weather would be cool or even cold for a while, but not for long, and soon the heat would return and the life of the savannah would revert to its drought mode. The edible fruits and leaves would vanish. The caterpillars would be hidden in cocoons and chrysalises, the swarming ants would have shed their wings and gone back to their tunnels, and the baby birds would have fledged and flown away.

More importantly, the seasonal water sources would dry up, and the widely scattered groups of our ancestors would converge at the sites of permanent water. In many places, as is true of the modern Ju/wasi, these groups would have shared a dwindling supply of plant food for the remainder of the dry season, the gatherers walking farther on every foraging trip, returning at night or at least every few days to the water, and finding less to eat as the season and the competition progressed.

At this time of year, an important activity would have been hunting. Hunting was not new to us. While we lived in the rain forests, we surely did a little hunting. Chimpanzees hunt often enough, if informally and opportunistically, and we would have had no reason to abandon the custom. While we still had the rain forest, we might be eating buds somewhere in heavy cover, then hear the soft voices of monkeys above us in the trees. We would hope that they were coming to eat the same buds. We would wait, keeping perfectly still, just our eyes moving, listening to the monkeys rustle in the leaves overhead. Then suddenly they'd be among us. We'd be ready. They'd scream when they saw us, of course, and try to escape, scattering up through the branches, trying to get to the thinnest branches where we couldn't follow, but we'd go leaping after them and might manage to grab a few. Perhaps we tried to kill them by biting their necks or swinging their heads against the tree, or perhaps we just started eating, because those who hadn't caught a monkey would be grabbing from those who had. Or they'd be following those with monkeys, reaching out their hands, begging for a share, as modern chimpanzees do today.

. . . .

The waterhole at /Gautscha as the dry season begins.
In the six thousand square miles known as Nyae Nyae, there were
only seven waterholes the Ju/wasi considered to be permanent.
These had not failed in living memory, even during drought.

Just because we later became savannah animals does not mean that we gave up the chase-and-grab mode of hunting. The prevalent notion that we suddenly took up some form of primitive weapon comes from looking at modern methods of hunting and working backward, imagining our lineage as using ever less developed tools, from the bow and arrow back to the spear, and finally back to the club and the stone. Better to think of us as the animals that we were, developing the skills we already had, just as other animals do. The cheetah, for example, did not suddenly appear as a cat who could run down prey at seventy miles per hour. No, the ancestral cheetah was a forest animal, a lynxlike cat that hunted by stalking and grabbing. With the loss of the forests, out on the plains, it evolved longer legs, a more streamlined body, and a somewhat better lung capacity as the stalking phase diminished and the grabbing phase became a long distance chase. The cheetah became a splendid hunter of the savannah.

As for us, we didn't suddenly invent weapons and we probably didn't even throw stones with deadly aim until our bodies became modified and our shoulders changed shape. Human beings with their wide, horizontally placed shoulders can wing out stones with deadly velocity, but the round-shouldered chimpanzees cannot. So at first, we surely kept on hunting as we had always hunted, the same way that modern chimpanzees hunt to this very day, because the method works quite well, certainly in heavy cover. We would notice something moving, perhaps sniff the air to learn what it was, then wait in hiding for it to come near or creep up and make a lunge for it, and if we didn't manage to catch it then we'd chase it until we did, or until it got away. This, of course, is the basic method for almost any kind of hunting, with hunters such as sharks giving more importance to locating the prey, and hunters such as cheetahs giving more importance to the chase.

Here is a passage from my diary about the chase-and-grab method of hunting.

Just then we saw a baby rabbit which two young boys chased and finally cornered in the roots of a shrub. One of the boys reached for it. It bit his finger. "What are you going to do with that?" we asked. "Eat it," said the boy. They then played with it for a while, chasing it and laughing. It was too young to run very fast, but it was very game and it tried for all it was worth every time they let it go. Finally one of the boys picked it up and walked off with it, carrying it, still struggling, draped around his neck like a hunter would carry a buck. One of the men then killed it, pinching its throat. It was later eaten by the boys, although it was just a morsel.

Although our body form adjusted to the developing savannah, our social arrangements probably stayed roughly the same. Of course we continued to live in groups, and would have encountered the problems faced by all groups during the hot seasons when many of us would converge on the sources of permanent water. At that point, hunting probably became more important rather quickly. If we were tied to water, we would use up the small game of the area in the same way that we used up the plant foods. However, the bigger the victims, the better off would be our large, underfed groups. As we extended our chase-and-grab methods, we became fast hind-leg runners in the process.

We seldom think of "early man" as running after animals. Some of the textbooks show our stereotype—a big muscle-bound guy in a leopard skin, standing with his knees bent, wielding a club or a spear. That, to us, is early hunting. Yet several important truths support the probability that we became big-game hunters by chasing animals, our potential victims getting larger as we modified our bodies for speed. We kept on doing what we had always done, getting better and better at it, having no reason to abandon a technique that worked so well for us. In the 1950s, the Ju/wasi of Nyae Nyae were still doing it, and doing it extremely well. I knew several men who hunted in this manner. But it wasn't easy, not everyone could do it, and it wasn't a method that people would develop as an afterthought, especially if they already had the bow and arrow.

The modern Ju/wasi had their famous poison arrows and were very accomplished in using them. So why would they continue to run down animals? At least one reason was that if you ran down the animal, you could eat it that same day: you didn't need to track it for many days while the poison did its work. Also, you didn't need a weapon. You were the weapon, you and your strong, athletic body.

. . . .

The task was difficult, of course—you had to run steadily, not just jog, for a very long way in the African sun (temperatures can reach 120°F in the shade), which made such hunting equal to the most demanding marathon races and therefore not for everyone.

But such was the Old Way. Virtually every species is challenged to push to the extremes. As prey animals get faster to escape their predators, for instance, the predators must meet the challenge by becoming faster to catch them. As a species we, too, would have tried to meet our challenges. Some scientists believe that hunting by running contributed to our present body shape (with perhaps the First People serving as the paradigm rather than, say, the overfed American couch potato). The biologist Bernd Heinrich, who himself is a highly successful marathon runner, suggests that running was indeed a feature of early human development. He points out that as the forests disappeared, we became bipedal and more gracile, until we had long thighs, deep lungs, and well-developed multipurpose feet that could carry us over everything from rocks to sand and mud. We kept cooler by shedding our body hair, acquiring more skin pigment to take its place, and retaining only little hats of head hair that became curly and lofty rather than straight and flat, creating air space to insulate our brains from the sun. In short, we assumed the best possible body for long-distance running in a hot climate. And why would we want to become runners? The most compelling reason was almost certainly to hunt.[1]

True, we sometimes hear the laughable suggestion that out on the savannah with no trees to climb, we became fast hind-leg runners to escape predators. This is hardly worth the trouble to refute, as many of our would-be predators reach speeds of sixty miles per hour, at least for a few seconds, which is all it takes. True, the predators would have chased the slowest of us, not the fastest, thus providing a selective pressure for greater speed, but if that had been the case, most of us today would be faster than these predators, which we most certainly are not. Then as now, even the fastest runner could not have escaped even from a marginally competent predator unless the runner had a big head start. Even in automobiles, we have trouble accelerating fast enough to outdistance the rush of a big cat. The ways people of the Old Way coped with predators will be discussed later, but unless you had no other option, running was not

. . . .

one of them. You'd never make it. You'd just excite the predator. You'd be showing how inadequate you were, how little confidence you had in your ability to defend yourself, and you'd be presenting your vulnerable back, making it easy for him to grab you.

The real question, then, is not why did we run, but what did we chase? Perhaps there were several larger species that were safe to hunt, that wouldn't turn on you and kill you. The most likely of these was probably elands, especially mature, bull elands, the largest of the antelopes.

Were elands around at the time? All the modern genera of bovids have been present since the Pliocene, including the antelope family, and are with us today with little or no modification. Yet to understand why some of the large antelopes fall victim to runners, it is important to consider their physiology. Many savannah antelopes, including elands, go for long periods of time—months or even entire seasons—without drinking water. They rest in the shade by day and eat at night, getting some liquid from the little melons that grow on vines throughout the savannah, also some liquid from morning dew. Most antelopes prefer browsing to grazing because they get a bit of additional moisture from the leaves of bushes and trees, as these plants, unlike the savannah grasses, have roots that go deep to where the earth still holds traces of moisture.

The antelopes also get moisture from fresh green grass, and they graze on it whenever they find it. Long, dry grass, in contrast, offers no moisture and little nourishment, so the antelopes more or less leave it alone. Yet even leaves and fresh grass don't offer much moisture for such large creatures. Therefore the bodies of these antelopes became specially adapted to withstand heat, so that they don't need to evaporate water to cool themselves by sweating or panting. Instead, they store the heat in their bodies, their metabolism falling as their bodies become hot and dry. For us, this would produce a fatal fever, and we would die of heatstroke, but the internal temperature of these antelopes can rise very much more than ours can, and it does them no harm.

Even so, the ability to do this is not infinite, and without water to drink, the large antelopes must try to overheat as little as possible.

Elands are particularly vulnerable to overheating, not only because of their size but also because they are more solidly built, with less surface area in proportion to their mass. Then, too, they are the only antelopes with fat in their bodies (a characteristic much valued by their predators, for whom every calorie is precious). Elands, in fact, almost seem to be a hot-climate version of Bergman's rule, well known to zoologists, whereby the farther north your species goes, the bigger the individuals become, with less skin surface to radiate heat and more body mass to retain it. This, of course, keeps north-ern animals warm, but to a heat-storing animal such as an eland, the more heat you can store as the sun burns down, the better off you are, so body bulk can offer some advantage.

However, with so much body mass and so much stored heat, a mature bull eland becomes vulnerable to a runner, who would have no chance at all to catch, say, a gazelle, which not only runs at fifty miles an hour but also has long, thin legs and a skinny, silvery-haired, heat-reflecting body. When an attacker approaches a gazelle, the gazelle disappears over the horizon. When an attacker ap-proaches an eland, however, the eland sprints off at thirty-five miles an hour and runs for a while, then stops and turns around. He has run far enough to discourage a lion (all cats except cheetahs are ca-pable of only short dashes, and cheetahs are too small to hunt elands) and he wants to see what has become of his pursuer. A charging lion would have stopped, winded and discouraged, but, far behind, a hu-man hunter will still be running. The bull eland will sprint off again, and keep running, but, with his reddish hair absorbing the sunlight into his big body, he is beginning to overheat, so again he stops for a look. Still the hunter is coming. The eland must force himself to keep running. Surely the hunter will give up soon, after coming so far in so much heat, so the eland stops again to look back, but still the hunter is coming, even gaining on him. Eventually, the eland can run no more. He falls to his knees, or just stands still, head low, legs wide apart, spent, dying. Then the hunter, with the last of his strength, can catch up and grab him by the tail, then kill him with a spear if he brought one, or he can push the eland over and lie on his neck to keep him from struggling and clamp his hands over the eland's nose and mouth to stop his laboring breath. In short, to catch and kill an eland on a hot day, all you really need is a strong, athletic, runner's body.

Needless to say, throughout our time as hominids we have been developing tools, many of which were designed to enhance our hunting success. Two and a half million years ago our ancestors at Olduvai Gorge were hind-leg walkers who used stones for tools, our *Homo habilis* ancestors struck knifelike flakes off the stones, and our *Homo erectus* ancestors sharpened the flakes even further, so that by the time we were fully human we were making sharp points, to say nothing of sharpening the digging sticks that had been with us all along, meaning that all men, not just the fast runners, could be hunting big game, and could do it in all seasons, not just the hottest seasons. But all of this took time, during which the well-known methods of chase-and-grab hunting and its sequel, hunting by running, would have helped to sustain us. The method continued until the 1950s, and conceivably could still be in use today.

As has been said, we knew several young men who hunted by running, one of whom lived among the people we knew best. His name was Short /Kwi, and once or twice a year, he might run down an eland. The best season for this, he said, was in hot weather after rain, because the muddy earth would squeeze up between the eland's hooves, causing the hooves to split apart, making running more difficult. The hooves of many antelopes are designed to speed along a solid surface, not to plod through mud. Short /Kwi's own strong, unspecialized feet had no such problem. More will be said about Short /Kwi later.

To show the difficulty of the practice, though, I offer the example of my brother John, strong and athletic at age nineteen or twenty, who, in the company of several equally young and athletic Ju/wa men, once tried to chase an eland, although their object was not to run the eland to exhaustion but simply to get near enough for a bow shot. This took place during the hot season before the start of the rains. The men came upon a small herd of young female elands and decided to hunt them. The elands ran off quickly, got far ahead, and hid in a clump of bushes, perhaps for shade as well as for cover. When the men got near them, the elands ran again, fast and far, to hide in another clump of bushes. The hunt proceeded like this until

*Using sticks to mimic the horns of the eland, the people perform the rite
for a girl's first menstruation. Elands are associated with the menarchal rite
of the !Kung-speaking people; specific music known as "eland music"
is sung by women during this rite, and never at any other time.*

the men were too tired to run anymore. The elands still had energy left and therefore they escaped. Being females and also young, they were smaller than the large, old bull elands most vulnerable to overheating, yet I include this description because I think it suggests the kind of stamina that might be needed to successfully run down an eland. Half an hour or so of fast start-and-stop running on the part of some athletic young men didn't begin to finish the job. Even so, there were men who did it, if with older, heavier elands.

One might ask if people ran after game in relays, as wild dogs allegedly do. (In reality they don't—the whole pack runs en masse, but sometimes a dog or two will sprint ahead of the leader or cut across if the prey animal is circling, thus giving the appearance of relay running.) Relay running has its uses, and perhaps our ancestors tried it. But for the technique to succeed, the victim must circle, which an animal may do if he has a home range and needs to stay within it or return to it. Elands do not have home ranges and have no reason to circle, no incentive not to run straight ahead. And of course it is the potential victim, not those chasing it, who decides in which direction they all will go. That being true, relay running would be futile.

Further compelling evidence that our species has been chasing elands for a very long time is offered by the elands themselves. In the 1950s most of the Kalahari antelopes had a flight distance of about one hundred feet, which was enough to protect themselves from a lion's charge or a Bushman hunter's arrow (the two distances being similar). But even today, an eland's flight distance from a person on foot is ten times as far, surely because the eland knows that a person can cover that distance and still keep going. The eland tries to leave as much space as he possibly can between himself and a potential hunter/runner.

The biologist Richard Estes, who has extensively studied the African antelopes, notes an interesting relationship between elands and people. "Elands fear only man," he writes, "and have the longest flight distance (300–500 m) of all African game. Might this be a habit acquired since the advent of firearms, or could it be that hunting peoples are able to run down an eland?"[2]

My thought is that runners are known to have been chasing elands for a considerable period of time, while people with firearms have been a significant presence only recently, yet where antelopes are hunted by riflemen, all of them know about rifles, and where they have never been hunted, none of them know, but only elands show the extraordinary flight distance.

Abundant evidence in the form of cave paintings and Bushman lore also shows a powerful relationship between people and elands, or, rather, a powerful fixation by people upon elands, particularly large bull elands, and although the paintings cast no light on pre-human activity, since humans, not prehumans, are known to have painted them, the pictures and lore are not without interest. For example, the Drakensberg caves in semidesert country in Namibia are filled with paintings of elands, not a few showing a rather close view of the rear end of an eland, more a runner's view than a bow hunter's. Other paintings show men holding elands by the tail with the elands showing no resistance but appearing to droop, lowering their heads, stretching their necks, and raising their noses to enable the clearest possible air flow, a position that strongly suggests fatal exhaustion. There is also a painting of a running eland looking back over its shoulder.[3] The rock art specialist David Lewis-Williams, who points out these paintings, has also told me of a painting in the Main Caves showing a man running after an eland. Dr. Lewis-Williams notes that this particular man is infibulated, meaning that a device is attached to his penis that prevents his copulating, which may suggest that this particular painting shows an event in the spirit world. The Nyae Nyae Ju/wasi of the 1950s (and since then, for that matter) did not practice or even talk about infibulation, so this painting seems remote from the life of the people we knew. Even so, there it is—a painting of a man running after an eland.

Elands are also associated with the menarchal rite of the !Kung-speaking people, the rite performed for a girl's first menstruation. Only very specific music, known as "eland music," is sung by women during the rite, and it is never sung at any other time. The musicologist Nicholas England studied this music extensively and found that it is by far the most ancient of all Bushman music. It uses the very ancient five-tone scale, it is very different from other Bushman music, and it occurs unchanged in widespread cultures that include the different language groups of Bushmen, the Ju/wasi and others, each of which also has, in addition to eland music, its own unique set of songs and music. Yet they all have the same eland music.[4]

How did this happen? Deep in the past, some people composed eland music, which spread with them as they separated, multiplied, developed different cultures and languages, and composed other music and songs. But during all that time, all of them kept singing eland music for the menarchal rite, as their mothers had done before them, and their grandmothers before that, in the hand-holding chain that goes back through time. To this day, all these disparate groups still sing eland music.

Interestingly, during the eland dance that the women perform at this time, they dance naked except for front aprons, with strings of ostrich eggshell beads draped over their buttocks to represent elands' tails, the part that would be seized by a hunter-runner.

During the menarchal rite, the women also represent the sound of an eland by clapping bits of metal together. A mature bull eland and possibly an old cow eland, the very animals that would have been chased by the earliest hunters, produce just such a clicking sound. Other antelopes, including younger elands, do not make the sound. (Reindeer make a similar sound, as a tendon snaps over the pastern, but reindeer don't belong in this story.) How the elands produce the sound isn't known, but it is presumed to be made by a tendon snapping over the carpal joint.[5] The scholars who know about music don't know about animals, and the scholars who know about animals don't know about music, hence interesting little facts such as the clicking sound being exclusive to the biggest, heaviest elands sometimes aren't brought to light.

Is there significance in the fact that the menarchal eland is a bull? Yes, but because of its size, not its masculinity. To us, of course, almost any kind of bull symbolizes the ultimate male, the phallus, and all that. But the bull-as-phallus has an agricultural aura and doesn't seem to have struck the hunter-gatherers. Large bull elands almost certainly inspired menarchal music because elands have fat in their bodies, and large bull elands have the most fat. So, rather than suggesting masculinity, the bull eland suggests that after the menarche, the woman will find fat, will live in plenty, and will not starve.

Even so, there is a connection between the eland and human fertility, because, of course, very thin, starving women don't menstruate and also don't conceive. Then, too, there is a connection between fat and sexuality, as body fat contributes to a woman's beauty. This might be hard for many Western people to understand, but that is because most Western people do not live with hunger. A group of stories collected by the folklorist and anthropologist Megan Biesele reveals the concepts of female beauty and desirability. The stories concern two sisters, a python and a jackal. Of the two, the python with her smooth, well-rounded body is the beauty. She is serene and slow moving, as are pythons—eating, as they do, rarely but heavily—and as a person might be who is well fed and secure. (Interestingly, the python and the elephant can be interchangeable in stories—the elephant also being fat and confident.) The jackal sister is just the opposite, thin and nervous, with a harsh voice and dry, scruffy hair, as someone might be who eats mice and the scraps left by others and therefore would seem to be chronically hungry, like jackals. The well-fed python sister is good, and the raucous, hungry jackal sister is bad, because extreme thinness is almost stigmatic to the Ju/wasi and can be a symptom of laziness and other failures. The stories end with the thin jackal sister dead and the fat python sister married to a large bird called a paouw or greater kori bustard, whom the jackal sister had also wanted for a husband.[6]

Still, it is hard to imagine a menarchal rite without a male image involved somewhere. Virile young men are excluded from these rites, but old men attend them, holding up sticks to represent eland horns and jokingly approaching the women, who ignore them and keep on singing. Would a menarchal rite have been a good occasion, in the distant past, for a virile man to be infibulated?

As has been said, elands do not limit themselves to home ranges. They don't have to worry about poaching the grass on the range of other elands but can go anywhere they like. This means that at any given time of the year, they can be found wherever the food supply is most productive. They tend to browse, but they relish new green grass, both preferences due to moisture, and they converge in large numbers where new grass is growing. Herds of one hundred or more grazing elands have been noted, not necessarily in the Kalahari, but in other parts of Africa.

This means that one way to find elands and all the large antelopes is to find green grass. And during the dry season, when our distant ancestors most needed the meat, green grass would have been found only where a rare, unseasonal rainstorm had produced it, or where a wildfire had burned off the dry grass. After a fire, new green grass grows to replace the burned grass, no matter what the season. In the dry season, antelopes watch the sky for unseasonal rainstorms, for heat lightning, which is a common cause of wildfires, and also for smoke, which indicates a wildfire. The animals would know that green grass might soon be in those places. Our ancestors surely knew that, too, and realized that after the green grass grew, they would find antelopes there.

In the 1950s, the Ju/wasi burned dry grass to encourage the growth of green grass. This, interestingly, was virtually the only way they manipulated the environment. Sometimes when the Ju/wasi passed a wildfire they would take a branch and spread the flames around a bit. In other places that had not burned for a while, they might set a new fire. Certainly, our ancestors had done the same. When did we begin to do it? Possibly around the time that we became big-game hunters.

In my opinion, many things come together around the likelihood that our very distant ancestors set grass fires to help their hunting, whether by running or with weapons. In dry times, our ancestors would have gathered around a source of water, putting heavy demand on the plant foods. And they would have wanted meat. Even chimpanzees seem to want meat. Also the dry, yellow grass would then be extremely flammable. Our ancestors would have known that large antelopes would arrive if fresh grass replaced the dry grass. All these things point to the possibility that our ancestors were setting grass fires before they used fire for anything else.

We didn't need fire for warmth any more than the animals did. The climate was mostly warm or hot, and we would have endured the cold times just as the Ju/wasi did in the cold season when their firewood supplies were low. Nor did we need fire for cooking because, like other animals, we ate our food raw as we had always done. And we probably didn't see fire as a defense against predators, because the sight of a savannah fire isn't frightening, and neither we nor the predators would have feared it. Fire on the open savannah is nothing like fire in a dry forest, where we might have been terrified of it—at first a flash of lightning, then the smell of smoke, and suddenly an inferno all around us, with roaring flames leaping from tree to tree faster than most of us could run. But fires on the sparse savannah are hardly worth noticing. Unless the fire reaches a heavy thicket, it has little more than grass to burn and therefore is not very hot. We could easily have avoided a fire in a thicket, and we would have treated a grass fire just as the animals did—we would have walked around it or waited for it to burn low, and then stepped over it. On the savannah, only the smallest animals fear wildfires, and birds are attracted to them. When birds see the smoke of a grass fire they fly right to it to catch the insects that are jumping out.

New developments such as hunting big game spur further developments to enhance success. There we were, all of us, camped somewhere near water at the height of the hot season, hungry, thin, and tired, traveling farther on every search for food. We would think with longing about elands, so big, with so much meat and fat. We might also have looked upon the dry-season grass with much regret, knowing that somewhere there could be fresh grass that elands and other antelopes were eating. We might have seen in our imaginations the big herds of one hundred or more elands. Even one or two elands would have been a welcome sight. We might have wished that fresh grass was growing at a place that we knew about, so that elands and other antelopes would be where we could find them. We might have watched the horizon for signs of smoke. We might have wished that we could cause lightning. Maybe we sang some songs or offered some prayers to bring lightning. Maybe these were not effective.

Meanwhile, we would have known that certain things have fire in them. We would have known that sparks jump out of rocks when you smash them together and flame comes out of wood when you heat it in a grass fire, just as heat rises in your skin when you rub it—the harder you rub, the hotter you feel. If you rub your hands together fast, you quickly see how hot they get. And if you put a stick between your hands, all you need is something underneath it so it won't bore a hole in the ground. Soon, smoke rises. There you have it.

That was how the Ju/wasi made fire. They used two sticks about twenty-five inches long, one of hardwood with a pointed end (the male stick) and one of softwood with a notch for tinder (the female stick). The fire maker would pin the female stick under his foot, set the point of the male stick in the notch with the tinder, and roll it between his palms until smoke rose and fire started. If another man set his hands at the top of the stick as the first man's hands reached the bottom, the rolling never stopped and fire came more quickly.

Although fire has been on earth ever since there was something to burn, our use of it has not been dated. At present, it is suggested that fire was first controlled by early *Homo erectus* about 1.6 million years ago, but this is from archaeological evidence that suggests hearths and perhaps cooking. In contrast, burning dry grass to encourage green grass would leave no archaeological evidence yet would be a simple and natural step to evolve from hunting antelopes.

The Ju/wasi told a story about the control of fire. The story has to do with cooking. In "The Raw and the Stolen," Richard Wrangham and his coauthors discuss the food-preparation practices of our ancestors, pointing out that cooking has enabled our species to extract more nourishment from food and allowed us to reduce our tooth and jaw size, perhaps leaving more room for our much-touted brains. Also, cooking may have profoundly rearranged our social systems by giving women increased access to nourishment, among other things.[7] Perhaps, then, it is not surprising that a story about fire should focus on cooking, because cooking, much more than the encouragement of green grass, was to become an integral part of our existence.

Long ago, according to the story, only one person had fire, a man named Kai /Kani. One day a god came by and saw Kai /Kani's children eating cooked food. They gave him some. He found it tasty and became angry that he and everyone else had to eat raw food. So he spied on Kai /Kani and saw him make fire by twirling one stick against another, repeating to himself, "Fire will come. Fire will come." Soon enough, fire came, and Kai /Kani cooked more food. So the god played a trick on Kai /Kani, persuading him to play a game that lured him far away. When Kai /Kani was far enough, the god ran to the place where the fire sticks were hidden, broke them into many little pieces, and threw them over the whole world, crying, "All the world will now have fire!" When Kai /Kani saw what was happening, he came back from the game. The god told him, "It is not right that you alone should have fire. From now on you will not be a person." And the god changed him into a small bird. Since then, fire is in every tree. People can get the fire out of wood and cook their food with it.

Such was our Pleistocene experience. We lived in groups; we could dig roots; we could find water; we could catch grubs, snails, tortoises, porcupines, and other small animals that were not fast runners (sometimes called "slow game"); some of us could run down large antelopes; and we had fire. We had lived on the savannah for a million years. During that time the world got warm again and wetter, and some of the rain forests returned. But for us it was too late. By then we knew how to live only on the savannah.

We could still climb trees, but we did not go back.

4

The Kalahari

It seems ironic to use the word *explore* to describe one's travels where people have been living since the Upper Paleolithic, and probably long before that. Suffice it to say that before the 1950s few outsiders had ever penetrated the interior, and those few kept right on going. None had settled there to interfere with the ecological balance, which remained as pure as any on the planet, as pure as the planet itself until the end of the Paleolithic. The ecology of that untouched interior included hundreds of thousands of indigenous plant and animal species, one of which was of course our own, the capable and fascinating Kalahari hunter-gatherers, who were known as . . . as what?

The five groups of Bushmen, each speaking a distinct language, had no collective name for themselves. This was one of the ancient features of their culture, deriving from the time when each little population of people, isolated from its neighbors by topography and territorial requirements, saw the people of other groups almost as if they were dangerous animals and felt nothing in common with them. The Kalahari hunter-gatherers were not, of course, alone in this opinion; the attitude is found throughout the world and holds that members of one's own group are the human beings while other people are less

My mother and an interpreter, Ledimo, talk with the Ju/wasi. I listen.
Note how the shape the group has taken conforms with the
shadow of the overhanging tree.

so. Many ethnic names (names such as Navajo and Bantu, for instance) mean exactly that: "the people."

Such was the way of the people we visited, the Ju/wasi. Their name for themselves, *ju*, means "person"; the suffix *si* makes the word plural, and /*wa* (also spelled /'*hoan*) has been translated as "just," as in "simply" or "only," also "worthwhile," "clean," or "pure," as water is pure if nothing bad is floating in it; also "right," "correct," and "harmless," as someone might be who shows his empty hands and says "*Mi /wa*" (I'm clean, I'm harmless) to indicate that he doesn't have a weapon.

Meanwhile, it also seems to be a universal truth that if we name other people at all, we name them pejoratively. In the past, the Ju/wasi saw no special similarity between themselves and the other groups of small-sized, brown-skinned hunter-gatherers who spoke related languages and lived on the savannah. On the contrary, although they were surely familiar with the names of the other groups, the Ju/wasi were inclined to call the other people *ju dole*, which means "bad person." (Although, like /*wa*, the word *dole* has other implications; when used in *ju dole*, it is pejorative.) The !Kung language spoken by the Ju/wasi had no generalized name that could include any group but their own.

Over time, some of the southern African grasslands were penetrated by Bantu pastoralists[1] with their herds of livestock, and after that, by English, German, and Dutch colonials, who probably first arrived as ivory hunters.[2] To all of these newcomers, African and European alike, the hunter-gatherers with their click languages must have seemed pretty much the same. If the various groups of hunter-gatherers failed to note their similarities, the Europeans and Bantus failed to note their differences, and called them all Bushmen or Basarawa or Bakalahari, or variants thereof, all names more or less pejorative, as would be the normal nature of any name that any one group of people gives to any other.

Not surprisingly, the Ju/wasi did not do much better when they tried to find a name for the Bantu and European newcomers. Just as the newcomers did not distinguish one group of Bushmen from another, so the Ju/wasi did not distinguish among the newcomers, and, after designating them as "red people" (*ju-s-a-!gaa*, or /*hu*, the so-called whites) and "black people" (*ju-s-a-djo*), they lumped them together with the predators, calling all of them, very simply, *!xohmi*, the word that they would use for lions or hyenas, meaning, interestingly enough, that like the lions and hyenas, the newcomers had no hooves. *!Xohmi* could possibly be translated as "nonungulates." To the Ju/wasi, the worthy beings of the earth were the Ju/wasi and the hoofed animals they hunted.

Meanwhile, another group of former hunter-gatherers, the Khoikhoi (formerly known to Europeans by the pejorative name of Hottentots, that is, "stutterers"), whose language, Nama, was related to the five Bushman languages, had acquired cattle and other livestock. This resulted from the arrival of the white and Bantu settlers, when many of the Khoikhoi gave up the old lifestyle of the savannah and began to farm. The Khoikhoi had a pejorative word in their language, *san*, to describe people who lived without farms or livestock—the word for people who lived in the bush and ate food off the ground. Anyone could be *san* if the description fit, and the Bushmen fit perfectly. Thus the Khoikhoi pejoratively called the Bushmen *san*.

Then along came the anthropologist Isaak Schapera to study the Khoikhoi. He chose to use the term *san* for the Bushmen just as his Khoi informants were doing, and he popularized a term of his own, *Khoisan*, for the speakers of these particular southern African click languages. Following his lead (but long after we began our work there) came anthropologists belonging to the Harvard Kalahari Research Group, sometimes called the Harvard Group, who also began to call the Bushmen the San, of course with the aim of honoring them and removing from them any possible stigma inherent in "bush." Then, too, these anthropologists liked the fact that the name San has no suggestion of gender, or male dominance, that once so comfortably fit our patriarchal concepts. The Kalahari hunter-gatherers had an egalitarian society, where the rights of women were equal to those of men. Still, the idea that a gender problem exists in the name Bushman comes from us and our own notions of gender and political correctness. To change the name satisfies the needs of our society, no matter how remote those needs might have seemed to the Bushmen. Unlike us, they lacked male supremacy in their culture and did not need to counteract it. In contrast, the concept of poverty and back-country squalor implied by the name San comes from a large group of people who live beside and among the Bushmen, and applies to anyone who fits the description.

The plan to follow the anthropologists and the Khoikhoi in calling the Bushmen the San had great success in Europe and North America, where San became politically correct and now seems standard in academic circles. But it did not catch on in Namibia or Botswana, where the Khoikhoi and the Bushmen live side by side, and where the Bushmen could have felt the stigma inherent in "san" even if the academics didn't. According to the anthropologist Robert Gordon, who is from Namibia, the word *san* is derived from the Nama word *sonqua*, which means "bandits," and would refer to stock theft when the groups collided. Dr. Gordon writes, "Contemporary use of the term San appears to be restricted to [Khoi] Nama speakers in Namibia, and its continued use by academics serves to further mystify the tragic situation of those labeled 'Bushmen.' In Namibia, everybody uses the term 'Bushmen.'"[3]

It was Hobson's choice, really. Are we going to call ourselves "The People Who Live in the Woods, in the Bushes"? Or will we be "The People Too Poor to Have Livestock Who Eat off the Ground"? Supposedly some former hunter-gatherers at a conference formally adopted the name San for their people, but evidently they did so without general consensus, because, as Dr. Gordon said, most Bushmen, especially those in the hinterlands, continue to call themselves Bushmen when they refer to themselves collectively.

The name Bushman eventually acquired panache. By the time I revisited the people in the 1980s, some had begun to own cattle, including an enormous white bull with long, curved horns whose testicles hung almost to his knees and whose bellowing voice could have been the Minotaur's, it was so thunderous. A more macho animal would be hard to imagine. His massive sides were scarred by the claws of lions who tried from time to time to kill some of his cows. The bull fought off each attack, shaking off the lions who clung to him and chasing them away from his harem. His owner was understandably proud of him and had honored his people as well as the bull by naming him Bushman.

. . . .

My family made many journeys to visit the Kalahari hunter-gatherers. Most of our time was spent with Ju/wa Bushmen, but we also spent time with /Gwi Bushmen, another language group living close to the Botswana border. Between 1950 and 1955, I made three visits and spent a total of two years (plus other visits later), but the rest of my family lived for many more years among the Bushmen, and my brother was to devote his life to their well-being.

It was my father, a civil engineer and retired president of Raytheon, the electronics company he had founded, who conceived of these expeditions. Never particularly conventional, he wanted to take his family to a part of the world that had not been explored. Born in 1889 to a farming family in Canada (he was born in the United States, but the family was in Canada), my father belonged among the frontier types who didn't like to see the smoke of their neighbor's chimney, and the idea of an enormous, pristine wilderness appealed to him strongly. To him, nothing was impossible, certainly not a project like penetrating an unexplored waterless wilderness all on his own, so he organized the expeditions, financed them, and led them, planning them so thoroughly and so expertly that no harm ever came to any of us, although we were often a month's travel and several hundred miles from the nearest outpost of the so-called civilized world, from any doctor or hospital, from any mechanic or spare auto part or source of gasoline, or from any known source of water.[4] We had no radio, so no contact with anyone outside. To whom would we appeal for help? The days when a helicopter would appear in the sky to lift you out of your difficulty had yet to come. Anyway, in those days there were no helicopters. Astronauts have a better chance of rescue than we did in the 1950s in the Kalahari, even though, if things go wrong, an astronaut's chances of rescue are not good. When it came to rescue, we were, in short, in the same situation that the Bushmen had been in for the past thirty-five thousand years. There was no "rescue." Our well-being was up to us.

But then, like the Bushmen, people like my father don't need to be rescued. Although we were far from medical care and spare auto parts, we were never far from food, or he wasn't. He brought to our project many useful skills, among them the ability to find his way anywhere and make a fire with wet wood using just one match—a skill that he insisted my brother and I also learn—and he was an excellent shot. He'd see a small object in the distance, recognize it as an antelope, reach for the rifle, *bang*, *flop*, and he'd go get the meat. (He made nothing of these skills, however, and because he was my wonderful father who could do anything, I took his abilities completely for granted. All men had them, I assumed. I soon realized that this was far from true, but not until after his death did it occur to me to wonder where he'd acquired these abilities. In his youth he'd had friends in the Micmac nation and spent time with them in the Canadian woods. He taught me and my brother certain soft-spoken phrases in Micmac with which, should the need arise, we could communicate with the Micmac about moose, so I suspect he had done a little hunting before he met my mother, who protected all animals, including earthworms and flies.)

From time to time, other people came with us—a photographer, a botanist, a zoologist, a musicologist, an archaeologist, a government official from Windhoek, a man who had traveled in the Kalahari to immunize people from smallpox, also a camp manager, a mechanic, and interpreters, including a wonderful young Bushman man named /Gani, who was with us almost from the start, and another wonderful young Tswana man named Kernel Ledimo, who had grown up among Ju/wasi at his father's cattle camp but had also gone to school and so was fluent in several languages, including English. He also spoke some German.[5]

Interestingly, no anthropologist wanted to join us, although my father tried hard to find one and would have paid his or her salary and all expenses. However, unlike the modern Kalahari, where the anthropologist/Bushman ratio often seems to be one to one, in those days no anthropologist took an interest in our project. The main task of learning the ways of the Ju/wasi thus fell to my mother, a former ballerina, later an English teacher at Mount Holyoke, who had no anthropological training whatever. But she persevered and eventually published a series of peer-reviewed papers in academic journals and also two scholarly books about the Ju/wasi, who came to like her so much that, in time, baby girls born in and near the Kalahari were being named Lorna or Norna. Reviewing her first book, *The !Kung of Nyae Nyae*, for the journal *Africa*, the anthropologist

. . . .

Alan Barnard wrote that "Lorna Marshall is one of the most sensitive, meticulous and unpretentious ethnographers of all time."[6]

She subsequently became known in academic circles as the grande dame of hunter-gatherer anthropology, complete with Festschriften in her honor and honorary doctorate degrees from prestigious universities, and, in the course of events, was commemorated by impressive obituaries with photographs in such important publications as *The New York Times.* A very moving story by Sy Montgomery was broadcast on National Public Radio telling how Lorna gave water to African bees, who swarmed by the thousands over her hands and arms when she began to wash her face in a basin. Moved by the desperate thirst of the bees, she floated little rafts of wood in the basin for them to stand on so they wouldn't crowd one another into the water, and she rescued those who fell in so that they wouldn't drown—all this with her arms almost hidden in bees. We also received a proposal from a well-known Hollywood producer for a film about her starring Jodie Foster.

(My brother and I were doubtful. We wondered if the producer truly envisioned, as he seemed to claim, a film about a middle-aged married woman doing scholarly research for an ethnographic monograph. We suspected white hunters and sexual peccadilloes, or, worse yet, ourselves portrayed as problem teenagers. We managed to suppress the film, even though that meant we wouldn't get to meet Jodie Foster.)

But all that came later.

While I was in the Kalahari, I took notes and kept journals and later wrote a travel book, *The Harmless People*, in which I tried to describe the delicate perfection of the enormous, pristine wilderness that the Ju/wasi knew so well. I wanted to give some account of their fascinating lifestyle and combat some of the overwhelming prejudices that then existed about them, because the Khoikhoi were not alone in seeing them as *san*. The white people agreed that they were lowly—they had no money, they didn't wear nice clothes, they had no dishes or furniture, they couldn't read and write, they didn't go to church or get married (meaning that the brides didn't wear white dresses and blue garters—I was once instructed to use the word *mate* for hunter-gatherer marriage), and they didn't want to work on white people's farms. Many non-Bushmen considered them dangerous. We were told that they would kill us from ambush with poison arrows, and we'd never even see who shot us. Fear of their poison arrows had much to do with the failure to map the Kalahari.

One didn't need to be in South Africa to hear these views. I heard them expressed in my hometown of Cambridge, where the average Harvard professor thought very little of the Bushmen. A famous architect and professor of art history once called them "monkeys" to my then-young face, while humorously scratching himself under the arms. Not many yards from his large and well-appointed Cambridge living room flowed the Charles River with its unsightly flotillas of raw sewage that in those days was discharged by the towns along its banks. The sewage gave off an odor to which the professor had become accustomed and didn't seem to mind. But having recently come from the dry savannah, I was seeing any source of water with new eyes and found the condition of the river disturbing. The Bushmen might not have had the benefit of Harvard educations, but at least they knew better than to put feces in their water, a refinement they shared with many animals. I hoped that from reading my book, some of my own people, such as the abovementioned professor, would realize that if they were compared to the Bushmen, they would not necessarily come out ahead. I hope I did right by that.

I made an important mistake in that book, however. I said that the Bushmen had been driven into the Kalahari by more powerful people, the Bantu pastoralists and the European farmers who wanted all the good land. This was the going theory at the time and seemed reasonable to me, at age nineteen, because in my experience everyone came from somewhere else, and also the Kalahari was a really tough place to make a living. I wasn't surprised to hear that no one lived there voluntarily.

But the theory was wrong, as the Bushmen themselves had tried to tell us. They said that their people had lived in the Kalahari since time began. At first I didn't take this at face value because they couldn't read, whereas I was in college. Printed material held that the Bushmen had been driven into the Kalahari and I, for one, didn't doubt it. Not surprisingly, however, scientific research was later to

. . . .

prove the Bushmen right and showed that people had indeed "always" lived in the Kalahari or, at the very least, had been there since the Upper Paleolithic and perhaps much longer, which also meant, of course, that Bushmen had also been living in the border areas of the Kalahari that the more powerful outsiders took as farms. Far from evicting all the local Bushmen, or most of them, the outsiders pressed them into service as unpaid laborers. If an area taken by a farmer had no resident Bushmen, or if they had escaped, farmers raided into the interior and captured Bushmen as slaves, sometimes taking the children, knowing that their parents would follow the tracks of the vehicles to get their children back. When this happened, the parents, too, were captured. The Bushmen taken by farmers became like the serfs of Europe, bound to the land, working for a foreign landowner whose life was as remote from theirs as the life of the colonizing farmer was from that of the Bushmen.

If Bushmen lived on the land a farmer was taking, the process of enslavement used by the farmers was also similar to that used by the European aristocrats (but possibly more brutal). The settler would appropriate a large piece of land, intending to make it his farm. The Bushmen who lived there would know nothing of his plans or, for that matter, of the settler himself. To their surprise he would suddenly appear and might try to chase them off as he would chase off wild animals, or he might try to press them into service, serf-style. Like the serfs, they had little choice. They needed food and water, and they couldn't just go somewhere else. For many Bushmen, there was no "somewhere else." Some people resisted, of course, but were quickly eliminated, usually by vigilante action on the part of the farmers because, in this newly opened country, a frontier atmosphere prevailed, and the laws of the colonizing powers meant little or nothing. Some white settlers even found sport in hunting Bushmen, hiding in hunting blinds near waterholes and shooting the Bushmen who came to drink.

Most Bushmen who were taken as slaves or whose land was taken over by farmers had no choice but to work on the farms. As the cattle displaced the wild game, as the farmer's livestock grazed the wild plants down to the sand, the food supply of the Bushmen would be decimated, and the former hunter-gatherers would have to work for food. The farmer would give them some rags of clothing

. . . .

5 2

and a ration of cornmeal but little else, unless a farm animal died, in which case, the Bushmen and the farm dogs could share the carcass.

The Bushmen of these farms were robbed of their world, where they had been at the top, and were dragged into our world at the bottom. The Bushmen of the interior, in contrast, still had their world—the world that, as an indigenous species, they had helped to form. It was the earlier world that we wanted to know, so we went to the interior to find them.

5

The Search

With a jeep as a pathfinder, a Dodge Power Wagon, and two army 6 × 6 trucks to follow, we loaded all our gasoline and water, our medical supplies, tools, food, and camping equipment, and enough spare parts to make another vehicle, and were ready to travel. There were about ten or twelve of us, including two mechanics and a man from the government in Windhoek. The government found it hard to believe that anyone would travel so far and go to such trouble and expense just to talk with a few Bushmen, and wanted to be sure that we were not prospecting for diamonds. (Months later, reassured, the official returned to Windhoek with my father, who made a trip out for supplies.)

We began our search by visiting outlying farms. Through our interpreters we interviewed Bushman farmworkers, especially the people whom the farmers called "wild Bushmen." The farmworkers knew of several possible places in the interior where groups of Ju/wa Bushmen might be living. Two of the farmworkers agreed to guide us to these places. The farmer agreed to let them come, and we were ready.

It was the month of July, and winter was starting—dry and warm in the daytime, dry and very cold at night. We left the last farm on a cart track that we followed into the bush until it vanished. Then we went forward, plowing through heavy brush, grinding over sand dunes. In about three weeks we had traveled two hundred miles.

"We are making a 200-mile trek through country in which there is no water," wrote my mother in her journal. "The trucks lurch and jounce violently. We find it best to stand up in the backs of the trucks all day holding on to the side. We climbed a ridge in the trucks, pushing right through the brush. I was impressed. I had heard about doing this, and had imagined it to a degree but not fully. We roared straight ahead, plowing down shrubs and brush higher than the trucks." Farther on, she writes, "Everything that grows here, it seems, has a thorn. You are heaved up into the air by a lurching truck, thorns sift under you, you crash down on them. Little ones work under your clothes, and there they are at night." She adds the following thought: "Fascinating quality of humanity, this undertaking of any amount of hardship, struggle, and danger, to come into country like this. Some men have made such trips for diamonds. Sometimes it has been gold that has lured men. For us it is Bushmen."

As her journal demonstrates, the going was rough. We tried to be careful, but often enough we would puncture a tire or break a spring, and we would stop to make repairs. When grass seeds plugged the radiator grills and caused the radiators to boil, spilling our precious water, we would stop to clean the grills with a metal brush and pour in more water. When we camped at night, I would push grass seeds out of the radiator grills with a readily available three-inch acacia thorn. The sandy stretches were difficult, too—we tried to find ways around them but couldn't always, and the trucks sank in up to the axles. The hotter the day and the softer the sand, the more likely we were to get stuck, which meant that in the hottest times of day we would be digging out the wheels and shoving brush and branches under them. Sometimes we could use our winch, but sometimes we all got behind the truck and pushed with all our might while the driver gunned the motor and the spinning wheels threw sand in our faces.

As we went, we looked for signs of people. The following is from my diary:

It was very cold last night. The south wind blew from the Antarctic all night long, sweeping the haze out of the sky, leaving the brilliant, hard, white moon. We moved on shortly after dawn, through this gorgeous dry rolling veld, by little forests, over outcrops of rock. We went through valleys and burned areas, and over plains so long you could see the trees in the haze miles away, like a distant shore, until we came to a dry pan where we hoped to find people. We found no people's footprints on the edge of the pan. A little way into the veld, which here is yellow pinkish grass like old bloodstains, we found high spring bushes with karu vines on them. We then walked all around the pan and found high ant heaps all grown over in a tangle with bushes. We climbed the ant heaps and looked around. And we found a tree full of weaverbirds' nests swinging in the wind but all empty, and we found a shoulder blade, all white, bleached and dry, of some large antelope. We even saw a little round mouse nest, also empty, hanging from the branch of a thornbush. We walked farther but found no signs of people, so we got back in the vehicles and drove for the rest of the day down a series of vast, long, narrow plains. There we saw the smoke of a veld fire on the horizon which might have been lit by people, so we left the plain and drove toward it, through heavy, low thornbush, until we reached the fire. We found a way through the wall of flames and found our way to the source, where we looked for a sign of what set the fire, but the burned area is very large and it is hard to be sure. The fire has run on and on and is now far away against the evening sun like the smoke from a train traveling away. It is very quiet and lonely here. We called for people but there is no answer. We have searched through about 100 square miles of veld and tomorrow we will search some more.

We slept all night under the frosty moon. We got up from time to time to feed the fire, and when it got light we cooked the remainder of last night's meat. When we woke we could see our breath, but when the sun came, it suddenly got warmer. We are on a rise of ground and you can literally see for miles. A range of mountains, which are about 13 in number, are far away on one side, and on the other, towards the south, the land falls

My mother and me and the truck that brought us to Nyae Nyae

*away and away and away, down and down, much farther than
anything I have ever seen before, until all the trees are ob-
scured, on and on, until the horizon looks like the ocean seen
from miles away, just a blue line a little darker and hazier than
the sky.*

The waterholes of the Kalahari are far from obvious. Wherever
we went, we looked for signs of water. A source of water would not
only have helped us to replenish our supply, but also would show us
that we were in an area where we might find people. My father
looked for baobab trees, which often grow near underground ledges
that hold rainwater. He also looked for small areas of green grass
among the dry, yellow grass bordering the large clay flats or pans.
Our aim, however, was to find a place called /Gam, which was
known to have water, so we didn't spend time (meanwhile using up
our water) making a thorough search. Our guides had difficulty
finding a way because, as they said, everything seemed different
when riding in a vehicle. They would have had an easier time if they
could have gone on foot.

Eventually, although we still had several hundred gallons of water in barrels in the backs of the trucks, my father rationed us to one
cup of water a day. We could wash in it first if we liked, he told us.
Knowing him, I am sure he had a point of no return in mind—when
we had used half the water, we would turn back, get more water, and
try again. His rationing was intended to postpone that moment. We
did not find water along the way, but because of his precaution we
still had enough when we arrived at a little place at the base of a
rocky outcrop where, deep in the sand, fresh water filled a hand-dug
hole perhaps two feet wide. This was /Gam. We were glad. Even so,
we would have had enough water to backtrack ourselves to our
starting point if, for any reason, we hadn't found /Gam. Those who
traveled with my father might have been a little dusty, but their
bones didn't bleach in the Kalahari sun.

Our guides had known about /Gam from other Bushmen. At /Gam,
a wealthy Tswana rancher kept about twenty head of cattle. The
rancher himself lived far away in the Bechuanaland protectorate

(now Botswana) but, having learned of the waterhole at /Gam from his Bushman serfs, he had divided his large herd into smaller herds and pastured one of these at /Gam, putting his relatives in charge.

In the past, the year-round waterhole of /Gam had supplied its original owners, a small family band of Ju/wasi. They, of course, lived in the Old Way, by hunting and gathering. The water at /Gam had been their water, their dry season source of supply. One of these people later told me about the arrival of the cattle. She said that late one afternoon they heard cattle bellowing, then saw a herd of cattle approaching from the east through the dry grass, necks stretched, hurrying toward the water. Behind them were some *ju-s-a-djo*, black people—two men, a boy, and a woman with a baby—driving before them a herd of goats and followed by two donkeys whose loads held, among other things, pottery jars with chickens in them, heads down. Evidently a chicken in this position doesn't know how to help herself and stays put. The men wore shorts and shirts and the woman wore a long, high-waisted dress and head scarf, the traditional costume of many African women, especially those in southern Africa, first adapted from the early Dutch settlers. The cattle had traveled many days without water and were critically thirsty. Crowding around the waterhole, they pushed one another for a place to drink.

Like most other farmers and pastoralists, the Tswana family saw no reason why the Ju/wasi of /Gam shouldn't let them use the water. The Tswana family spoke a little !Kung, having lived with Ju/wasi on the Bechuanaland side of the border, where, years earlier, the Bantu pastoralists had taken over Bushman lands, Bushmen and all, just as the white farmers had done in South West Africa. The Tswana family would have learned !Kung from their Bushman serfs. Perhaps they asked permission of the Ju/wasi at /Gam to use the water. Perhaps the Ju/wasi gave permission just as, later in our travels, other Ju/wasi at other waterholes gave us permission. The Ju/wasi were generous and empathetic, and also were intimidated by the farmers and pastoralists at the far edges of their land. They would not have wanted to refuse.

All we knew was that by the time we came to /Gam, the Tswana people were in charge. It was they who courteously gave us permission to camp and also to refill our water drums. They also invited us to stay and rest from our travels. We accepted gratefully.

. . . .

/Gam was pleasant, tucked under the north side of a low ridge, facing the winter sun. At a reasonable distance from the waterhole, the Tswana family had built three substantial little huts with grass thatches and had made a nice chair and a table with wood from the little local trees. Beyond the tiny village was the cattle pen, around which scratched the hens and a rooster. A skeletal dog would emerge from the bushes from time to time and try to snatch the one of the hens, never successfully, because the rooster was aggressive and always fought him off while one of the people threw stones at the dog. The starving dog would slink back to the bushes and wait to try later.

The Tswana family was very good to us—the young wife was a gentle, kindly woman of about my age. She was Herero, not Tswana, and her name was Kavesitjue, which means "Submission to the Will of God"—a concept that may have come from Christian missionaries or perhaps from Islam, a word that also means "Submission to the Will of God," although Islam was not a strong presence in southern Africa in those days. We both spoke a little broken Afrikaans, and with no more than this we became friends. We both had pierced ears and became involved with safety pin earrings. At /Gam, I was given the name of Kothonjoro. I am not sure who named me, but Kavesitjue told me that it was a name for a person who laughs. She said that although I was always laughing, my heart was sad. That might have been true. I missed my boyfriend, later my husband. Kavesitjue's heart might also have been sad. A woman alone, with only men and a boy for company, she was far from her mother and sisters, her family and friends, out there in the back of beyond, and I know she was lonely. I gladly would have stayed at /Gam and pursued my friendship with this interesting person, but my father decided to move on. As far as our work was concerned, it was not a good place, he felt. To live among hunter-gatherers was our goal, and the presence of cattle, a dog, and other relics of the world beyond the savannah could not help but affect the lifestyle of the Ju/wasi.

He was right. It is not possible for true hunter-gatherer life to take place in an agricultural or otherwise developed setting, if only because, in one way or another, the presence of domestic animals (and, to a lesser degree, domestic plants) greatly affects the local plants and wild animals. Perhaps the culture of the Ju/wasi themselves would not be affected by a pastoral setting, but then again, perhaps it would. Few people realize the significance of an environmental setting to those whose survival is governed by it, but my father did. Context was too important to ignore.

But where would we find other people? We wanted to ask advice from the Ju/wasi at /Gam—they who best knew the thousands of square miles of the Nyae Nyae interior. We asked around, but most of the people didn't answer. The reputation of white people had traveled even to /Gam, and they didn't trust us. Nor, I suspect, did they trust our Bushman guides and interpreters, who to them were *ju dole*, the bad people, not Ju/wasi, the pure, worthwhile, harmless people.

But then, one evening, two Ju/wa people, a man named /Kwi and his wife, //Kushe, walked into our camp to see us. /Kwi, we learned, was better known by his nickname, Lazy /Kwi, which turned out to be a joke name that he had given himself. Once when asked to join a hunt, he declined because he was sick. But not wanting to say that he was sick, he said he felt lazy. The name stuck. In reality he was an excellent, willing hunter, and very far from lazy.

That evening, he sat on his heels at our campfire, his hands cupped under his chin to shade his eyes from the firelight. From this shadow he watched us politely for a moment, waiting, then spoke through our interpreter to say that his wife, //Kushe, didn't like to stay at /Gam. To the north was another permanent waterhole, the place of her family. She was going there and he was going with her. He offered to lead us there.

We were encouraged. These two young people were clearly of the Old Way, very much the hunter-gatherers. Each just slightly more than five feet tall, they were brown skinned, short haired, slender, strong, and graceful. They had come in single file, the man first, and they stepped carefully. When they sat down they sat on their heels, knees up, legs folded tightly. Both were barefoot. Lazy /Kwi wore a simple loincloth made from a soft piece of leather, nothing more. //Kushe wore a small leather front apron, a small leather back apron, hair ornaments made of ostrich eggshell beads, and a large leather cape over her back, tied at the shoulder and around the waist to form a pouch, where, as we soon noticed, a baby was sleeping. The baby, about eighteen months old, wore a little necklace, a leather string with one bead.

We were grateful that Lazy /Kwi and //Kushe were willing to guide us. We gladly accepted their offer. They stayed for a little while, then stood up and left as quietly as they had come, and as we were packing our trucks in the morning, they came back with their things. Lazy /Kwi brought a hunting bag—the cured whole skin of a duiker tied off at the neck, open at the rump, with the forelegs tied to the hind legs as a double shoulder strap. In it were a short spear, a bow and a quiver of arrows, and a pair of fire sticks. His only child, the baby boy, rode astride his shoulder, holding on to his head. His wife walked quietly behind them carrying a digging stick—just a long, straight, peeled branch sharpened at one end. As she passed, I glanced into the pouch of her cape and saw the most wonderful things—two blown ostrich eggshells, still beaded with drops of water and stoppered with tight plugs of grass. These were her water bottles.

We had tents, cots, sleeping bags, folding chairs and tables, maps, a compass, cameras, film, recording equipment, reference books, notebooks, pens, ink, pencils, disinfectants, antivenin kits for snakebites, brandy, cases of canned foods, boxes of dry foods, dishes, cooking pots, frying pans, knives, forks, spoons, cigarettes, matches, spare tires, auto parts, inner tubes, tire patches, jacks, toolboxes, winches, motor oil, drums of gasoline, drums of water, bars of yellow soap, towels, washcloths, toothpaste, toothbrushes, coats, sweaters, pants, boots, sneakers, shirts, underwear, socks, reading glasses, safety pins, scissors, a sewing kit, binoculars, bullets, a rifle.

The Ju/wasi had sticks, skins, eggshells, grass.

This trip, too, seemed endless. We took turns driving. Everyone but the drivers rode on top of the trucks, where we had to duck overhanging thorn branches but hoped we would be cooler than in the cab. Lazy /Kwi and //Kushe had never ridden on a vehicle before and at first //Kushe was afraid. But Lazy /Kwi seemed confident enough, taking his cue from the rest of us, especially from our guides and interpreter. //Kushe took heart from him. They rode in silence, watch-

≠Toma returns from a foraging trip carrying a net lined with skin
and filled with nuts. A gathering party of men and women would walk for
several days over waterless country to pick clean the nut groves or the
groundnut patches and would carry home their harvest in big leather bags
that could hold from fifty to one hundred pounds of nuts.

ing the bush go by. We had been traveling for almost a month before we came to /Gam, and the scenery was much the same as it had been all along the journey. No animals showed themselves in the heat of the day, and with not much to see, the days became monotonous. Also the terrain was very rough. The trucks lurched horribly, giving us backaches, and although we went slowly we broke an axle when a truck dropped through an aardvark burrow, and we had to spend a night on the way while we replaced the axle. Thanks to my father, we had spare axles.

In the afternoon of the second day our vehicles lurched over a rise of ground and we saw before us a vast, shining salt flat ringed with low dry bush and yellow tussock grass. It was a pan from which the shallow water had evaporated, leaving the lake bed white and dry, stretching to the north and west for almost a mile. The lake bed or pan was the most conspicuous feature of the landscape—that, or else three baobab trees on its eastern rim, two of them about two thousand years old and one hundred feet high, both so big that five or six people together couldn't reach around them. But the most important feature was barely visible. Marked by a few green reeds below a rocky ledge in the southeast corner of the pan, it was the waterhole. We asked Lazy /Kwi if the place had a name, and he said, "/Gautscha."*

/Gautscha means "Place of Buffalo." At first I did not find this remarkable. Why wouldn't buffaloes live there? Kudus did, giraffes and ghemsboks, too, and so did duikers and steinboks. I didn't know at the time that the savannah antelopes did not need to drink water, or in other words were water independent, nor did I see all that much difference between the antelopes and buffaloes. Of course there could be buffaloes.

But my assumption was too hasty. Buffaloes didn't live there. Like most other animals, including elephants, rhinos, and zebras, buffaloes need to drink water fairly frequently. This means they need significant amounts of permanent surface water within reasonable distance of sustainable grazing. /Gautscha did not meet that description. So why the name?

When I was nineteen, everything that the Ju/wasi did or said

---

*Anthropologists and linguists spell this name /Aotcha. On paper, that looks like Ay-ot-sha, so I'm using a common anglicized version.

seemed wonderful. That a place without buffalo had been named for them anyway was fine with me. Probably the Ju/wasi just liked the name, I thought. But many years later it struck me as strange to name a place for an animal not found there. Could the name commemorate something?

People had hunted buffalo there, we later learned, on the very rare occasions that buffalo visited during the rains. But buffalo visited other places, too, also rarely. Besides, events that were even more unusual had taken place at /Gautscha, events fully as characteristic of the place as any of the buffalo visits, or more so. For instance, a line of pegs ran up one of the baobab trees, hammered in by the people to form a one-hundred-foot ladder from the top of which they could spot distant game. Twice, we were to learn, men had fallen to their deaths from this ladder. Few other places had baobab trees, and fewer still had ladders. So the incidents could almost have been unique to /Gautscha. Even so, /Gautscha was the Place of Buffalo, not the Place of the Baobab Ladder.

At last it struck me that the name /Gautscha could be old. But how old? The grassy, sandy bushveld plains of Nyae Nyae were bordered to the east and west by several long valleys, the dry beds of prehistoric rivers known as *omarambas*, which ran northeast for about three hundred miles to the Okavango River and its giant swamp. Over the millennia, the Kalahari has known successive climate phases, and at some time during the deep past (possibly prior to a cool, dry period eight thousand years ago), these rivers were running. Sustained rainfall sufficient to fill the rivers would have made an excellent habitat for the water-dependent elephants, zebras, and buffaloes. Ju/wasi were there at the time, watching these animals and hunting some of them.

Could a name continue for so long? !Kung is an ancient language and has even been called the First Language. Studies of genetic separation between the !Kung speakers and a population of former hunter-gatherers in Tanzania known as the Hadza, whose languages are very closely related, indicate that these two groups separated fifty thousand to one hundred thousand years ago. Since then, their genetic composition changed, but they kept their language. The research suggests, among other things, the extreme antiquity of !Kung.[1]

. . . .

The Western world has names such as Novgorod (meaning New Town), and Newcastle, although these places have not been new since the ninth and sixteenth centuries, respectively. The places are permanent, they have been in use without interruption, and their inhabitants don't change their names just because the adjective no longer applies. Quite possibly a similar rule applied to /Gautscha, and if so, a name from the ninth century could seem recent. Such was the stability of the Old Way.

We got out of our trucks, prepared to meet the /Gautscha people—the heirs to this tremendous antiquity. But it seemed that no one was around. I glanced about for Lazy /Kwi and //Kushe, but they had disappeared into the quiet, sunlit veld. "Gone to bush," said one of the interpreters uneasily when their absence was noted. He and our two guides would look over their shoulders from time to time, as if they thought that someone might be watching them. None of these men was from this area, and not all of them were Ju/wasi, so their presence might seem questionable. I, too, wondered if people might be watching us from a hiding place, yet I saw nothing but the veld, stretching away on all sides. Had we come so far to find nobody?

It was afternoon. Choosing a place within reasonable distance of the waterhole, we set up our camp. We were, after all, at a place where people were known to be living. Our guides said that people had been camping there previously, but they certainly weren't there at the moment. We considered the fact that unseasonal rain had fallen earlier, meaning that water might still be present in hollow trees and little soaks, and it came to us that the people could be living somewhere else in the veld and didn't yet need to come to the permanent water.

The thought was daunting. That night, we made plans to travel on, but first we would wait for a while in case Ju/wasi should be present. So we waited for two days while our guides and interpreters looked here and there without much enthusiasm. To learn if anything, such as smoke from a campfire, could be seen from higher up, I climbed the two-thousand-year-old baobab tree—so enormous that it took a long time just to walk around it and find a place to start the climb. The skin of the tree was smooth and grayish pink. Once up inside it, I found an entire little ecosystem in its massive branches—bird nests, bats in a hollow where a branch had fallen off, a tree snake, a beehive, and squirrels with greenish fur. Great, fuzzy, clublike fruits hung from the tips of the branches and a little ladder of pegs ran up the side—the ladder, we later learned, from which people could see distant game. I didn't climb the ladder, but from a branch not halfway up the tree I could see for miles, across the wide white pan and beyond, to the empty, rolling bushveld. But I didn't see the smoke from an encampment.

On the way back to our camp, however, I happened to notice something moving, and saw a small leather bag hanging from a string against an archlike empty space framed by grass and bushes. The little bag was swaying gently in a breeze. I was puzzling over this phenomenon when I saw that near our camp, two Ju/wa men were standing, speaking to my father and some of the rest of us through our interpreter. They were dressed like Lazy /Kwi in simple leather loincloths. Both were empty-handed, having left their bows and arrows behind to show their peaceful intentions.

If such a meeting could ever again be repeated in today's troubled world, someone surely would have been lurking in the bushes ready to let fly a poison arrow, with someone else crouching in the cab of a truck, aiming a rifle, ready to fire a shot. But such thoughts never entered our heads in those days, even though some of our group, someone such as myself, may have displayed a raised palm— our way of sending the peaceful message. Hello there. My hands are empty, at least this one is. We are harmless.

The shorter of the two men was doing the talking. His name, he told us, was ≠Toma. His manner was amiable, somewhat reserved but confident. He stood leaning back a bit with his feet slightly apart and his arms crossed, his hands in his armpits—the very picture of someone who is sure of himself and is informally considering a situation. The other, taller Ju/wa man seemed less confident. With his feet closer together, not planted apart like those of his companion, with his arms held stiffly at his sides, he added a word every now and then, but in a lower voice.

Of course I had no idea what either man was saying. At the time, I knew only a word or two of !Kung. But if I had been called upon to describe what these men were to each other, I would have said that the first man was the leader even though we already knew that the Ju/wasi didn't have chiefs or headmen. Still, he was a kind of leader, just the same. Unarmed, wearing only a loincloth, faced with vehicles for the first time in history, and worse yet, faced with a large group of strangers, not knowing what the vehicles were or why the strangers were standing there, not even knowing which of us were males and which were females, but knowing full well that white people were extremely bad news, he cordially, modestly, politely radiated the fact that he was in charge of the situation. Perhaps Lazy /Kwi and //Kushe, the couple from /Gam, had reassured him. Perhaps he was bluffing. Or perhaps he really was unafraid. The second man, his taller companion, glanced from us to him from time to time. He was relying on ≠Toma.

Through our interpreter, my father introduced us and explained what we were doing there, saying that we had learned of the Ju/wasi and wanted to know them. Would they allow us to camp nearby? Could we use the water? Could we talk with them in friendship?

We could, said ≠Toma. We could camp there and use the water. As for talking with us, he said he couldn't answer for others, but he would be glad to talk with us. The interpreter then asked the other man to tell his name, which he did. His name was Gao Feet. These two men, we later learned, were brothers-in-law. Their wives were sisters.

As we were speaking, we noticed that a few other people had quietly materialized and were sitting on their heels at a distance to listen. What they heard cannot have been encouraging. The government official, unfamiliar with recommended anthropological practices and fed up with our family's attempts at courtesy, was rudely ordering the two Ju/wa men to call in the rest of their people. He also told them where to place their camp. (Fortunately, the official later stood back—my father must have gotten to him.) The two men heard him out politely but did not leap to obey.

The rest of us meanwhile were watching the newcomers, noticing three young women, two of them with babies. We noticed an elderly woman wearing many necklaces of ostrich eggshell beads, and also a boy about fifteen years old who, when he stood up, hopped rather than walked, using a long stick as a crutch. Then two little boys, perhaps six and eight years old, appeared from among some bushes. (Almost thirty years later, one of these little boys, ≠Toma's eldest son, Tsamko, would say that the sound of the approaching vehicles had terrified him. The loud noise had sounded like lions.)[2] Behind them came a young girl about eight years old wearing strings of ostrich eggshell beads and ostrich eggshell hair ornaments. As all this took place, one of the women who was listening to us stood up, reached into the pouch of her cape, and removed some small green melons, which she set down one by one, seemingly in the nearby patch of bushes. Looking more carefully I saw that she was placing them beside an arch made of branches. Then I looked even more carefully, and saw that the arch was the opening of a little nestlike shelter. Then I saw other shelters. Then it came to me that we were standing in the people's camp. At last I realized that the little bag that I had spotted earlier hanging in the archlike empty space had been hanging in the opening of one of the little nest shelters. We no longer needed to wonder where the Ju/wasi of /Gautscha were living. We were there.

Thinking back, I treasure that moment. I treasure the friendships that began that day, that have lasted through three generations and will last as long as any of us are left alive. I treasure the names that the people soon gave us, enclosing us, bringing us among them—naming my parents for ≠Toma's parents, my brother for ≠Toma himself but with the distinguishing name of Cheeks or Longface, naming me for his wife's sister, Di!ai, at her request. "Good fortune attended us then and after," wrote my mother. "≠Toma's reception of us was one of the greatest portions of our good fortune."[3] I treasure the memory of those slender, brown-skinned men coming forward to

deal with us while their women and children kept out of sight—
a scene as old as our primate experience. If we had been gorillas,
≠Toma would have been the silverback. And I treasure the memory
of not noticing the little nest shelter—the *tshu*, as it was called—but
only the small bag hanging from it, as if suspended in the air. This
was what the Old Way looked like. Bushes and grass.

6

Place

When we first came to /Gautscha, I would have described the people as three men and their families. I assumed, of course, that ≠Toma, Gao Feet, and Lazy /Kwi owned the place, and that we would need their permission if we wanted to stay. The latter was true enough, but the former was my cultural perspective and, as often happens when one interprets someone else's culture in the light of one's own, it was skewed.

In fact, during our first encounter with the /Gautscha people, the actual owners were hiding while ≠Toma and Gao Feet dealt with us. Back in the bushes, anxiously watching, were the elderly grandmother, her two daughters, her brother's two daughters, her little grandchildren, and her adolescent son. These people were the *kxai k'xausi*—a firm, nailed-down expression that has been translated as "owners who possess." The grown men, in contrast, were not the owners. They had come from other places and married the owners. Of all the men present at /Gautscha at the time, only the adolescent boy was an owner, and he, too, had been hiding in the bushes. His name was Lame ≠Gao and he was partially disabled with a withered leg. We were to learn that when he married (which he did seven years later), he would go elsewhere to live with his wife's family.

≠Toma, !U, and their children

When in time it dawned on me that none of the full-grown married men were owners, I was taken aback. Were the Ju/wasi matrilocal?

At first it seemed unlikely. All societies that I knew anything about were patrilocal—living with the families of the husbands—including my own. Women moved away from their families to live with their husbands and their husbands' families, not the other way around. Surely, I told myself, the picture we were getting of women owning territory must somehow be wrong. The women had no weapons, so if their territorial rights were threatened, they would be unable to defend them.

When we started our real work there, after the government official and our guides from the farms went back to their homes with my father on a trip for supplies, our formidable numbers were reduced. All those remaining were polite to the Ju/wasi, or we tried to be, and we perhaps did not seem quite so imposing. So this was the time that we began our task of trying to speak !Kung and understand Ju/wa culture. One of my first efforts, with the aid of one of the interpreters, was to probe the question of women and territory more deeply. Sitting on the ground with two or three women who were kind enough to talk with me, I named the men of /Gautscha. Were these not the real *kxai k'xausi* of /Gautscha? Were not the women their mothers and wives?

The women looked uneasily at one another. Our practice of asking questions had its own negative implications, suggesting that we were suspicious and lacked trust. Perhaps the women thought I didn't like the idea and were not sure how to answer. Meanwhile, Lame ≠Gao was standing at a distance, listening. When he heard the question, he called my name, "Di!ai." This came too early in my sojourn—I heard him but didn't at first take in what Di!ai meant. He then tried "Nisabe," the Ju/wa version of Elizabeth, to get my attention. This word I knew, and as I turned to look he started toward us, his withered leg hooked around the long stick that he used as a crutch, lifting his foot forward with each step. It took him some time to cover the ground between us, but soon enough he was standing over me, looking down. "I am the *k'xau n!a* [the big owner]," he said firmly. "Me and them." He pointed with his lips at his mother, his sisters, and his cousins. "Them. Me. I am the *k'xau n!a*. We are the *kxai k'xausi*." He tapped his chest and repeated himself, insisting.

. . . .

"I see," I said, but I didn't. He was a boy among grown men who were much more physically capable than he. They could hunt. He could not hunt, or not well (although despite his leg he had once successfully hunted). He also lived, it seemed to me, in a very simple society where surely, at least to some extent, might made right. How could he own something as important as a *n!ore*—the Ju/wa term for such a landholding—the place that gave his people the necessities of life? I smiled politely at Lame ≠Gao but didn't exactly believe him. As a college student well versed in pop psychology, I thought he might be trying to make himself appear more important, perhaps to compensate for his leg.

I often review that experience in the light of what I have learned since. It is another of my favorite memories—a profound picture of the Old Way. And when I think of it, I think of lions, a group of whom also lived at /Gautscha, depending, as did the people, on the /Gautscha waterhole. At night we heard them roaring. "Lions!" I would say to myself, until it came to me that on the rather rare occasions when we saw them, we saw lionesses, not lions—an indication that, in matters of social organization, the Ju/wasi and the lions had certain things in common, and that the clues to anthropological puzzles are not always found among our own kind. I didn't know it at the time, yet on reflection it now seems clear that at least at /Gautscha, the women held the *n!ore* with their children and grandchildren, and the lionesses of /Gautscha did the same. Again, it was the Old Way.

As we looked into the situation more deeply, we learned that ownership of a place was conferred in a rather straightforward manner. You had the right to live where you were born, assuming that your mother was not simply passing through at the time of your birth. You had the right to live with your group, they who were the *kxai k'xausi*. You held a *n!ore* strongly or weakly, as the Ju/wasi put it, depending on whether you stayed there or not, depending on whether close relatives stayed there. If you didn't stay on your *n!ore*, and if your relatives were no longer there or no longer living, you would hold the *n!ore* weakly, and after time your ownership would fade.

If you were not an owner or connected to an owner, you

couldn't simply plunk yourself down on the *n!ore* of others without their invitation. We, in fact, had been apprised of this by our interpreters and guides. Because they themselves were not from the area, the question had been particularly important to them. Under other circumstances in southern Africa in those days, a black man could hardly be held responsible for what his white employers were making him do. But such immunity would not apply deep in the interior, where the Old Rules had not been overcome. Certainly in earlier times the hunter-gatherers of the savannah had conflicts over scarce resources—the aspect of our prehistory that makes us leery of strangers to this day. The Old Rules about intrusion, which applied to us, applied even more importantly to our guides and interpreter. These men obviously were also of hunter-gatherer families, but not the right kind. What if they seemed to be mounting some kind of challenge? What if they were an advance guard come to survey /Gautscha with a takeover in mind? No wonder our guides felt uneasy to live among *kxai k'xausi* without permission.

How would the rules of ownership be enforced? I hate to think. We never saw them enforced because nobody broke them. Yet the possibility seemed to be in the backs of people's minds. For instance, as part of a study conducted many years later, the anthropologist Polly Wiessner showed an arrow made by one group of Bushmen to men of another group. They reacted strongly and spoke at length about how they would feel if they found an animal killed by such an arrow, because it would mean that strangers, invaders, were hunting on their lands.[1]

We, too, made a similar observation. My brother and I witnessed something like an incursion in 1953 when we were traveling with four Ju/wa men through a windswept reach of empty bush desert near a nondescript place called N/am Ta Kwara, which means "Here Is Nothing." There, one of the men came upon the tracks of three strangers—a man wearing leather sandals, a barefoot woman, and a child. The strangers were Bushmen, but the four men with us didn't know them. This was most unusual. These men recognized tracks almost as easily as they recognized faces, and they also knew the whereabouts of their own people. To find strange tracks was astonishing.

Fifty years later I still remember this event. A catch in the breath, a very subtle note of repressed concern in the voice of the man who made the discovery, as well as the tension in his body as he looked down at his find, made my hair rise. For a moment, I thought he saw a snake. Who were these strangers? Why had they come? Where were they going? The tracks said nothing more. The four men examined them briefly, then said we could resume our journey, which we did in grim silence. I didn't hear more about the three strangers, and being naïve at the time, I forgot about them. My mother was the anthropologist, not me. So now, fifty years later, I presume either that the presence of the strangers was explained eventually, or that their journey carried them so far that their presence was no longer of concern. Even so, that a few dents in the sand in a seemingly limitless expanse of wilderness savannah would cause anyone the slightest anxiety spoke volumes about *n!ore* and strangers. Such was the Old Way.

In time, we made a survey of all the groups of Ju/wasi in the Nyae Nyae area of South West Africa (now Namibia) and the adjoining area of Dobe in Bechuanaland (now Botswana)—nineteen groups or bands, averaging about twenty-five people in each—and found that about half the people were living on the *n!ore* of the wife and half on that of the husband. A fluid arrangement of this kind was most advantageous, largely because survival is the main concern of any population living in the Old Way, and everything that enhances survival is practiced. The fluidity of the Ju/wa system, whereby you could live not only where you yourself had rights but also where your kinfolk and your in-laws had rights gave most people access to a widespread food supply, which could be life itself in times of drought or famine.

Even so, to "own" as the *kxai k'xausi* would "own" was a very different position from that of a visiting family member, and obviously was very important. For now, it is enough to say that although the system allowed both men and women to live in the *n!ore* of their birth, the *kxai k'xausi* in residence usually seemed to be women and unmarried boys. I wondered why.

The reason may be older than our species but may have come about after the savannah took us over, because our ancestors, the chimpanzees, are usually patrilocal,[2] so that the females leave their groups to join the males, as do the vast majority of people. Interestingly, however, the matrilocal arrangement is common enough among other species, including other savannah primates. It even occurs among chimpanzees when the mother's landholdings are advantageous, in which case her daughters, who otherwise might leave, may stay with her.[3] And the matrilocal arragement is conspicuously present among lions, whose territories are held by prides composed of sisters, daughters, mothers, and aunts, and all their young children including their almost grown but still immature sons. The adult male lions associated with a pride are not related to the females but are born elsewhere to other prides, which they leave as they mature, to find females they can call their own.

In a patrilocal culture such as ours, with our profusion of male scientists, it was once assumed that any group of female creatures was the harem of the male in their midst. Yet tightly knit groups of females on a home range that they share with a husband or two from elsewhere—a male who is living with the females to father their children and perhaps to help discourage intruders—are found among animals as diverse as pilot whales and savannah baboons. If the Ju/wasi were essentially matrilocal, they wouldn't have been breaking Gaia's rules.

Their marriage customs had much to do with their matrilocal arrangements. With only about 550 people in all of Nyae Nyae, great care was taken to avoid the marriage of close relatives, thus the choice of marriage partners was limited. Many children were betrothed while young, almost inevitably to someone from a group or band that occupied another *n!ore*. A girl could be betrothed while she was still a baby, usually to a boy in his early teens. Needless to say, the couple refrained from sex until the girl was sufficiently mature, but sex was hardly the reason for marriage. A young man was expected to hunt for his wife's people and to continue hunting for them preferably until he and his wife had three children who could walk. This rule, like many similar Ju/wa customs, was somewhat amorphous, and more will be said later about the Ju/wa birthrate. For now it is enough to say that children were usually spaced about four years apart and were usually about six before they could travel far unaided.

This meant that a man could live with his wife's people for fourteen or fifteen years if all three children lived, and longer if they didn't. By the time he had fulfilled his bride-service obligations, his own hunting skills might be cresting and he might be at an age at which his own daughters, if he had them, would be betrothed. He might be thinking about the sons-in-law who would help to feed him and his wife as they grew older. Integrating a son-in-law took time, because unless a young man had already lived in his wife's *n!ore*, he could not immediately make a contribution as a hunter. He could hunt, of course, or he wouldn't be getting married, but when he went to his in-laws to do bride service he would need to learn the landscape of his new home so that he wouldn't get lost—no easy task given the enormous, rolling distances with only the sun as a point of reference. For the first few years, therefore, he would not be going out on his own to do long-distance hunting. At first, his contribution would be as a member of someone else's hunting party—mostly to help with the tracking and to carry home the meat. Many a man considered his wife's *n!ore* to be his permanent home, where he would eventually be joined by sons-in-law who then would hunt with him.

In actual practice, people were quite flexible about residence and pretty much lived where they liked. A man could take a break from bride service if emotions or conditions demanded it. He could also get divorced or, because the Ju/wasi allow polygamy, he could take a second wife, and because bride service was required for every marriage, he would do bride service for her, even bringing his first wife with him if she agreed. Even so, the pattern often resulted in women staying with their relatives on their *n!ore* while men married out and moved away.

Meanwhile, as Lame ≠Gao had told me, the Ju/wasi had an interesting custom pertaining to the *n!ore*. The oldest male among the owners had a special name—the *k'xau n!a*, the "big" or "old" owner (the word *n!a*, meaning "big" and "old," is a term of respect). Normally, no woman held this title, which was said to pass from a man to his eldest son. Only if a *k'xau n!a* had no son would the title pass to a daughter. When we came to /Gautscha, Lame ≠Gao was the Big or Old Owner, just as he had told me. No such title graced the oldest man of the group, or the most influential, or the best hunter—only the oldest male among the owners held it. No special privileges came with it, just obligations, at least in theory, because the *k'xau n!a* was supposed to be more generous than others. Perhaps he was. Perhaps he wasn't. His role was to personify the ownership of the *n!ore*. The Ju/wasi had several little customs that didn't quite fit the contemporary picture. Perhaps the *k'xau* role sprang from one of these. Could it have been a holdover from an earlier time, when the divisions between men and women were perhaps a bit greater? At any rate, by the time we learned of the title, the role of the *k'xau n!a* was essentially symbolic.

What is a territory or a *n!ore* to a group like that? Not what it would be to us, a carefully delineated piece of property that can be bought or sold, with marked-off boundaries. A Ju/wa territory belonged to those who were born there, whose rights were acquired through a parent who was born there, on back through time. The ownership could not be transferred, and the land had no formal boundaries but faded off into no-man's-land on the far sides of which other, different groups might hold equally extensive territories. Thus the importance of *n!ore* derived less from its condition as a tract of land and more from the plants and animals that lived on it, the firewood that could be found there, and, most important of all, the water.

If a waterhole went dry, as in the driest times more than half of them did, the group of people who had been using it would set off in single file for one of the other waterholes where some members of the group would be owners, or else relatives of the owners. And when they arrived, they met their relatives there, who would share the food and water. Thus a *n!ore* was not property, it was life, and the concept of *n!ore* was deep in the soul. The territorial antelopes were said to have *n!oresi* (the plural of *n!ore*) to which they always returned if hunters chased them. When a person died, he was seated in his grave so that he faced his *n!ore*.

We knew only one nuclear family, a married couple and their four children, who did not have a *n!ore*. This was the family of a lame man named !Kham. As an adolescent, he had suffered a bone disease, perhaps the same disease that had affected Lame ≠Gao, but it had withered both his legs. He moved with the aid of two long, forked sticks, planting them on the ground like crutches, holding them by the forks, and swinging his body between them. His wife,

. . . .

Be, was a tiny little woman, scarcely four feet tall, and their four children were also very small for their ages, although seemingly in good health. (Was this also of the Old Way, whereby among many other species those of lowest rank are often the smallest? The Ju/wasi did not have rank, or not overtly, but a *n!ore* and its food supply certainly gave the owners and their descendants a very great, inherited, biological advantage over those who did not.)

!Kham's little family group had no strong connections to any larger unit, no living parents or siblings, which meant essentially that they were homeless. So they lived by visiting others, crossing from the south of Nyae Nyae to the north, a journey of about one hundred miles, then crossing back, camping at night, gathering small amounts of food along the way, stopping for a time with one group of people, moving on to another group, making themselves useful by carrying messages and gifts that the people of the various groups sent to one another.

!Kham and his family seemed welcome enough during their visits. They stayed in the background, however, always quiet and self-effacing. The people whom they visited would include them in any important sharing, and in this way they occasionally ate meat, because, of course, !Kham could not hunt. They would not stay with any one group for very long, not wanting to erode their welcome. After a while, they would resume their slow, endless journey, !Kham laboriously swinging himself between his crutches, the rest of his family behind him. "Their hold on a group and a place," wrote my mother, "was the most tenuous we knew."

She also wrote, "My feelings about Bushmen who have become landless and unattached are very concrete and personalized when I think about !Kham and his family."[4]

The pull of the *n!ore* was very strong upon the /Gautscha people, as we learned when we returned to /Gautscha the following year to continue our work. We arrived late in the day and found no one there. We started to set up a camp, and presently people began to appear, then came to greet us. More people appeared, then more people, and then began to pour out a terrible story.

After we left, the rains had come and were especially good that year, so good that a large herd of buffalo made one of their rare visits to /Gautscha. The people saw the herd on the far side of the pan, which was filled with water. Although the people well knew how dangerous these animals were, it didn't occur to the men not to hunt them, so ≠Toma and several other men went after them. ≠Toma put a poison arrow into the bull. The herd ran off. The men returned to their camp and came back later to track the wounded bull, and after a time, they found him lying down. An enormous creature, he still had plenty of fight left in him, and most of the men stayed back, but ≠Toma felt that the hunt wasn't getting anywhere, and, grasping his spear, he rushed forward and hurled it into the bull with all his force. The bull lurched to his feet and gored ≠Toma in his abdomen, wounding him terribly. Bleeding badly, he was helped back to camp, where people thought that he would die. Others sang over him, trying to draw the pain and injury away from him, trying to stop his bleeding and chase away the spirits of the dead that had come to take him.

At about this time, far away in the farmlands, a white farmer was hearing of us and our work. He heard that we had gone home but that we had found Bushmen in the interior. He decided to come after them, to get himself some farmworkers. He assembled a helper or two, probably his sons, and then in his truck he followed the tracks our trucks had made on our way out. The people of the interior had never seen or heard any vehicles except ours, and when they heard the farmer's truck coming, they thought it was us, returning to them in their hour of need. They came to meet the farmer, and only when they saw him did they know that he had nothing to do with us.

The farmer captured many of the people and made them get into the back of his truck. Among his captives was ≠Toma, who was too weak to resist. The farmer took these people back to his farm. Those he had not managed to capture, among them Lazy /Kwi and his wife, //Kushe, could hear the motor of the truck long after it was out of sight. But no one knew where it was going.

At the farm, the Ju/wasi were made to work—all but ≠Toma, whose wound was still open. The farmer was not the worst of his kind; he was a rather nice person who meant well despite what he

. . . .

had done. Capturing slaves was not something that he and other farmers considered to be wrong. In his eyes, he was even benefiting the people, giving a home and jobs to those who, as he saw it, had none. He dressed ≠Toma's wound with disinfectant and bandages, and after several months, the wound healed. Meanwhile, ≠Toma and the other captives had been discussing their situation. They disliked the farm, even though the farmer gave them cornmeal every day and otherwise was fairly decent to them. ≠Toma suggested that they go home.

Some were afraid. Farmers had been known to wreak terrible vengeance on Bushmen laborers who tried to escape. A certain farmer, for instance, had punished one of his Bushman laborers by tying his feet behind his head and his arms behind his back, then tying him to a tree and leaving him there overnight, then returning the next day and beating him until he was tired, then resting and beating him some more. The people from /Gautscha must have heard similar stories from other Bushmen on the farm, and they knew what a chance they were taking. Also, they were very far from /Gautscha. But those who were willing to take the risk gathered together with ≠Toma and waited for dark. They left in the night and traveled by moonlight. By morning they were far away.

The kindness of this farmer had its limits. When he saw that they were gone, he went after them. He guessed what direction they had taken, and he went that way, too. But in that enormous, silent landscape the sound of the motor preceded the truck by half an hour. The Ju/wasi heard him coming. Being small and dark skinned, carrying next to nothing but their well-adjusted babies, who wouldn't betray them by crying, they simply vanished into the long grass and let the truck go by. Then they kept going.

Did they complete the journey? The savannah hunter-gatherers could track a fish through water and navigate like migratory birds. With someone as brave and capable as ≠Toma in the lead, the little group of travelers could have found their way home from hell, living off the land along the way. They could, and in a manner of speaking, they did. Of course they completed the journey. Eventually they arrived at /Gautscha. How the farmer had underestimated them!

When they told us the story, pointing out that some of them had stayed behind, my father got back in his truck and headed off to visit the farmer. But first, he went to the colonial government and reported him. Capturing and enslaving people was illegal, and my father insisted that the government take action. At first, the government officials declined. They knew that the farmer had broken the law, but they also knew that he needed farmworkers and because times were hard, he probably couldn't afford to hire other people. Also, according to the government officials, the Bushman farmworkers liked to be on the farms. They were better off there. The farmer would feed them and give them clothing. Out on the veld, they could not always find food, and they had no clothing. And if the Bushmen didn't want to stay on the farm, they were free to leave, said the government officials.

My father thought differently. He knew how intimidated the Ju/wasi would be in that situation, and he knew what other farmers had done to other people who tried to escape. My father believed that the Ju/wasi would not be speaking for themselves in this situation, which was why he had come to speak for them. Besides, he had some things that the Ju/wasi didn't have, such as friends in high places, a knowledge of the way of the world, and money with which he made phone calls to high-ranking officials in Pretoria who understood the importance of international publicity and pressure and could force the local officials to keep their own laws. Before long the local officials were agreeing to accompany my father to the farm, if only to get rid of all the problems that my father was making for them.

There they caught the farmer with his slaves red-handed. This became one of the first cases in the history of the country in which a white man was punished for capturing slaves, a landmark case, really, because the farmer was found guilty and fined a punitive amount— not as much as my father would have liked, but punitive nevertheless. The rest of the captives who were still at the farm got into my father's truck, and he brought them home to their *n!ore*. Despite the daily meals that the farmer had given them, and despite the medical help he had given to ≠Toma, there was no other place that they wanted to be. Far from it. Some of the people wept with joy to be home in their place with their kindred, reunited.

In the late 1990s, the Peabody Museum of Harvard made as its main exhibit a display of hunter-gatherer life. Upon entering the museum,

At the front of the line walks the sister's lineage.
At the rear of the line walks the brother's.

the visitor was greeted by a huge, blown-up photograph of a group of Ju/wa women with their children and babies. The photograph was surely taken by my father during that second year that we stayed among these people. I don't often get a chance to visit the museum because I live far away, but one day I happened to walk in. To my surprise, there in front of me were the familiar, much loved faces of the /Gautscha women, on display not because of who they were but because they inhabited a beautiful photograph. They were the women and children who had come out to meet us on the day that we arrived at /Gautscha.

My father was no longer living, nor were most of the women, nor was the only boy in the photo—the little two-year-old son of //Kushe, who is riding in his mother's cape in the photo but who grew to manhood only to be killed in a tragic fight. But there they all are in the photograph, happy, young, and vital, wearing their leather clothes and their ostrich eggshell ornaments, walking east in single file. It is a warm day in the dry season. The women are passing just south of the waterhole, which does not show in the picture, and are on their way back to their encampment. They may be singing as they walk.

≠Toma's pretty young wife, !U, is their leader. Carrying her baby daughter, she is followed by her elder sister's daughter. Then come two of her cousins, then come her mother's two nieces, also sisters— an unmarried widow named !Ungka and her younger married sister, //Kushe, the woman who came with us from /Gam.

The order in which the women walk speaks of relationships and ownership. Two ancestors, unseen, are there in essence in the photograph—the sister and the brother who together once owned the *n!ore* of /Gautscha. At the front of the line walks the sister's lineage. At the rear of the line walks the brother's. And even though the museum had other reasons for displaying the photograph so prominently, and didn't mention the relationship of these women to one another or to the land over which they are walking, the photograph shows the owners who possess. *We are one thing, this place and these people*, says the photograph. Who would have thought that half a century later, an unnoticed whisper of the Old Way would turn up on the far side of the world?

7

Hunting

The *n!ore* of any group of people included water and certain vegetable foods, but it also included miles of low bush, high bush,
short-grass plains, long-grass plains, tussock-grass plains, and groves
of different kinds of small trees, most of them thorny acacias. These
were the habitats of a varied population of large animals who did
not need to drink water, or not much water, including giraffes,
warthogs, ostriches, and, most important of all, at least eight, perhaps nine kinds of antelope representing four of the water independent antelope families. Giraffes get moisture from the leaves they
eat, so that they, too, can be reasonably water independent.

These were the animals people hunted. Wildebeests and elands
were animals of the open plains, and the Ju/wasi would hunt for
them wherever grasses and low bushes were growing.

The territorial antelope, in contrast, had *n!oresi* just as people
did, a fact that people acknowledged by using the same word for
these territories that they used for their own. As the Ju/wasi knew
the *n!oresi* of other people, so did they know the *n!oresi* of the territorial antelopes, and went there to hunt them. Among these were
gemsboks. With their wide feet and pale hair reflecting sunlight, they
tended to hold large *n!oresi* on grassy dunes and open plains because

heat did not bother them particularly. Kudus also had *n!oresi*. With their reddish brown coats and pale stripes that look like bars of sunlight on dry leaves, the kudus tended to live on *n!oresi* that included dense thickets where they became invisible. Hartebeests held *n!oresi*, too, as did steenboks and duikers, whose small bodies overheat easily so that they need shade. They kept to the thickets in the daytime and emerged onto the plains at night.

The importance of the large antelopes cannot be overstated, even though they were by no means the people's only source of meat. They were not even the best or the easiest source of meat. Far from it. Protein foods were readily available as "slow game"—the tortoises, snakes, snails, and baby birds that are often found by people who are gathering. In the bushes at the edge of /Gautscha pan, for instance, ≠Toma found a nest with naked pink baby birds, all with their beaks gaping wide, hoping for their parent to feed them. ≠Toma put them in his hunting bag and brought them back to camp. The man named Lazy /Kwi, who had come with us from /Gam, found a python at the waterhole and bashed its head in with a stone, then gave it to his wife's mother, who threw the front part of it over her shoulder and dragged it to the camp, where she flung it down so that the people could decide what to do with it. It was nine feet long, not exceptionally large for a python, and the people decided to cook it for the children. The baby birds were also given to the children, as were many of the snakes, lizards, and tortoises that people came upon in their travels, and the mongooses, rabbits, partridges, and guinea fowls that young boys sometimes caught in snares. The animals who became "slow game" were important to the diet but were not considered to be important animals.

Another source of protein was meat stolen from other predators, who themselves stole meat, robbing carcasses when they had an opportunity. This was not as dangerous as it sounds because no one, neither the people nor the other predators, would attempt a robbery unless they thought they had a clear advantage. In Nyae Nyae I was twice present when Ju/wa men took kills from the big cats, once from a leopard and once from some lions. The leopard had killed and eaten most of a small antelope at the edge of a thicket, into which he vanished when three Ju/wa men approached. They unceremoniously picked up the remains of the antelope and left, not even bothering to look back to see if the leopard was going to accept this treatment.

He did. Being solitary and not very big, leopards are often the victims of robberies. If possible, they carry their kills up into the forks of trees to prevent such losses. But the surroundings of this leopard didn't include substantial trees. As the so-called big cats go, leopards are perhaps the most eager to avoid trouble. Thus the leopard must have felt he had no choice but to let the Ju/wa men walk off with his food.

Interestingly, the lion robbery was not very different. One year in the dry season, my brother, myself, and four Ju/wa men were traveling across some open long-grass plains ringed by bushes when we noticed vultures on the upper branches of a thorn tree, looking down. Obviously, they were looking at a carcass that was still being guarded. Otherwise, the vultures would be down with it, eating it, not sitting in the tree.

Unfazed by this clear information, the Ju/wa men approached in what seemed to be a nonchalant manner (I stayed behind), and in no time they emerged from the bushes with the ribs, spine, and hind leg of a hartebeest, all with meat still on them. Lions had made the kill, they told me. Where were the lions? Evidently they had not wanted an encounter with the men, so they had kept out of the way. Since some of the meat was still on the bones, there may have been no more than one or two lions, who may have been fairly well sated.

But how had the Ju/wasi known this? How had they known that they could stroll right up to a lion's meal and remove it with impunity? And if the lions had gone, why weren't the vultures eating? I have no answer for this, unless a piece is missing from the puzzle. Perhaps the lions were feeling full and had temporarily lost interest in the carcass. In that case, perhaps another predator was eating it, a predator small enough to give way to the men but big enough to keep the vultures in the tree. I have no choice but to guess, because at the time I was so impressed by the courage of the Ju/wasi, and so relieved that the lions hadn't come charging out of the bushes, that I forgot to ask.

Of course, robberies worked both ways, and lions also took kills from the Ju/wasi when they could. If hunters shot an antelope and were tracking it but didn't find it quickly, lions might find it first. Once, in the most dramatic instance of all, a pride of lions tried to take a wounded wildebeest that had been shot by a group of four Ju/wa hunters who had been tracking it for several days. My brother, who was with the hunters, witnessed the following event and filmed it. The hunters came upon their wildebeest in the afternoon, only to find her lying down, sick with poison and surrounded by twenty-five or thirty of the /Gautscha lions—the entire pride. The bushes were alive with lionesses. A big lion with a heavy mane was with them. Several lionesses were standing beside the wildebeest, evidently trying to think of the best way to kill her without being hooked. The wildebeest kept turning her head, keeping the lions in view, and this was inhibiting them. It would not have stopped them for long, though, as everyone knew.

The four hunters paused to consider the situation, then advanced slowly but deliberately in a row, never taking their eyes off the lions, picking up small rocks and chunks of earth and tossing them toward the nearer lions. In firm but soothing tones, the hunters kept saying, "Big lions, old lions, you must go now. This meat belongs to us." Despite the respect shown by these words, the lions were displeased. They rumbled considerably, but the hunters slowly advanced just the same. Although the men were polite, they were not deferential and seemed very sure of themselves. However, as my brother said later, in reality they were acting. Actually, they were understandably nervous, as was my brother.

The lionesses near the wildebeest were not too sure of themselves either, but unlike the hunters, they didn't try to bluff. Instead, they ingenuously began to turn their faces aside, unwilling to look the hunters in the eyes. The male lion was in the bushes at a distance, waiting for his wives to make the kill, but when he saw what was happening, he also turned a bit sideways, then turned more, then turned tail. After all, the lionesses were only his wives, not his kin or his allies. They might very well stick up for one another, but they had no special reason to stick up for him. He was, as it were, alone in a crowd, and he acted accordingly. He left the area.

Taking a cue from him, the lionesses in the background followed him, and soon the lionesses in the foreground did too. With no supporters, they must have felt exposed, and soon they were hurrying. In moments, all were gone. As far as the hunters were concerned, that was the end of it. They turned immediately to the wildebeest, who had been watching all this. They speared her, killed her, cut her up, and carried home the meat.

Thus the people didn't need to hunt in order to get protein. Yet they hunted all the time. Hunting was exciting, desirable, and extremely important. Even the act of robbing a carcass, exciting as that could become, was not the same as hunting. In fact, there was nothing like hunting. Our species seems to have an atavistic urge to hunt such as is found among the carnivores. That our impulse is atavistic can be seen in the reaction shown by some of us—not all of us, surely, as we have been overfed and sedentary much too long, but some of us—when, say, we notice a deer at the roadside. *Oh wow! Look at that!* Our eyes fly open, we draw a short, sharp breath, and our bodies tense. Physically speaking, we are ready to run forward. No matter how often this happens, our reaction is always the same and does not fade with time or repetition. This means that it was put deep inside us by Gaia and is not under voluntary control. Upon seeing a deer, most of us today would reach for a camera or simply enjoy the glimpse of wildlife, but evidently Gaia would want us to give chase. When our bodies ready themselves without our volition, we are preparing ourselves to do just that.

Our relatives the chimpanzees are much the same, suggesting that Gaia imbued us with this feature at the same time that she imbued them. "When chimpanzees kill a monkey," write the primatologists Richard Wrangham and Dale Peterson, "the forest comes alive with the barks and hoots and cries of the apes, and aroused chimpanzees race in from several directions."[1] Surely the scene would have been much the same when our ancestors caught monkeys. Surely catching monkeys was more stimulating than plucking the grubs and caterpillars that were our daily fare. Red meat was hot, and the bodies of the monkeys were active and struggling. When you grabbed them, they would open their mouths very wide and their

≠Toma once said of himself,
"From the day I was born, I was born for meat."

pupils would grow huge and black, and they would stare straight into your eyes. You could smell their fear and feel their hearts pounding. To pick up a caterpillar and put it in your mouth, that is nothing. To catch an emotional, terrified monkey who is twisting and trying to bite you, that is something big.

The Ju/wa men hunted by running, or some of them did, but the all-important, meat-producing, socially encouraged, communally recognized hunting was done with bow and arrow. Not all men can run down antelopes, but virtually all men could bow-hunt, including the young Lame ≠Gao, who lived at /Gautscha. They could and they did, every one of them.

Interestingly, the five kinds of antelopes whom they most commonly hunted, and also giraffes, were considered to be unlike other animals because they shared a certain quality with human beings. The quality was called *n!ow*. Predators did not have *n!ow*, nor did elephants or African buffaloes, nor did any small animal. Even the gods did not have *n!ow*. *N!ow* (discussed more fully later) is a concept completely absent in Western culture so that there is no reminiscent feature to invoke. *N!ow* connects those who have it to the cosmos and it has to do with weather. *N!ow* occurs only in human beings and (although the Ju/wasi might not have put it quite like this) in nondangerous, water-independent ungulates weighing roughly 300 pounds or more. In Nyae Nyae these were giraffes (1,500–2,400 pounds), elands (970–1,300 pounds), kudus (370–565 pounds), wildebeests (440–550 pounds), gemsbok (350–390 pounds), and hartebeests (277–315 pounds).[2] Duikers, much smaller (40–45 pounds), could have been a possible exception, as these might also have *n!ow*, said the Ju/wasi, but if so it was poorly developed. When hunters went into the field, giraffes, elands, kudus, wildebeests, gemsboks, and hartebeests were the animals they hunted. If something else presented itself, they would take that too, of course—a warthog, perhaps, or a steenbok or an ostrich—but no other animals were as important or desirable as the six big-game animals.

Any one of the six animals was more than an ordinary group of people could eat at one time, but the meat was never wasted. The people would cut it into strips and dry it in the sun. The dried meat would feed many people for a long time. Also, the skin was big enough to be made into a blanket or clothing. So surely the enhanced importance of the six big-game animals came from the fact that any one of them provided, among many other useful items, one large skin and a long-term food supply. With a leather cape around one's shoulders and enough meat to last for a long time, there was little else that anyone could want. Of course the people preferred to hunt big game.

In all of Nyae Nyae, the best and bravest hunters were probably ≠Toma and the the man named Short /Kwi. ≠Toma once said of himself, "From the day I was born, I was born for meat." Not everyone, barefoot and wearing nothing but a loincloth, will throw a spear from close quarters into one of the world's biggest, fiercest, most dangerous animals, and on the day he speared the buffalo and was gored, ≠Toma became known as Male ≠Toma, although people more usually called him ≠Toma Word because of his wisdom, and occasionally called him Stumpy ≠Toma because he was short. Yet the nickname Male stayed with him for the rest of his life. The name Male is with ≠Toma still, so that long after his death, those who remember him continue to use it, because of their respect.

Short /Kwi was the man who ran down elands. He was small, slim, and unassuming, a little over five feet tall, and was probably not yet twenty when we met him. Sitting among others, wearing what all men wore—a plain leather loincloth—he could be the very last person one would notice. However, in that company of extraordinary hunters, no one was quite as successful as he. He was as cool as he was capable, which he showed one day on an open plain where he had been looking for ostrich eggs and was attacked by the ostrich. This might not sound particularly dangerous, because an ostrich, after all, is just a bird, yet an ostrich is eight or nine feet tall, weighs two hundred to three hundred pounds, and can run at forty miles an hour. A single kick from its well-armed foot can eviscerate a person. As the ostrich charged, Short /Kwi calmly dropped to one knee, whipped out an arrow, and smoothly shot the ostrich in the heart. This meant that he knew exactly where an ostrich's heart was, even as it was running at him, because if he had missed by even a fraction of an inch, the ostrich would have been on top of him. But although precise aim is not required with poison arrows, since a shot placed almost anywhere will do, Short /Kwi's shot was faultless. The ostrich fell dead right in front of him, and he dragged it back to camp.

On another occasion, when Short /Kwi and other hunters had been tracking a wounded bull wildebeest, they came upon it lying down but still very much alive. Short /Kwi threw his spear, which pierced the wildebeest's side. Short /Kwi was then empty-handed, but the wildebeest was still living. Short /Kwi needed to retrieve his spear, so he ran at the wildebeest, and as it lunged up to gore him, he leaped over its back, yanking free the spear as he flew by. My brother was there with a camera and wanted Short /Kwi to repeat the maneuver so he could capture it on film, but Short /Kwi declined. If he did it again, he said, the wildebeest would remember and would be ready to hook him.

Perhaps because he was so young yet so unusually capable and therefore in some danger of arousing the envy of others, Short /Kwi sometimes went off to hunt alone at his *n!ore*, the place called Nama, the small pan with the waterhole in which hyenas had drowned. Or perhaps he went because no one else was living there, and the hunting was particularly good. Only his young wife, their baby daughter, and his wife's mother went with him. They went when the savannah was hot and the rains were starting, and would stay there for as long as Short /Kwi felt like hunting.

It was at Nama that Short /Kwi ran down elands. Once he killed an eland, a warthog, and a duiker all in the same day, then stayed with the carcasses to guard them while his wife and her mother walked to /Gautscha to bring others to carry back this bounty of meat. Over a three-year period, it was my calculation that Short /Kwi provided his people with at least eight large animal carcasses, which, when dressed out, would yield two and a half to three tons of meat.

Hunting was a test of character and strength as well as ability, as from start to finish a hunt could last a week or longer, sometimes much longer (in contrast to a runner, who would finish a hunt in less than a day if he succeeded at all). During lengthy hunts, the hunters might eat very little, if anything, and they often traveled very far, under extreme conditions. My mother writes of an occasion when "the hunters hunted for eight days without success in heat so exhausting they had to lie covered with sand through the middle part of the day."[3] A constant problem for hunters was water, because their hunts often took them very far from reliable sources, and they did not carry ostrich eggshell water bottles as travelers did on long journeys and as women did on gathering trips. Yet they knew every source, including hollow trees, and were always aware of how far they were from each of these sources. Before leaving for a hunt they would drink prodigious amounts of water, until their stomachs were bulging, and would do this again on returning, and in between would choose water over food if the two sources were not together. They managed this so well that no matter where their hunting took them, no one died of thirst, although all hunters suffered because of it.

Even so, for all the difficulties, all men and boys were enthralled with hunting. "Ju/wa men talk endlessly about hunting as they sit together repairing their equipment or poisoning their arrows," wrote my mother. "They recount over and over memorable episodes of past hunts, hear each other's news about recent hunts, and make plans. Little boys play at hunting from the time they can walk and they practice shooting throughout their childhood." Their toys were miniature bows with arrows made of thorns, which at very close range they would fire into empty melon rinds or into the large, slow-moving scarabs that were present in almost every campsite. On knees and elbows, the little boys would creep up behind a scarab and shoot it full of thorns. The struggling beetle would lie dying while the boys crept after another. This had nothing to do with slow game. This was hunting.

"At adolescence," continues my mother, "the boys begin to hunt with their fathers. They learn the skills of tracking and stalking and begin to participate in actual hunts. They continue through their manhood till they are gray-haired old men who can no longer endure the exertion of the hunt. A young man may not marry until he has killed a big game animal (preferably a large antelope, although a duiker or steenbok will also suffice) and proved himself a hunter." He will then have a small ceremony performed for him. Perhaps his grandfather will do this for him, making tiny cuts on his arms and face and chest and rubbing a paste of fat and ashes in them to give him strength and good vision, and, as my mother concludes, "so that he will not be lazy," so that as he sits at his fire he will ask himself, "Why am I still sitting here at my fire? Why am I not out hunting?"

At /Gautscha, the men tended to form small hunting parties of three or four, each led by a man who was generally acknowledged to be one of the best hunters. One group was often led by ≠Toma, who usually hunted with his brother-in-law, Gao Feet. Both of these men were excellent hunters and trackers.

Another group was led by Short /Kwi, and a third was led by a man named Gao Beard, also a renowned hunter. Two or even three groups might go hunting at the same time, taking different directions, but there were no rules about this. Men hunted when and where they liked, including on the territories of other Bushman groups if they dared.

However, the territory of any group was so big that men could hunt for weeks on end and never be off their own territory or see even a trace of another person. These factors tended to keep territorial infringement at a minimum. Then, too, it was generally agreed that if you shot an antelope on your own hunting lands and followed it onto the hunting lands of a different group, the owners would probably be understanding about it, assuming they knew you were there. You might give them a gift of meat, but you didn't have to. Even so, at /Gautscha each of the leaders had his own preferred hunting area—Gao Beard to the west, ≠Toma and Gao Feet to the east and northeast, and Short /Kwi usually in the area around the place called Nama.

The modern notion that you just wander along until you see an animal to shoot is strictly from the movies. The savannah antelopes, of course, have been hunted by our kind for hundreds of thousands of years, and they know how to avoid us. Yet however cautious an animal may be, almost everything in the environment, from odors to broken leaves to the tracks of other animals, can tell a hunter just as much about a potential victim as its own footprints and droppings, and the areas over which the men hunted were so enormous, each containing so very much to notice and to remember, that a man did best to hunt in the country with which he was most familiar. The predators often do the same, for the same reasons.

The hunting party would chose a direction and set off, carrying only their spears and their hunting bags, in which they put a bow and arrows, a short digging stick, a pair of fire sticks, perhaps some of the grubs from which they got their arrow poison, if they had any grubs, and perhaps some tinder stuffed into a small tortoiseshell. They walked in single file until they got to the area in which they planned to hunt, then spread out a bit, walking quietly, speaking in very low voices if at all. If they thought game was near, they might alert one another with clicks, omitting the vocalized parts of the words, as the click sound scarcely travels and animals don't find it alarming.[4] The hunters might also use hand signs to communicate— the first and second fingers up and bent to show the bent horns of a hartebeest; these same fingers up, spread, and curved for a kudu, or up in a V for gemsbok; or the thumb and little finger up and curved for a wildebeest, for example. (The click is probably better—it involves just a faint, natural sound but no movement.)

The time of year and type of terrain would determine, to some extent, the kind of antelope they hunted. Wildebeest, for instance, were present in large numbers during the migration and then would be on open plains. The wildebeests who didn't migrate, or those who had somehow become detached from the migration, also were usually in the open, although they took cover in the hottest times. Kudus could be found at any time of year, usually in heavy bush. Elands could be found by day in groves of big trees, while hartebeest were creatures of edges, favoring grassy areas near significant cover. Gemsbok, in contrast, being very well adapted for heat with their silvery-gray, sun-reflecting hair, were often on grassy dunes or open plains or in the shade of large, solitary trees at the edges of those places.

No hunt was easy, but some were luckier than others. The following is an excerpt from my diary—the "we" is my brother, myself, and a young /Gwi hunter named !Gai, from a group that lived far from /Gautscha:

There, a long way from us, we saw a herd of eight wildebeests standing up to their bellies in the yellow grass. !Gai said he was

. . . .

*going after them. But they were three or four hundred yards
away, and that flat, grassy country is very difficult to hunt in, it
is so open and flat. Even so, !Gai bent over so that his back was
below the grass tops, and holding his bow in his fist, he ran
bent over, touching the ground with his fingers every now and
then, keeping to where the grass was long and thick, staying
downwind, weaving his way toward the herd.*

*The wildebeests suddenly put their heads up. He was near.
Probably they had caught a whiff of human odor, because they
all pointed their noses straight at me and my brother. I believe
that this was part of !Gai's plan—if the wildebeests caught a
whiff of human scent they would think it was ours. They knew
that my brother and I were there—they just didn't know about
!Gai—and because my brother and I were so very far, the
wildebeests knew we didn't threaten them, so they didn't run.
Suddenly, right under their noses, !Gai rose up out of the grass
drawing his bow. The wildebeests bolted, heading for some tiny
little trees on the horizon, ever so far away. But even at that
short distance, !Gai's arrow missed. It just dropped. When he
came back we saw that his bow had broken—it had cracked in
two as he drew it for the shot.*

Normally, the bow doesn't crack, the arrow flies true, and usually hits the animal. The arrow was made in three sections so that
after it struck and penetrated, it came apart and the shaft fell to the
ground. Thus the antelope could not grab the shaft with its teeth and
pull out the poisoned arrowhead. The hunter could usually hear the
arrow hit—it made a *thunk*. Also the animal often cried and always
wheeled and ran. Then began the longest, most exacting part of the
hunt, the tracking.

The tracking ability of the Bushmen is legendary, and rightly so.
I happened to be traveling with three Ju/wa men who had occasion
to track a hyena across a wide slab of bare rock. How they did it I
have no idea. They were not simply following the line of travel, because out on the rock, the route of the hyena made a curve of about
one hundred degrees and emerged about one hundred feet away on
sandy ground on the far side of the ledge at a place that I, for one,
had no reason to anticipate. The three men had anticipated it, how-

ever, perhaps because of heavy bushes that grew there, which the hyena must have noticed while partway across the ledge, and headed for their cover.

The feat seemed effortless. The trackers thought nothing of it and, being at the time unfamiliar with the general ignorance of white people regarding the natural world, they were mildly startled by my amazement. To us, however, the ability of the Ju/wasi to track a wounded antelope if the antelope is with a herd seems equally amazing. To recognize the tracks of, say, a kudu who is traveling with six or seven others, all about the same size, is a feat that must be seen to be appreciated, especially because none of the tracks are clear footprints. Mostly they are dents in the sand among many other scuffed dents made by the other kudus.

Without the marvelous ability to track, the hunters could not complete a hunt and would lose the meat. When they heard the arrow hit, when the herd bolted, they all would go to the scene and examine the ground for information. They would find the shaft of the arrow. If more than one hunter had loosed an arrow, they would know whose arrow had struck. (This also seemed almost miraculous, as the arrow shafts, which were hollow reeds, looked exactly alike to me. But yes, each one could have had a scrap of twine tied on it, perhaps to strengthen it, and obviously, they were not alike.) After identifying the arrow, the hunters would examine the tracks of the victim so they would know them later.

That done, they would then go back to their camp, or if that was too far, they would make a fire and prepare to spend the night. If some kind of food such as melons or berries had presented itself along the way, the hunters might have taken time to eat a few bites, but in most instances they merely went hungry. The next day they would revisit the scene and follow the tracks, which often would be covered by those of other animals, either made at the same time or later. Sometimes the herd that included the victim might mix with another herd. The two herds might travel together for a while, then split again but not into the same groups as before, to go off in different directions. The hunters would study the tracks of both herds until they could make a determination. For this they would also consider the terrain. If it was hot, the victim might have gone with the herd that went into the trees. If one way led up a slope, she might have chosen the easier direction. Even the tiniest sign, such as the tracks of a beetle superimposed upon a footprint of the victim, would have meaning to the hunters, especially if the beetle was of a type that moved about after the day had reached a certain temperature. Thus great skill and much knowledge went into tracking, but almost always the hunters correctly identified and followed the tracks of the animal who had been shot, and not some other. If they were wrong, the great effort was for nothing.

At first, the victim would not feel sick. Her tracks would look like the others. But the following day, as the poison did its work, she would be weakening. Her toes would drag. She might stumble. All this time, the hunters would be following, stopping in the late afternoon to make a fire and wait for morning, picking up the trail the next day. Sometimes, at this point, they used magic—one of the extremely rare occasions that these utterly pragmatic people did so. The man whose arrow had hit the antelope would push the point of another arrow down into the wet spots where the quarry had urinated to further weaken her. After two or three days the antelope would be so weak that she could walk no more. The hunters might find her dead, or standing alone in some bushes, trying to hide, or lying down, too weak to stand. Then they would kill her with their spears.

If no more than three men had been tracking, while two of them were removing her skin and butchering her body with their knives and spear blades, the third might go back to the main camp to get helpers to carry home the meat. A larger hunting party wouldn't need help. They would build a fire and cook the liver to strengthen themselves after the long ordeal, during which they might not have eaten, and then would cut the meat into strips that they would load onto long poles or carrying sticks that they might cut for the purpose, two men carrying on their shoulders a pole loaded with perhaps one hundred pounds of meat, perhaps more. They didn't always bring the head—a heavy object with little meat on it—but if they did, it, too, would be carried on someone's shoulder, horns down, jaw against the sky.

At camp, they were greeted with joy. My mother describes such an arrival. "One time when the people had been many days without meat and were anxious about the hunters' success, an eland was killed, and the hunters were sighted moving toward the encampment in a dark, lumpy, bobbing line in the golden grass, their carrying-sticks loaded with meat. We heard the sound of voices in the encampment, rising in volume and pitch like the hum of excited bees. Some people ran toward the hunters, others crowded together at the edge of the encampment, some danced up and down, children squealed and ran about, the boys grappled and tussled together. I venture to say no women have been greeted in this manner when they returned with vegetables."[5]

When dividing big game, the hunter did not distribute the meat. That role belonged to the person who provided the arrow that actually killed the antelope, or, in other words, the owner of the poison that had its effect. By the Ju/wa system, anyone could own an arrow or arrows (although only the hunters used them), so that an old man or a woman or a boy like Lame ≠Gao, the *k'xau n!a* of /Gautscha, who had little chance of ever being much of a hunter, could give an arrow to a hunter and become the distributor of important meat. This custom emphasized the importance of these foods, as it was intended to enhance fairness. Anyone could find slow game and vegetable foods, anyone could set a snare, but only the strong adults could bring food in quantities large enough to feed the entire group. Without the formal system of sharing, the same people, the strongest people, would always be distributors, and over time, unfairness could emerge. My mother put it this way: "There is much giving and lending of arrows. The society seems to want to extinguish in every way possible the concept of the meat belonging to the hunter."

The donor of the arrow would make the first distribution, raw and on the bone, to the hunters and the owner of the arrow if the arrow had been lent to him. He would also keep some for himself. He and the other recipients would then redistribute meat, still raw—a man giving first to his wife's parents, then to his own parents, his wife, his brothers and sisters, his wife's brothers and sisters, and to other relatives who might be present. And, as my mother writes, "Everyone who receives meat gives again, in another wave of sharing, to his or her parents, parents in-law, spouse, offspring, siblings, and others. The meat might [by then] be cooked and the quantities small."[6] As people ate, they would share again, and soon enough, everyone would have a share and would have eaten.

Meat united people. A meal of life-giving meat was meant for all. On the day that Short /Kwi came home dragging the heart-shot ostrich that had charged him, the women in the camp stood up and started dancing, just from the joy of seeing the meat and from having a man like Short /Kwi living among them, bringing a bounty of life-giving food to share with his people. My mother wrote: "Women bring most of the daily food that sustains the life of the people, but the roots and berries of the Nyae Nyae Ju/wasi are apt to be tasteless and harsh and not very satisfying. People crave meat. Furthermore, there is only drudgery in digging roots, picking berries, and trudging back to the encampment with the heavy loads and babies sagging in the pouches of the leather capes; there is no splendid excitement and triumph in returning with vegetables. The return of a hunter from a successful hunt is vastly different. The intense craving for meat, the uncertainty and anxiety that attend the hunt, the deep excitement of the kill, and finally, the eating and the satisfaction engage powerful emotions in the people."[7]

Many years later and on the other side of the world from the Kalahari, I was at a dinner party, sitting across the table from an art collector. She politely asked what I did, and when I told her that I was writing a book about hunter-gatherers, she immediately instructed me not to romanticize the past, not to idealize the hunter-gatherer lifestyle. Surprised, I assured her that I didn't plan to but wondered what aspect of the past concerned her.

The people with artistic genius concerned her, she said. How, when limited by their lifestyle, could such people realize their potential? The great artists would find no means of self-expression. Therefore, people are better off today than they were back then. Unless of course, she added, the hunter-gatherers had managed to express themselves somehow. Did they whittle, perhaps, or make carvings?

I pointed out that the hunter-gatherer lifestyle had not limited the Paleolithic artists of the European caves or the South African rock shelters. The Ju/wasi we knew in the 1950s didn't paint, however, and (to answer the question) they didn't make carvings. But after all, I pointed out, they moved camp from time to time, carrying their possessions with them. Not even a very artistic person would be inclined to create a lot of statues that added to the load.

Then what about jewelry? asked the art collector. Perhaps genius could be expressed through personal ornamentation. Well, there again, the hunter-gatherers didn't have much use for jewelry. The people wore ornaments, to be sure, made with ostrich eggshell beads, each bead perfectly shaped and drilled in the middle, but, since every bead was the same size, shape, and color as every other bead, the biggest challenge to artistic genius could be deciding how long to make the string. Beadwork was normally seen as a secondary occupation, something to do with the hands while chatting. People very much enjoyed sitting together in the shade, making and stringing beads and talking, and they made some beautiful ornaments this way, but the work was more craft than art and could not be said to express individuality or to generate creative passion.

Talk turned to other subjects, but I began to have trouble listening, because the art collector's question, which had seemed lightweight at first, suddenly began to seem more interesting. At least, by assuming that artistic genius would be found among the Bushmen, the art collector showed them vastly more respect than had the architect at Harvard so long ago who likened them to monkeys. How indeed had the artistic geniuses expressed themselves? An obvious answer might be that they didn't, or at least the Ju/wasi didn't, because they so strongly believed in equality. No one should be more important or have more food or possessions than anyone else. No one should stand out above the rest. The "big man" persona was unknown to the Ju/wasi, who would have been horrified by the self-aggrandizement of such artists as Picasso, say, or Frank Lloyd Wright, whose personalities were products of modern times if nothing else and who, no matter how accomplished they may have been as artists, would not have lasted a day on the savannah, where the ideal person not only kept a low profile but also was expected to care for others.

Even so, the qualities that make great artists might indeed occur in any population, and if so, how, in the Old Way, did these qualities emerge? One answer is that the Ju/wasi expressed their art through music (about which more will be said later). But also, at least to me, the spirit that powers art seemed also to inspire hunting. Among the Ju/wasi at their fires at night, men told stories of hunting. All other stories were expressions of the culture, sometimes cautionary tales and often funny, usually familiar to everyone, and told to us at our request, but never, at least in my experience, were they told at night as people sat around their fires. The stories that were told were mythlike accounts of actual hunts, and these were told over and over.

One could tell from afar when hunts were the subject of discussion. Men told of them in special voices, sometimes almost chanting. Often, no one else would be speaking because all were listening. *Ai! What? Is that an ear? Yes, an ear! There's his ear against the sky, he's in bushes, just there, the edge of the bushes. I watch it. Yes, it moves, he turns a little, a little, hi! he lifts his head, he's worried, he sniffs, he knows! He looks, I'm down low, down low, just very quiet, down low, he doesn't see me! He's safe, he thinks. He turns around. I am behind him. I creep forward, eh! I creep I creep, I am just that far, eh! just that from me to there, quiet, quiet, I'm quiet, I'm slow, I have my bow, I set the arrow. Ai! I shoot. Waugh! I hit him! He jumps. Ha ha! He jumps! He runs. He's gone! I shot him. Right here, just here the arrow went in. He jumped, he ran that way, going that way, but I got him.*

As hunting inspired the stylized stories of the Ju/wasi, so it inspired graphic art at its inception. When Paleolithic people painted on the walls of their caves, they didn't paint grubs or baby birds, and they didn't paint nuts, roots, or berries. No, they painted large mammals, mostly ungulates, many with projectiles sticking out of them. They were big-game hunters, just like the Bushmen. They were artists who knew about hunting. They were hunters who knew about art.

The natural world is all about hunting. Virtually every wild animal hunts, or is hunted, or both. Even elephants are hunted—today, of course, only by people, but at one time young elephants were hunted by sabertooths and other giant cats. As for us, we were hunters before we were people. We were hunters before we were mammals. We were hunters before there were plants to eat and therefore before we had choices. The will to hunt is deep in the brain, down there with art in the cave of the unconscious. That the two would join is not hard to imagine, especially in the minds of those who live with hunger. What better art form could there be than a successful hunt and its result—strong men together in a dark, lumpy line bobbing toward you through the golden grass, carrying a massive head with spiral horns and hundreds of pounds of meat?

8

Gathering

For all the excitement of hunting, for all the importance that people placed on meat and especially on the meat of big game, the mainstay of the people's diet was vegetable food, and most of it was gathered by women. I found it interesting to compare the vegetables we ate, especially the ones we brought with us, to those found by the Ju/wasi. We had potatoes, sweet potatoes, onions, and carrots, plus dry beans, canned pears, and canned peaches. The Ju/wasi ate about eighty kinds of plants, including twenty-five kinds of roots,[1] seven or eight kinds of berries, five kinds of nuts, sixteen or seventeen kinds of fruits, three or four kinds of melons, four kinds of leaves of which two resembled spinach, eleven kinds of tree gum, and two kinds of beans from pods. They also ate palm hearts.

For the Ju/wasi, these foods fell into two categories. Some, like the meat of big game, belonged to the group and had to be shared. Others belonged only to the individual who found them, to be shared at the individual's pleasure. Vegetable foods to be shared were mangetti nuts, marula nuts, and the ground-growing nuts known as *tsi*. In this, these foods resembled the meat of big-game animals, which always required sharing. Like big game, nuts and groundnuts were usually found far from water, and to get them was the work of strong adults. A gathering party of men and women would walk for several days over waterless country to pick clean the nut groves or the groundnut patches, and would carry home their harvest in big leather bags or tied up in their leather capes that also served as bags. They might carry some of their water in ostrich eggshells, but, at least on nut-gathering forays, might also find water in hollow trees in the grove, water left over from the rains. Hollow trees were therefore an important feature of these groves. We visited a mangetti grove in which there was a large hollow tree that supplied twenty-five people with water for four days. This tree and others like it were owned by individuals, often inherited from a parent. Because none of the Ju/wasi would take the water without the owner's permission, the owner and his party could count on finding water in the tree when they arrived at the grove. Using the water very sparingly, the people might spend the first night at the grove, spend the next day or two knocking down the nuts and filling their bags, spend one more night at the grove, and then start back to their encampment, each person carrying fifty to one hundred pounds of nuts, enough to provision their group for a long time.

A major harvest of this kind was very much like a successful hunt for big game, and such major bounty was shared in the manner of big game, if without as much excitement. As the owner of the arrow, not the hunter, made the first divisions of the animal killed by the arrow, so the owner of a bag made the first division of the nuts, no matter who gathered the nuts or carried the bag. This sort of food gathering was surely of recent origin ("recent" in geological time), because without large skin bags, such a harvest could not take place, and before people could obtain large skins by hunting big game, there were no large skin bags.

Palm hearts were also shared. These luscious items were uncommon, found by chance during long-distance hunts. During the time I spent in the Kalahari, only one palm heart was found and divided, to my knowledge. My conscientious mother dutifully recorded the unusual event. Hunters noticed a palmetto, and, at the end of the successful hunt, went back for it, chopped out the heart (a good-sized item perhaps two feet across), and brought it home with the meat. There being no arrow or bag to predetermine the ownership of this palm heart, the hunters themselves cut it up and handed out the slices.

The meat of big game, large harvests of nuts, and large, delicious windfalls such as palm hearts were profoundly welcomed by all concerned, but months could pass before the people obtained these kinds of foods, foods that required sharing. Most of the time, people ate the berries, roots, and slow game obtained by ordinary, everyday gathering, usually but not necessarily done by women, and almost always within a day's trip from where the people were camped. These foods belonged to the category of foods that did not need to be shared. The finder could eat them on the spot or share them with others—whatever the finder wanted. This was a firmly stated rule. No matter whom you asked, the answer was always the same. Ordinary, everyday foods belonged to the person who found them and were shared at that person's pleasure.

Here again, to those of us in industrial societies, this aspect of a hunter-gatherer culture seems as simple as it is unfamiliar, and is therefore hugely underestimated. Yet this particular rule may very well be the oldest encoded rule in human history—encoded because all people knew it precisely and were unanimous as to its existence and meaning. There it was, perhaps somewhat out of joint with the people's almost obsessive sense of equality and sharing, but there nevertheless. Its probable antiquity is seldom noted in anthropological circles, where it is attributed to the equality of women. The rule suggests that women were not the subordinates of men and were not forced to feed anyone. If a man wanted berries, roots, or slow game, he had to get them himself unless his wife volunteered to get them for him. Anthropologists consider the gatherer rule to be a positive statement about the status of women, and rightly so.

But surely in a larger picture, the rule had little to do with gender. Perhaps the most interesting aspect of it was that however clearly and firmly stated that rule might be, it was rarely invoked. In daily matters, sharing was the way of life. Everybody shared. So perhaps to understand this particular rule, at least as it applies to creatures like ourselves, we should once again imagine ourselves holding our

Roots were by far the most important staple food of the Ju/wasi.

mother's hand while she holds her mother's hand, but this time we don't stop with the chimpanzee. Beyond her the line continues, not now for five million years but for forty million years, all the way back to the Eocene, when the hand-holding mother was something like a bush baby.[2] She, too, ate plant foods and slow game (which in her case would be mostly larval insects), and she would share her finds or not, as she chose, probably not, thus observing the rule invoked by her modern descendants. Thus this particular rule of the modern hunter-gatherers seemed to belong to the Very Old Way.

Perhaps it is not surprising that so apparently simple a rule would be underestimated. Most of us in the modern world, including the anthropologists, have little concept of such continuity or such stability. Yet these characteristics are the very fiber of the Old Way, wherein the margins of survival are narrow indeed, so that habits that have stood the test of time remain in use unless change is needed. "If you find it, it's yours" was a preverbal rule that in time found its way into language.

By far the most important staple foods of the Ju/wasi were roots—the twenty-five kinds of bulbs, rhizomes, corms, and tubers. The other foods were either small, such as berries, or scarce, such as truffles, or seasonal, such as certain fruits or the spinachlike leaves. Roots were the everyday meal, and even in some cases were sources of water, as at least one kind of root was chopped up and squeezed only for the juice. For the Ju/wasi as for the people of the past, roots were excellent nutrition, and best of all, unlike fruits or berries, could be noted in one season and gathered in another, as few other creatures were competing for them. (Usually, fruits and berries were gathered on the spot before the birds could eat them. Here, the thing to remember was where the berry bushes grew, so that one could return to them the following season.)

Digging roots might be significant, but it isn't easy. The Ju/wa women did not conclude their gathering trips with any display of triumph. Instead, as my mother, quoted earlier, put it, they would come "trudging back to the encampment with the heavy loads and babies sagging in the pouches of the leather capes."

. . .

I for one was awed by gathering. I could imagine myself with no more than a stick and five cups of water, out in the wilderness, day after day, year after year, trying to find enough food to feed a family. So I often went gathering with the /Gautscha women. The following scene describes one of the first gathering trips that I accompanied. The episode begins on a warm night as the dry, hot season is starting. Two groups of Ju/wasi are camped at /Gautscha at the time, and both camps are set back from the waterhole on either side of a grove of trees and bushes. I go to the camp where the people I know best are living, the people who met us when we first came. Although the sky is quite bright from starlight and the new moon, both camps are dark, in the black shadow of the trees. Even so, red light from the little fires reflects from the undersides of the branches and from the people's faces. In the camps, the people have long since pulled up most of the grass, so that the earth is bare around the grass shelters, none more than ten or twelve feet apart, that face in different directions. The fires are in front of the shelters and are small, each no more than a few sticks, butt ends together, each producing its little flame. Here and there are small piles of branches, the wood to keep the fires going through the night. Some people are roasting small amounts of food in the coals of these fires—a few nuts or a root cut in half. Some people have nothing.

The two pairs of sisters who are the *kxai k'xausi*, or owners, of /Gautscha have built their shelters side by side. One of the elder sisters is Di!ai, the woman for whom I was named. She hands a few sticks of firewood to her younger sister, !U. !U has recently given birth to her third child, a baby girl, and Di!ai has been looking after her, bringing food and firewood as !U regains her strength. !U is right in front of her shelter lying on her bed, a pile of dry grass covered with a skin cape. Another cape covers her and hides the baby.

I am sitting near Di!ai, trying to understand the conversation. Although I will eventually learn enough !Kung to stumble along in the language (other members of my family will do much better), at this point I am at the stage where the Ju/wasi either address me in baby talk or raised voices, or both. I can understand a bit better than

I can speak, however, and get the impression that the women want to go gathering in the morning. Evidently the two pairs of sisters will be going, as they go almost everywhere together. Struggling with !Kung, I ask if I can go, too. They all laugh mildly. What have I said? Di!ai then looks at me to see if I am paying close attention, and, with her eyes on mine, she shouts, "It's far!"

I grin ingratiatingly to show I still want to go and ask when they will leave. Di!ai points at the sky, showing where the sun will be then. She means to leave at midmorning. To me, this seems late in the day to be starting a long gathering expedition, and I assume that there has been miscommunication. I thank her and plan to be ready early, not wanting to be caught by surprise as the group leaves, because few things are as unobtrusive as a group of Ju/wa women leaving an encampment. There they are, at the edge of the camp. Suddenly they have vanished, and the bushes aren't even moving.

From their fires, the other two sisters who are owners of /Gautscha overhear the conversation and speak as if they, too, are going. I go back to my tent, about fifty feet away, and go to sleep. I get up early to be ready and go to Di!ai's grass shelter. She is by no means ready. She isn't even thinking about going. I sit down. The sun climbs up the sky, and time passes.

Much later, it was to come to me that the probable reason for a late departure was to give the predators, especially the lions who also lived at /Gautscha, plenty of time to get back to their own encampments under shady trees and go to sleep, but at the time the late departure puzzled me. As an American with elements of a rural background, I saw no other option than to get up before dawn and get the work done. If you didn't have your laundry washed and on the line by sunrise, you were something of a slut, in my limited experience. But rural Americans didn't contend with predators.

So at the Ju/wa camp, we sit around not doing much of anything until almost midmorning when the sun is at forty-two degrees. Di!ai then goes to the waterhole to get a drink and fill an ostrich eggshell. Fearing that she will leave from there to meet the others somewhere else, I wait with the others at the camp—the last thing I want is to find everyone gone and have to go scouting after them.

In all, six women are planning to come, four from one camp, two from the other. These woman are now considering their children.

Taking children on a gathering trip is no easy matter. Infants are not a problem, as they ride safely in their mothers' capes and can be nursed just by being hitched around to reach the breast while the mother keeps walking. The older children are no problem either. They play with one another all day anyway, and otherwise look after themselves. The problem is the little children who are more or less knee-high to adults, whom the Ju/wasi call "knee children." Knee children must be watched, and they tire easily but are heavy to carry. This morning, the women with older knee children, those who are no longer nursing, are looking around to see if someone who will not be going can watch them. Two of the young boys, ages about four and eight (the ages of the Ju/wasi, even the children, could only be estimated), are immediately eliminated from the gathering party. Their grandmother is present, their father, too, and the eight-year-old can watch his little brother. Di!ai's two boys are not so lucky. The younger boy is two, the older boy is five, both still nurse, and they are rivals. This morning, as Di!ai is sitting by her shelter, her legs stretched out in front of her as she sharpens her digging stick, her two-year-old feels hungry. He sits on her right thigh and begins to nurse. Holding her breast with both hands to keep the nipple in his mouth while his mother's arms are moving, he eyes his brother, who is coming toward them. The brother plunks down on his mother's left thigh and in a proprietary manner takes her left breast. He also begins nursing. Reaching around him, Di!ai continues to sharpen her digging stick, but her two boys are in the way and she is frowning. Already she seems stressed.

Suddenly she lifts her head and calls to her daughter, a girl of eight or nine. The girl is sitting on her heels by her grandmother's fire, where she sleeps at night. Di!ai tells her that she must join the gathering party. In a high, soft voice, the girl says she's sick and can't go. Di!ai flares and speaks bitterly to her daughter. The daughter ducks her head and says nothing but stubbornly doesn't stand up. The boys on Di!ai's lap have begun to kick each other. Di!ai looks down at them, then puts her elbow between them to keep them apart.

Soon she gets up slowly and gently spills the boys. They stand at her side. They know they will be going with their mother. The other women are also standing. Their capes are tied, their digging sticks are in their hands. They are ready. Di!ai again speaks sharply to her daughter. The daughter starts to cry but reluctantly obeys, takes a digging stick, stands up, and is ready to follow.

Di!ai's boys want to be carried. They look up at her, asking. She picks up the younger boy and puts him on her hip. The older boy seems disappointed. I offer to carry him if he likes. He doesn't like. He wants his mother to carry him, but she isn't going to, he can see that, and reluctantly he lets me lift him.

To lift a Ju/wa child is an interesting and wonderful experience. An American child is heavy by comparison and comes up off the ground like a sack of grain with arms and legs dangling—dead weight. A Ju/wa child almost lifts himself because he participates in the action with his arms and legs ready to clasp you so that the two of you instantly fuse as if you were a magnet and he a little piece of steel. And you don't have to hold him up—he clamps himself right on you and holds himself in place. You need merely to keep an arm around him. I love to carry Ju/wa children and would like nothing better than to carry this little boy, but he has second thoughts about me and after a moment he wiggles to get down. He will walk, he has decided. I had once put ointment in his eyes, which surely he remembers negatively, although it cured an infection. But also his mother has said something to him that I didn't understand. From the fact that his head droops briefly, my guess is that she criticized him for babyish behavior.

Off we go. The women stride along in single file, Di!ai in the middle of the line carrying her younger son, her daughter ahead of her, her older boy behind her, me behind him. We are on a threadlike trail that leads into the bushes. We walk for a few minutes until we are on the far side of the bushes. There, all the women step off the trail and fan out so that they are at a distance from one another. Those who are carrying children put them down, then all the women spread their legs, bend their knees, push back the skirts of their capes, lean forward slightly, and urinate. They do this very neatly. No urine touches their feet or their clothing. The children wait politely. Finished, the women shake their clothes a bit to rearrange them, pick up their children, and resume the trail.

The place is a latrine of sorts. At a respectable distance from camp, it is the first place that is open yet out of sight. Interestingly, no feces are noticeable, and no fecal odor. I do, however, spot a dung beetle, a scarab, on the trail ahead. She is laboriously coming toward us. Surely she and her kind explain the cleanliness of the area and all Ju/wa campsites. Scarabs are the janitors. When a fecal mass appears, one of these giant beetles inevitably visits it, inspects it, selects a piece, then backs up to it and, standing on her front and middle legs, raising her back legs, she begins to kick it. The dung ball rolls. On and on she goes, backing the dung ball uphill and down to a place of her choice, where she crawls over the ball to lay her eggs, then digs a hole and buries it with dirt. She may then return to the source for more. The faintest scent of dung attracts these beetles— even a fart. Scarabs can fly—not easily with their heavy bodies, but they fly. If you are in the bushes, squatting, you may hear a buzz, then a thump, and look around to see a scarab standing behind you, waiting. The Ju/wa children play a game about this, waving their hands while singing "*zein*," a droning sound that imitates the incoming flight, then dropping their hands to imitate the awkward landing. Scarabs keep an area almost pristine, which may be why the ancient Egyptians were so taken with them.

The line of women passes the scarab. No one seems to notice her, but everyone steps around her. Almost everything the Ju/wasi do is intentional. If they take a life, even if only a scarab's, it is because they mean to do it. We go on our way south while the scarab goes north, unharmed.

Our next stop is in a grove of six or seven berry bushes growing by the trail. More accurately, the little trail has led us to these bushes. Each bush is about six feet tall, with tiny, dry leaves and sparse, thin branches. On the twigs are a small number of berries. A flock of little sparrows sits at the tops of the branches; the birds have been eating the berries. They wait for a moment to determine our intentions, then fly up all at once when they see that we are going to pick berries.

The women carrying children put them down, and everyone begins to pick and eat, talking quietly as they do so. Di!ai hands me a few berries. Unless invited, I do not eat the foods of the Ju/wasi. Our expedition has brought its own food, and we purposely do not compete for local foods with the Ju/wasi. But Di!ai has invited me, so I eat what she gives me. The berries are not much bigger than blueberries, but they are hard and dry, with brick-colored skins, yellow pulp, and a big seed inside. They are also tasteless, but as long as an item is palatable and not poison, the taste doesn't matter. Each woman eats a few handfuls of the berries, seeds and all, and some of the women put a handful or two into the pouches of their capes. Then we move on.

Now begins the real trip. We walk about four miles, maybe farther, at a pace that for a while keeps the knee children almost trotting. Eventually, their mothers swing them to their hips and carry them. No one carries Di!ai's older son, although I would have done so. He trots along on his own, taking two steps to an adult's one, looking up from time to time at his brother who now is riding in the pouch of his mother's cape, looking down at him triumphantly.

The day is hot, the sun is in the zenith. We are all perspiring, although in the dry air, perspiration evaporates so quickly that I, for one, scarcely notice. The veld is very quiet—I hear the faint footsteps of the barefoot women as their heels hit the soft earth. I hear their breathing, the slight, rhythmic rattle of their ostrich eggshell ornaments, and the swish of their leather clothing. No one speaks. We pass through a grove of acacia trees with tiny leaves and ghostly, light gray bark, and we emerge at the far side onto a plain where long, pale yellow grass is growing. Scattered through the grass are small thornbushes, like brambles. I see a shrike on one of them.

We are no longer on a trail. Instead, we are making one. It appears behind us in the grass as we cross the plain. On the far side of the plain is another grove of widely spaced thorn trees where more thornbushes are growing, and we head for that. At the edge of the trees, the women walk more slowly, then stop. Their body language—a slight relaxation as they turn toward one another and reach into their cape pouches for their ostrich eggshell water bottles—tells me that we are at our destination. Tucking their capes behind their knees, they sit down on their heels for a short rest. It is early afternoon. Di!ai's sister, !U, nurses the new baby. Seeing this, Di!ai's younger son also wants to nurse. Di!ai changes her position and sits cross-legged so he can sit on her lap.

I look around for a clue as to what we are after and see nothing at all. No vines grow along the ground, the thornbushes have no berries, the thorn trees have no nuts or fruits. I wait, listening to the women talking, catching very little of what they are saying.

Suddenly Di!ai calls me. "Namesake!" she says. "Come!" I don't yet know the word *namesake*, but something in her voice makes me know that I am summoned, and I do know the word for "come." We exchange a look. *Who, me? Yes, you.* So I comply. The women are walking slowly among the thornbushes, examining the ground. I follow Di!ai. Soon she squats in front of a bush and reaches out to pinch a little grasslike bit of stubble about an inch long. Looking up at me, she wiggles it, then says something I don't understand. I feel quite stupid. What can she be saying about this little nothing, in thousands of square miles of desert plant life? She is, of course, showing me the broken-off stalk of a vine and telling me its name. I catch on at last and repeat the name. "Eh," yes, she says wearily and starts to dig. I had, of course, asked her earlier to tell me the names of the plants that people ate. She has just done so. I don't know how to be helpful, so I simply watch. She chops away at the earth, blow after blow with the digging stick, then scoops the loose dirt with one hand, then chops again. When the hole is about six inches deep, she rests for a moment, then chops and scoops some more. The subsurface portion of the vine appears in the hole. She keeps chopping. The hole is now a foot deep in hard, brown earth, part clay, part sand. She finds a lump of dirt or a dirt-covered stone and removes it. Around us I hear the distant chopping of the other women. All are digging. Di!ai rests a second time and rubs her shoulder. It must hurt. She is frowning. She changes her grip on her digging stick and continues chopping. Her youngest boy looks into the hole, watching his mother's progress. Her older boy has gone off somewhere. We hear his voice, faintly. He is playing with the other knee children. His mother keeps chopping.

Now the hole is almost two feet deep. She chops more gently. "Eh," she says, "come, look." I look and see a smooth, light brown something at the bottom of the hole. It is the top of a large root. She chops into it with her digging stick and removes a small yellow piece, which she tastes. I learn later that she wants to know if this root is still in its rainy season mode, shriveled and bitter from the effort of making its vine, or if it has entered its dry season mode, filled with nourishment and edible. She gently chops around it. Evidently this one is edible. She deepens the hole until the length of the root is exposed. She then gives it a tug, but it doesn't move, so she digs some more around its sides and tugs again until it comes loose.

She strains to lift it out of the hole. It looks like an enormous brown turnip and weighs about six pounds. She slaps it a few times to shake off the dirt, puts it in the pouch of her cape, and stands up, leaning on her digging stick. We again exchange glances. She turns and walks off to another place under another bush about ten yards away, where again she squats and starts digging. Another root, obviously. Had she known it was there from an earlier visit? Had she noted some sign of it from afar? I can't tell and haven't the words to ask her.

This time the hole is deeper. It's a different kind of root. As she digs, she names it. I listen to the *chop, chop* of her digging stick and watch her thin arms working. She rests, rubs her sore shoulder, again changes her grip on the digging stick, and keeps digging. At last she exposes the top of the root. It is bigger and much darker than the first, with long rootlets like hairs growing out of it. She digs around it, scooping with her hands, then brings it to the surface, a huge dark brown thing, almost shapeless. She hasn't tasted this one—evidently she knows it to be edible. This root too she puts into her cape. The new root must weigh nine or ten pounds, so now she is carrying about eighteen pounds plus her son, also about eighteen pounds, plus her ostrich eggshell, still almost full of water, about four pounds. She herself is only five feet tall and weighs about ninety pounds. She stands up slowly. Already the load in her bulging cape is more than a third of her own weight. She strides off to the next place where she intends to dig, and there sits down to nurse her little boy. As he sucks, she takes out her ostrich eggshell, removes its grass stopper, and has a drink of water.

It is now midafternoon and very hot. The sun has been blazing down all day. Di!ai is sweating and wears a facial expression that I have come to know—she grins while frowning, a look of exasperation. When her child is finished with her breast, she gently stands him on his little feet, but before she starts to dig, she shows him the stalk that marks the root—just a wisp of plant tissue, dry and almost white in the pale grass—and names the plant as she had named the first plant for my benefit. Interested, he watches. Then his mother

starts to dig again, chopping more slowly than before because, evidently, the heavy work is making her shoulder more painful. Her child is absorbed with her work and makes digging motions. When his mother lifts the root out of the hole, she holds it up and names it. By the time this boy is old enough to learn how to hunt, he will know the names of all the roots and also how to find them. As American children learn written words, the Ju/wa children learn botany.

The next root is very deep and takes ten minutes to expose. It is the same kind as the first root Di!ai tasted, but this one looks a bit wrinkled, and when she takes a bite, it is bitter. Annoyed, she spits out the bite and throws it back into the hole, looking at me meanwhile to be sure I get the picture. She then leaves that place and its hard-earned deep hole with the bitter root still down inside, and goes to another place where she starts digging for a fifth root. She secures it after a fifteen-minute effort and moves on to get yet another. As she hoists the sixth root out of the earth and slaps off the dirt, she hears the other women calling to one another from far away, their voices almost lost in the enormous sky. She calls to them. They answer her. I believe I hear the word for "camp." They are thinking of starting back. Di!ai is ready. She has already walked about six miles this day, dug six deep holes, and moved several cubic yards of earth. She is tired.

Before beginning their return journey, the women all sit down together to rest for a few minutes and drink some of their water. Then, their capes bulging, they heave themselves up and start home, again in single file, the knee children walking. But these little boys are tired too and in time will need to be carried. Never mind. We keep walking. I would like to help, but the Ju/wa women, who are probably the most self-sufficient people on earth, don't expect help. Again, it is the Very Old Way. You find it, you own it. And you carry it.

We circle to the side of the grassy plain, taking a different direction from the way we came. At the edge of the plain the women notice five small striped melons lying on the ground on a vine. I know what these are: *tsama* melons. They look like little round watermelons and they are, as I had learned, the ancestors of all domestic squashes and melons, which revert to this ancestral form if left to pollinate freely. There are not enough melons for everyone, so Di!ai and I take none. !U will share her melon with Di!ai later.

Gathering

By now the sun is partway down the sky. We stride right along, knowing that the afternoon sunlight, however bright, is nevertheless limited. We notice the tracks of a big kudu, probably a male. He came from the southwest and went into some bushes to the east. The women take a quick look at these tracks. When they get home they will tell the men. But they don't spend much time with the tracks—the sun is going down fast.

The knee children can't keep up, and when they slow down, gaps appear in our line. Their mothers pick them up. I offer to carry Di!ai's older boy, but he wants his mother. She takes him on her hip. Her load by now is about eighty pounds. Even her daughter, who didn't want to come in the first place, is carrying a heavy bundle and is tired. She is what the Ju/wasi call an "old child," meaning a young preteen or teenager, but she is doing a woman's work. Even so, Di!ai has further plans for her and calls a halt. We stop. Di!ai removes her younger son from the pouch of her cape and, holding him by the upper arm, hands him to her daughter. Making no complaint, the young girl takes the child on her back and we start off again. The sun above the horizon shows about an hour of daylight left, and we have covered only two-thirds of the distance. The strong, ground-covering pace of the women remains the same. We try to keep it steady.

I wouldn't mind getting home. Like the other women, I have eaten nothing all day except the berries. However, unlike the other women, I unwisely didn't bother to bring any water so I am quite thirsty. I am also tired even though I did no digging, am not pregnant or lactating, have no knee child to worry about, and carry nothing but my notebook. Nevertheless, I am thinking of camp and of being in my tent, resting. I am therefore mildly disappointed when we stop again. Now the women are looking at a large dead tree that has fallen over, and I realize why we are taking a different route. We have been heading for this very tree. The women go to it and struggle to break off its branches. This will be their supply of firewood for the next few days. They break off every branch they can, two women together pushing to break off the larger branches, then load the wood onto their shoulders. Here, at least, I can be of some help, and I take a load of branches that I will give to the women when we reach camp. We walk away. The sun, a red ball, is on the horizon, a sight of great meaning for those of the Old Way on the African plains. We are thinking of lions. Within the next hour they will get up and move around. But it is impossible to walk faster and the women do not try.

Night falls quickly at 20° south latitude. Soon the sky in the east has turned deep blue. In the west, the crescent moon is showing and long red streaks of sunset clouds lie over the darkening horizon. The air is cooling noticeably. The first stars appear. We trudge on, not speaking. Even the children are quiet, perfectly quiet. Then the new baby whimpers, a tiny sound, and her mother hitches her around to nurse on the move. In the silent veld I feel the night wind rising and hear the whisper of the grass and the footsteps of the women. A bat flies over us. A little later we hear a flock of guinea fowls calling intermittently as they fly, one by one, up to their roost in a tree. Later still a jackal calls and another answers. The first jackal calls again. The world of the day is closing. The world of the night is opening. We keep walking.

Just as all the stars appear, we hear voices and see firelight on the undersides of branches up ahead. We are there. The women drop their loads of firewood by their grass shelters, then unload the pouches of their capes, removing first the children, then the ostrich eggshells, then the striped *tsama* melons, then the many heavy roots, then the berries. Di!ai gets some branches and breaks them up, then borrows a coal from another woman's fire (a coal that she carries in her bare hands) and uses it to light her own fire. She feeds it with twigs and blows on it until it is burning. She then sits down beside it, calls me over, and asks me to rub her sore shoulder. At last I can be of some real help. I gladly rub her shoulder.

That night the women split open some of the roots and lay them on the coals, and by the time the crescent moon has set, every family is eating.

9

Poison

The discovery of underground foods and the practice of digging for them led to one of the most significant findings of humankind—the grubs that yield Bushman arrow poison. These grubs are the pupating larvae of certain beetles that infest some but not all marula and commiphora trees. All in all, there were three kinds of poison beetles from the families *Diamphidia* and *Polyclada*, each with its parasite, also poisonous.[1] Their poison is as deadly as any known substance, as lethal as mamba venom or botulinum toxin. A few drops will kill an animal the size of a cow, and a single drop will kill a person. Once the poison gets into the blood, death is inevitable. There is no antidote, nothing that anyone can do. In recent years, after the Ju/wasi no longer lived in the Old Way, after poverty, overcrowding, disease, poor diet, and substance abuse had taken their toll, not a few people committed suicide by stabbing themselves with poison arrows. In angry despair they jabbed arrows into their thighs to begin the fatal process, and although their weeping relatives ran to help them, to snatch out the arrow and suck out the poison, and although some of the suicides soon changed their minds and bitterly regretted their actions, it was too late. No one survives a poison arrow.[2]

On a global scale, the discovery of this poison is often viewed as a side issue, important only to the Bushmen, without relevance to the rest of the world. Yet this marginalizing view may be quite wrong, as the discovery of poison may have played a significant role in the development of the bow and arrow. True, the people of Paleolithic Eurasia are usually credited with the bow and arrow.[3] However, the weapon may have originated as two unrelated objects, the bow beginning as a musical instrument and the arrow beginning as a thorn or a porcupine quill.

The bow as a musical instrument is not a far-fetched notion—the use holds to this day. The Ju/wasi we knew in the 1950s frequently played music on their hunting bows. With the tip of the bow inside his mouth, tapping a stick or an arrow on the bowstring, changing its length and thus its tone with his finger, a man (always a man because women didn't carry hunting bows or, among the Ju/wasi, even handle them) would produce very soft music, barely audible to those nearby, but audible to him, because his mouth was the resonating chamber. Noise on the savannah is never good—if the Ju/wasi are any example, our ancestors were quiet people—so what better instrument for a tracker who wants to pass the time by playing a little music without drawing attention? We knew a youngster in the 1950s who, using his mouth as a resonator, played a tune on a blade of grass, which was perhaps the earliest of all instruments and makes the bowstring, by comparison, look almost as complicated as machinery.

When great inventions are discussed, the branch bent with a sinew tied to both ends is never among them, probably because the item speaks so strongly of the Old Way. Yet this elegant invention of an unknown hunter-gatherer thousands of years ago was to become a bow and arrow, then a crossbow, a musket, a rifle, a cannon, and, eventually, a rocket. People kept right on tinkering with it and eventually went to the moon aboard a modified version of the branch bent with sinew.

Meanwhile, the same branch and sinew also became a lute, a harp, a guitar, a zither, a mandolin, a violin, viola, bass violin and cello, a harpsichord, and a piano. These and their worldwide rela-

A few drops of poison will kill an animal the size of a cow.

tives are also versions of the branch bent with sinew and had their origins in the Old Way.

Perhaps the original bow had nothing to do with hunting, but the original arrow was almost certainly a dart of some kind, and on the African savannah was almost certainly a device for injecting poison from the grubs. However, darts were not necessarily used as projectiles, or not at first. In the earliest times, darts were probably used as the Ju/wasi we knew in the 1950s continued to use them—poisoned and planted upright in places where animals would sit on them. Megan Biesele finds reference to this practice in a story in which the jackal woman kills her sister by putting poison arrows where she sits. It's not an unusual idea. The Ju/wa people whom we knew would poison something sharp, usually an arrowhead, and plant it in the nest of an ostrich. But any pointed item, such as a long, sharp acacia thorn or the quill of an African porcupine would do. To sit on her nest, the ostrich bends her legs, lowers herself slowly, then drops down heavily for the last few inches. If something sharp is sticking up among the eggs, the ostrich is pierced by it. The planted-dart method of hunting seemed ancient indeed and could be used against any unsuspecting animal whose resting places were predictable.

The next step, of course, would be to find a way of propelling the dart into an animal who is on the move, rather than waiting for him to sit on it. Surely before we were human beings we were throwing things at animals, braining our victims with stones (unlike our other primate relatives, our arms and shoulders are especially adapted for throwing—we are, if you will, animals who throw), so that the idea of throwing a dart could not have been much of a stretch.

Nor is the idea of shooting a poisoned quill from a musical bow. If musical bows already existed, then the power of the bowstring would be understood. And if you are holding the bow in one hand, the wand you are using to tap the string is in your other hand. The tip of a porcupine quill (as well as many other items) if bound to that wand would lend itself beautifully as a projectile. In the 1950s, the Ju/wasi spoke of just that—using porcupine quills as arrowheads.

Thus the bows and arrows that Ju/wasi make today are reminiscent of the distant past, as competent in design as they are simple in materials. The Bushman arrowhead continued to be something of a dart, a tiny point on a shank or foreshaft, the point originally made of bone or wood or stone but more recently made of flattened wire,[4] set into a carefully shaped bone midsection, which in turn fits into the shaft, a hollow reed. When the arrow hits the target, the midsection comes loose and drops off with the shaft, leaving the dart portion of the arrow embedded. Thus, the arrow itself is simply a device for delivering a dart.

The bow is also elegantly simple—a branch cut from one of several kinds of trees, scraped smooth, tapered at both ends, rubbed with fat, and strung with a bowstring made of long sinews from the legs of large animals. The pull of the bow is about twenty-five pounds, and the arrow weighs less than half an ounce.

Commonly when we think of Paleolithic hunting equipment we think of spears, sometimes viewing the spear as the ancestor of the arrow. And when we think of the bow and arrow, we think of large bows with pulls of fifty to seventy pounds, able to send a spearlike, stone-tipped arrow through a bison or an Irish elk. Indeed, a bow and arrow is so useful that it could have been developed at several different times and places, but if the savannah scenario has anything to it, then the powerful bows and big arrows came later, the inventions of people who didn't live within traveling distance of marula trees and couldn't find grubs that yielded poison.

The spear is another matter—the Ju/wasi had spears and knew how to use them. Interestingly enough, however, their spears were almost peripheral objects. Ju/wa hunters made spears about three and a half feet long, the shaft a strong, straight branch of hardwood with a blade made of cold-hammered metal obtained in trade. This, too, says something about the antiquity of darts or arrows, which are highly developed and made from many different things. The spear blades, in contrast, were made only of traded metal, with no ancient, nonmetallic predecessor on hand and no substitute on the sidelines. Surely, then, the importance of darts and arrows traditionally exceeded the importance of spears, at least as far as the Bushmen were concerned.

This was certainly true in the 1950s. The Ju/wasi gave their spears relatively little attention, nothing like the attention they paid to their arrows. Nor did they find much occasion to use a spear, which was mainly for dispatching a victim already dying from arrow poison. A man might use his spear to reach high into a tree to detatch a bit of gum that was oozing through the bark, and he might possibly fling a spear into something the size of a porcupine or aardvark, but more likely he would kill such an animal by clubbing it—clubbing the victim does not break the skin and can be accomplished with a stick. A man might use his spear as a knife—he might bite into a chunk of meat and use his spear to detatch the bite from the larger piece, sawing away with the spear blade just millimeters from the tip of his nose. Then, too, a man would use his spear in self-defense against a dangerous animal if to do so was absolutely necessary, although spearing a large, aggressive animal is always a perilous activity.

Surely people have had some sort of spears for a long time, even longer than stone spear heads would indicate. A sharpened digging stick can be a kind of spear, which means of course that the spear descends from the earliest tools that we first learned to use in the rain forest. Spears are important tools for fishing—a fishing spear is of course a harpoon. But fishing wasn't an option for many of the savannah hunter-gatherers, especially for those in the waterless reaches, so the importance of spears was mainly limited to dispatching victims.

Do archaeological studies reflect these preferences? Not entirely, nor may they ever. Although the African earth is laden with stone objects, including tiny arrowheads, their presence does not exclude objects made of other materials, by any means. Bone, wood, big thorns, and porcupine quills are not as durable and may not turn up as readily in the archaeological sites, but all surely were present in the distant past, just as they were present in the 1950s in Nyae Nyae. Bone and wood are easier to work than stone but can be made just as sharp and hence are just as effective, although in the long run bone is much better than wood. And in the past, both were more readily available than were some of the better kinds of workable stones, because wood of course is everywhere, and every large antelope yields two scapular spines from which its hunters can make bone arrows. As has been said, arrowheads made of bone (and one or two made of wood) were used in Nyae Nyae when we first visited. Arrowheads made of cold-hammered wire were preferred, but bone arrowheads were very much present. Bone, in fact, was part of every arrow, always as the midsection, if not always as the arrowhead. Every Bushman arrow in Nyae Nyae contained this small bone segment, and still does to this day.

Interestingly, although the people of /Gautscha made bone arrowheads, earlier residents of /Gautscha had not confined themselves to bone or wood. Small stone arrowheads and other little stone tools lay scattered around on the surface of the ground just beyond the waterhole. The archaeologist Robert Dyson, who briefly accompanied us in 1951, identified them as belonging to a late Stone Age Wilton culture. The /Gautscha Ju/wasi knew about the stone points but didn't know who made them. They had always been there, the people said.

Seemingly, their ancestors made them. "The places with the largest and most dense surface scatters," wrote the archaeologist John Yellen about such ancient Nyae Nyae sites, "are just those where today Bushmen establish their dry season camps."[5] This is not surprising. The people of /Gautscha continued to use stone tools, not for arrows, to be sure, but as weights to stretch sinew, as hammers and anvils to crack things open—nuts for the nutmeat, for instance, or bones for the marrow—or as sharpeners for their metal knives and arrows. I once watched a man use a sharp-edged stone in a very old way—to gently scrape small imperfections from the shaft of a bone arrow. The Ju/wasi sometimes covered graves with stones to prevent animals from digging, and Khoi hunter-gatherers in other parts of the Kalahari made short stone walls that, as an inexperienced park ranger in Etosha National Park once told me, were hunting blinds. To me, this seemed unlikely. The people we knew did not use hunting blinds, which might work once but would be nothing more than warning signs after the resident animals realized what might be behind them. Each "blind" was about the length of a person, so I thought that the stone piles made by the Khoikhoi might be graves. But who am I to say? Anyway, when making spear blades, knives, and arrows, the Ju/wasi of the 1950s did not use stone but preferred materials such as wire and bone that were more easily worked.

Whatever the history, the bone users didn't leave much behind by way of bows and arrows. The same would be true of the Ju/wasi we knew in the 1950s. On the rare occasions that their biodegradable items got broken, the pieces were tossed aside wherever the owner happened to be standing. Or if the owner died, the items were broken up and scattered on the grave. Sometimes the broken bits were destroyed by mice, sometimes by wildfires, leaving little behind to help an archaeologist.[6] But too little archaeological work has been done in this area, sad to say. The only thing that can be said for sure is that for 150,000 years, at least some of the hunter-gatherers lived so lightly on the savannah that they did not produce much of an archaeological record. The people we knew in the 1950s, with their wood, bone, and sinew, were leaving next to nothing, yet there they were. The same is true of the nonhuman residents of the African savannah. It is knowledge, skills, and customs, not objects, that endure.

As for the poison grubs, although their earliest use may never be accurately dated, their discovery surely took place long ago. Digging for grubs belongs to the earliest part of human prehistory. Somewhere in the very distant past, our ancestors would have used insect larvae as a dependable source of protein, as do many animals including chimpanzees, but the Ju/wasi whom we knew in the 1950s did so only occasionally, and only then if the larvae were tasty, like certain sweet caterpillars. (These were called *gum*—the *u* as in *put*—which was also the name of sweet ants and the sweet gum that oozes from a tree.) When at our request the people listed the foods they ate, larval insects were seldom mentioned. Over the aeons, and given ways of getting protein in much larger quantities, people have tended to move away from grubs as food items, hence grubs have dwindled in importance.

So how and when did people discover the poison? If its use can't be dated by stone arrowheads (except that large stone arrowheads suggest a culture that lacked poison), then what might help to find an answer? The discovery is the kind made by those who spend their time exploring and memorizing every item in their environment with profound attention to detail. In the United States, black bears do this, moving carefully through a forest, noting every plant and insect, being able to recognize a plant whether it's a naked stalk in winter, or a flower in spring, or a berry in summer, or a few dry leaves in the fall.[7] If you remember the naked stalk and come back in a few months, you'll be rewarded with berries. Chimpanzees have similar abilities. The primatologist Richard Wrangham calls chimpanzees excellent botanists.

When in midlife I came to think of certain animals as botanists, I also thought of the people of the Kalahari, who had named almost every plant that grew and knew its properties, who would recognize a plant in one season and come back for it in a later season, either because it became edible seasonally, or because they were saving it for later when they needed it, so that a gathering expedition was not so much a search as a long-term harvest. Surely the earliest people were no less capable than American black bears and chimpanzees—all belonged to the Old Way, and all needed the same kind of knowledge for the same reasons. Surely the earliest people, or the ancestors of the earliest people, gave their environment the same kind of examination and handed down their findings from generation to generation. "The old people told us," was the explanation that the modern Ju/wasi gave for their profound environmental knowledge. "The old people showed us," would be the explanation of chimps or bears, or hominids without language. I'd say that it would be hard to find another explanation.

Profound examination seems to be the only way that anyone could learn of the poison grubs, as they are the larvae of beetles about whom nothing draws attention. The adults live in marula trees, which people visited for the nuts, but not all trees are infested with beetles, not by any means. In the trees that are infested, the beetles are small to average in size, plain looking, and of ordinary shape—a small oval body with plain short legs and plain antennae, at least to the naked eye—much less colorful or noticeable than thousands of other kinds of beetles found on the savannah. Nor do the poison beetles interact in any way with people. They don't compete for human foods, they don't bite or sting, and their hard little bodies—mostly carapace—cannot be particularly edible. Every time I saw these beetles, they were just standing around on the leaves of a marula tree, which was their specialized habitat. One would think that people would have no cause to investigate them.

What's more, if anyone did, very little would be learned from the adults, because the poison, according to the Ju/wasi, is obtainable only from the pupae, and normally these are not available for human observation, because during the pupating process, the grubs are out of sight. The larvae hatch on the leaves of the tree but crawl under the bark, and thus hidden go down the tree to the roots and out into the sandy soil where they pupate in casings they make from the earth that surrounds them. So they spend their pupa stage as sandy brown lumps in lumpy brown sand, deep among the roots of special trees that people visit seasonally, but only to gather the nuts. Nothing much grows under the trees, so people have little incentive to be digging. How then did they find the grubs?

The question has no obvious answer. Yet find them they did, which gives rise to an even more difficult question. How did they learn that the grubs were poisonous? Perhaps from eating them, although the poison must enter the bloodstream directly to be fatal. The people of Nyae Nyae safely ate the flesh from the arrow wounds of the animals they killed, even though the flesh was black with poison and would still hold residual poison from the arrow.

Meanwhile, a grub would have done nothing to suggest the presence of poison, because the grubs as pupae are passive. While in their pupa casings they don't need to eat or defend themselves, so they don't bite. When removed from their pupa casings they don't fight back—they do nothing more than twitch helplessly once or twice. Anyway, the poison is in the grub's body, not in its mouth. To get the poison, the grub must be removed from the cocoon, its insides must be mushed without breaking its skin, its head must be carefully twisted off, and the deadly innards must be squeezed out like paste from a tube. There seems to be little in the procedure that could be accidentally stumbled upon—the operations are not everyday activities that people do spontaneously.

Then, too, even if a person or animal somehow got injected with the poison, the connection between the juice of the grub and the death of the victim would be less than obvious, because the poisoning process is so slow. An animal victim would be long gone and far away before death overtook it, and a human victim—probably the creature upon whom the effects of poison were first noted—might easily live for at least a day after exposure, and could live longer. No matter—the discovery was made and would win acclaim for the discoverers if their names were known or if they had lived in a Western nation. However, the discovery was not made by people in white coats in a laboratory, but was the achievement of forgotten hunter-gatherers a long time ago, out on the veld, under a tree. It demonstrates, perhaps better than any other bit of acquired information, the profound environmental knowledge of the Old Way.

One day in 1955 we went with three Ju/wa men to visit a certain tree that they knew was infested with *Diamphedia* beetles. The tree stood alone in an open, rather nondescript landscape on grassy, sandy ground, and had been quietly dropping its leaves, which lay curled and scattered underneath it. The men scuffed aside some of the leaves to expose a number of dents in the sandy earth showing where, at an earlier time, other people had also been digging for poison. But because adult beetles still lived in the tree, more grubs had become available. The men sat down on their heels, took their digging sticks out of their hunting bags, and started digging.

The earth under the tree was a heavy, almost sticky, coffee-colored sand. I sat beside one of the men, Gao Feet, to watch the process, and was surprised at how clear the sand was. No stones halted his progress. Gao Feet simply chopped slowly with his digging stick, pausing now and then to scoop out the loosened sand. When the hole was about twenty inches deep, he reached down and withdrew a little round item made of the very sand he had been digging. It was a poison grub in its pupa casing. Gao Feet had spotted it immediately, but as far as I was concerned, it had been invisible. Gao Feet held it on his palm to show me, then set it aside and kept digging, scraping at the sides of the hole. Soon another pupa tumbled out of the dirt, then another and another. Gao Feet moved to a different spot and started a new hole. In fifteen or twenty minutes, he had found all the pupae he needed, about twelve or thirteen. Perhaps finding the beetles and learning about their poison was a miracle in the first place, but after watching the process that afternoon, finding the grubs even when one knew what and where they were also seemed almost miraculous—two or three brown pupa casings per cubic foot of brown sand seemed to describe their density.

Gao Feet put the pupae into a container made of the curved tip of a kudu's horn (it looked like a powder horn) and capped it with a little leather cap made of an antelope's scrotum. This and his digging stick he put back into his hunting bag. He finished by brushing off his fingers. Together the three men had found about thirty-five grubs in five or six holes. Many more pupae may have been in the sand, but no effort was made to find them. When the men had as many grubs as they needed, they were ready to leave, so we went.

Soon after this, the men poisoned their arrows. The grubs don't need to be used immediately, although the poison itself weakens after a while, becoming "cold," as the Ju/wasi put it. But for a very long time the grubs are so potentially dangerous that usually they are not left lying around, but instead are applied to the arrows. A possible explanation for this is that the process put the poison in a controlled condition and simplified the number of items that needed watching, so that only the arrows needed to be monitored, not the arrows and also the grubs. If the explanation is accurate, early application would have been one of the many deliberate safety measures taken by the Ju/wasi to protect the community from accidental poisoning.

In addition to using the grubs soon after gathering them, the people poisoned only the shanks of the arrowheads, not the points, so if someone got scratched or pricked simply by handling an arrow, no harm would come. The arrowhead had to be sunk far enough into the victim so that the shank entered the wound. Furthermore, arrows were stored in quivers, point down, and the quivers were hung in trees as high up as a man could reach, out of reach of small children. The Ju/wasi would no sooner leave a poison arrow lying around unattended than we would leave a live hand grenade in a kindergarten. (A diorama in the Iziko Museum of Cape Town troubles me. It shows a Bushman camp with a hunter in the middle, about to shoot an arrow. Although he stands in the middle of the camp, he is raising his bow as if he were planning to let fly the arrow. A similar diorama of our culture would show a man brandishing a pistol in his living room with his family all around.)

During the years we spent in Nyae Nyae, every man, woman, and child (with one notable exception, mentioned later) observed the rules of safety. No instance of carelessness was ever noted, and for as long as anyone could remember not a single human death in the entire Nyae Nyae region resulted from carelessness with grubs or arrows—not one. What's more, the care was so ingrained in the culture of everyday life that it seemed effortless. Very rarely did anyone make anything of it or talk about it. They just did it, as easily and naturally as breathing. It was part of the Old Way. I'd offer a comparative example from our society if we had one, but we don't. We certainly don't treat guns with such competence. But then, the loss of just one human life is a terrible thing in tiny communities such as those of the Ju/wasi, where everybody is essential, where people rely on one another in the struggle for existence. We in the Western world give human life plenty of lip service, but in reality, we as individuals don't matter much and the feelings aren't the same.

I often watched men poisoning their arrows and made notes in my journals such as the following entry from July 1955, at which time I watched !Gai, the young hunter who had stalked the wildebeests. About fifty feet downwind from the grass shelters where his group was living, he built a little fire and sat on his heels beside it with his hunting bag. That day, he poisoned just one arrow—a bone arrow—although normally a man might poison up to ten arrows at any one time. !Gai had ten grubs and used them all on this one arrow, the shank of which, when !Gai was finished, wore a shiny, faintly orange sheath, the crusted poison paste.

According to my journal, the day was windy and cold. It was good to be beside a fire. !Gai's first act in the poisoning process was to spread out a small piece of leather as a work surface. Then he took up his arrow, looked down its length to check it for straightness, and sharpened the point with his knife. Then he gently scraped the shank, cleaning it of any residual matter. Then he was ready to apply the poison.

Before he begins, he inspects his fingers carefully. Then he delicately opens a little brown cocoon and pulls the grub out with his fingernails, pinching it very delicately, not breaking the del-

icate skin. Another grub he drags out with a straw. The grubs are large and pale yellow with black spots. They are shiny, with very shiny black heads. Exposed, the grub struggles very feebly, giving one slight, almost imperceptible convulsion, then lies alive but motionless, curled into a U. !Gai picks up each grub and lays it over his thumbnail, and taps it gently to break up the insides. Then he twists off the head and squeezes the insides of the grub onto the shank of the arrow, smearing it evenly with a straw.

After !Gai had poisoned his arrow with paste from ten grubs, he propped it near the fire to dry and asked his wife to bring him a *tsama* melon that she had found earlier. He chopped an opening in the top with the sharp end of a digging stick as we might open a Halloween pumpkin, then reversed the digging stick and used the blunt end to pound the insides of the melon to a pulp, then put coals from the fire into the pulp, which hissed and steamed, then put the melon, coals and all, on the fire, and when the liquid inside was hot he used it to thoroughly wash his hands. Then he dried his hands with grass, put the arrow, point down, into his quiver, put his quiver into his hunting bag, dropped the digging stick in beside it, folded the empty carcasses of the grubs into the piece of leather, and stuffed them down beside the digging stick. The job was finished.

What !Gai eventually did with the carcasses of the grubs I neglected to put in my journal. Normally, people burn them, but perhaps on that day the wind was too strong and variable. Even the smoke of burning grubs can be dangerous, as I learned one cold winter day when a man, after poisoning his arrows, was burning the grubs. While I was standing about twenty feet from the fire, the wind changed and shifted the smoke so that it drifted past me. Not being as aware as the Ju/wasi, I didn't pay much attention, and anyway, I liked to stand in smoke as a way to keep warm. Someone called a warning, and I moved, but too late—some of the smoke had blown across a raw place on one of my fingers. At first I thought nothing of it, but after a minute or two I felt pain in my hand. The pain grew and moved up my arm. Worried, I mentioned it. One of the men seized my hand and smelled it—poison in a wound makes a faint odor—then quickly sucked the raw place as one would suck a snakebite.

Well, here I am, fifty years later, telling the story. How much of the poison had entered my hand, wafted by a little smoke across the raw place on my skin? A few molecules? Surely not more than that. And with such a tiny dose, would anything terrible have happened to me if no one had helped? Apparently the man who sucked the raw place thought it could. Nowadays, medical theory sometimes holds that venom cannot be removed by sucking, that there are better ways of dealing with injected poisons, but the Ju/wasi thought differently. Who knows better, them or us? Anyway, I'm grateful to the man who helped me. The pain had reached my elbow. It's hard to imagine the power of that poison.

10

Dangerous Animals

Since rain forest times, we have contended with predators. Many of them are as big as or bigger than we are and can run faster. Our fists and feet are too soft to deliver meaningful blows, we have no claws, and over time our teeth have become too small to act as a deterrent. In danger when alone, unable to fend off predators without assistance, we find safety by living in groups, so that many eyes are keeping watch and so that we can help one another if the need arises. The danger of predators explains why the Ju/wa women virtually never went gathering alone and why their babies did not cry. A baby's crying, after all, is a distress signal, telling the world that it needs help. Prolonged crying suggests that the baby has been abandoned, that no one is there to defend it. What predator would not prick up its ears at an invitation like that? The young of most species who live in the Old Way are also notably silent, for the same reason.

The presence of predators explains why, when the Bushmen traveled, they walked in single file, always with one of the men in the lead and usually with another man bringing up the rear. This way, the leader kept watch for a predator in ambush, and the man at the rear kept watch for a predator who might be trying to sneak up from behind. The women and children walked in the middle and were safe. We are, after all, primates, and our men were the silverbacks, the protectors.

In addition, the presence of predators and also of poisonous snakes explains the activity patterns of the Bushmen. The people tried always to be in an encampment by late afternoon, before the sun was setting, and did not move about again until the sun was high in the morning. This way, they used the day when the sun was hot, when the predators were sleeping in the shade and the poisonous snakes were in their burrows.

Since rain forest times, our most persistent predator has been the leopard. As the lynx is to the snowshoe hare, so the leopard is to many of the primates, creeping quietly into our encampments at night, trying to secure a victim. One night in Nyae Nyae, a leopard crept up behind a man who was sitting with his wife at their fire. The leopard seized the man from behind, at the nape of his neck. His wife leaped to her feet, snatched up her digging stick, and whacked the leopard so hard on the head that he let go of his victim. By this time all the people in the encampment were aroused and on their feet, and the leopard, bruised and outnumbered, ran off into the dark. In another encampment at another time, a leopard successfully killed a sleeping man and dragged him into the bush. On yet another occasion, a leopard killed a man in broad daylight although the man was fully armed and alert to his surroundings. He was hunting alone, as men often did, and the leopard must have been behind him. A study of causes of death among the Ju/wasi, conducted in later years by my brother and a colleague, Claire Ritchie, showed that leopards were traditionally a predator of the Nyae Nyae population. Even so, the living arrangements of the Ju/wasi, and their profound understanding of their environment and all that was in it, protected them. In my experience, visits by leopards were considerably more frequent than their successes, which perhaps explains why they did not try more often. They did better by hunting other kinds of victims.

Despite their preference for primates, leopards are easily discouraged. They know that they are smaller than other major predators, and unlike lions and hyenas, they are all alone, without support in times of trouble. Hence they live by stealth, exposing themselves

to danger as seldom as possible. To avoid being robbed, they some-times hoist their victims into trees where other predators can't reach them. They also climb trees for their own protection. Richard Estes reports that even a dog as small as a terrier can tree a leopard in the daytime and tells of a leopard who was driven off by a yapping jackal. One often hears the expression "lion hearted" but not the ex-pression "leopard hearted." If leopards cause fear, they also feel it.

We saw four leopards in the surroundings of Nyae Nyae. All were afraid of us. Once during the rains I saw a leopard's face in some leafy bushes. Our eyes met, he pulled back, the leaves closed over him, and he disappeared. Another time, at the height of the dry season on a scorching day on an open plain, we saw a crouching leopard who completely filled a spot of shade cast by a small, soli-tary tree. Although it was noonday, and he was in the only shade for miles around, the moment he saw us he went bounding off into the blistering veld, relinquishing the life-giving shadow before learning whether or not we posed any danger to him.

Once after a cold night, when we were traveling past a certain ledge of rock, we saw a leopard lying on his back, his thighs open, exposing his white belly to the morning sun. Horrified at the ap-pearance of our vehicle, he flung himself over the rim of the ledge and vanished in the landscape below.

And once, to the west of Nyae Nyae, I saw a leopard who evi-dently wanted a drink of water but knew that lions also used the wa-terhole. The lions did not seem to be present at the time, but they certainly had left their odor on everything, so the leopard may have assumed they were still around. Head high, body tense, making no effort to conceal herself, she slowly and carefully inched toward the water. She'd take a step or two, then wait a long time, looking and listening, then take a few more steps, but after almost fifteen minutes of this, she still had too many doubts about her safety, and she changed her mind and left without drinking.

I mention these sightings to show the caution of leopards—their furtive nature, their lack of confidence. Even so, they dared to hunt people.

Hyenas also preyed upon people, but they were not as secretive as leopards. We rarely heard leopards coughing or calling, but we very often heard hyenas, as they are social animals and must communicate with one another. Usually they do this at night when they are up and about, making a rising, falling, whooping call, not very loud. Spotted hyenas sometimes made the high, vibrating, excited call that unrealistically has been likened to laughter—a call that they use when they are distressed or are being chased, probably meaning that the calling hyena had tangled with hyenas from another group, or with a lion. But because the hyenas were active mostly at night, we rarely saw them. I used to take one of the trucks to the waterhole at night and watch to see who drank there, and although I never saw lions, who came long after I had gone (although we would see their tracks in the morning), I once became aware of the shadowy forms of two brown hyenas who had crossed the pan together and were walking purposefully but silently to the water. When they noticed the truck, a big, dark item where nothing had been before, they stopped short, then changed direction slightly so as not to approach the truck head-on but instead to pass by it very slowly, heads low, tails partly raised, radiating hostility and suspicion and calling softly with short, low-pitched whoops as if simply to relieve their feelings. Or perhaps they were addressing the truck, suggesting that it leave the waterhole. When nothing happened, they circled the truck in silence, then left without drinking, as quietly as smoke, each taking a different direction. I stopped trying to see them after that because I didn't want to deprive them of their chance to drink, or to put them in harm's way from the lions by making them come at a time not of their choosing.

Once I was walking alone about a mile beyond the northwest corner of /Gautscha pan when I came upon a high bank in which was a hole about three feet in diameter. It seemed to be a den. Just as I approached to take a look inside, a large spotted hyena stepped partway out. She stood very tall, her ears up but not rigid, her head high but slightly averted as she looked me over. I was entranced. The hyena was beautiful and unafraid, completely in command of the situation, very clearly the owner of that small part of the planet. I could have stood there all day looking at her, but she, apparently, did not want me to do that. She raised her lip slightly and showed me some of her teeth. *See these? Leave now, and I won't hurt you,* her manner said.

So I left, slouching a little to show her that my mood was casual, moving away at an oblique angle—an important protocol for leaving the vicinity of a large predator, a protocol that we had been carefully taught by the Ju/wasi. You don't want to present your back, and you certainly don't want to run. You want to seem indifferent and confident. Satisfied with my behavior, the hyena backed up into the den.

That was the last I saw of her, but that was not my last encounter with hyenas. One night a few months later, I was in my tent at the far edge of camp (a small, one-person tent such as a backpacker might use) reading a book by the light of a candle, when another spotted hyena, smaller than the first, quietly pushed his head through the open door flap. His yellow-brown eyes met mine. Our noses were almost touching. "What is it?" I asked. The hyena hesitated for a moment, then averted his eyes and modestly withdrew, leaving as quietly as he had come.

There seemed to be nothing to fear. I turned back to my book. Someone who had heard me speak asked what was happening, and I said that a hyena was in the camp. However, no one else reported seeing him. Why had he come? Perhaps the candlelight had cast my silhouette through the tent wall, showing those outside that someone inside was lying down. He was probably just checking to see if I was awake and in good health. When he saw that I was, he left.

Hyenas scavenge, of course, for which they are famous, but also they are excellent hunters, hunting alone or in pairs, always for the most easily captured prey—an animal who is young, old, or in any way disabled. Hyenas determine this by rushing at a group of antelope to see who leaves most slowly. Like the Ju/wasi who run down elands, hyenas for all their warm fur have extraordinary stamina and will jog along behind a targeted victim for miles until the victim is overcome with exhaustion. By this time the hyena has probably been joined by family members, who then, like wild dogs, simply take bites out of the victim, a process that eventually results in the victim's death. The only potential prey that hyenas avoid are those who are too fit or too big to tackle.

This category, of course, does not include all human beings. Hyenas have been known to enter encampments at night and take bites out of sleeping people. Terrible as it is to consider, what the hyena wants is a few bites of meat, even if he can't have the whole victim. As has been said, when hyenas catch up to victims, they take bites rather than trying to bring the animal down, although they do that too, if they can. Thus their treatment of us is not untypical. Even so, they also kill people when possible. At /Gautscha one night, a hyena caught a sleeping girl by the foot and, instead of biting her, tried to drag her into the bushes. She was rescued and the wound healed, fortunately.

A survey made by my brother and Claire Ritchie on causes of death in the Nyae Nyae population suggests that hyenas took relatively few human victims,[1] yet I sometimes wonder if the survey reflects the full number, because most of the victims taken by hyenas were enfeebled, alone, and near death anyway, so that their deaths might have been attributed to their condition and not to whatever might have happened to them during the very last moments of life. My mother, for example, was told of a woman, perhaps the victim of a stroke, who lay unconscious in her people's camp. The people said that "her body was dead," and a bad smell exuded from her, even though she was still breathing. Feeling that there was nothing more that they could do for her (and unwilling to stay near a corpse or even near a grave because of the dead person's departing spirit), they broke down her grass shelter, placed the grass and branches over her, and left. When they returned the next day, they found that hyenas had eaten her. If her death was included in the survey, was it attributed to hyenas, or to whatever put her into a coma?

We knew of four or five people who had been killed by hyenas. Unquestionably there were others as well. While a certain group was making a long journey during the dry season, an older man suffered a serious burn on his leg. As the group continued on its way (as any traveling group must do in order to reach water in a timely manner), the man could not keep up with the rest, and when night came and the group made its encampment, the man was not with them. The others did not want to travel at night to search for him, but they went back for him in the morning, only to find that he had been killed and eaten by hyenas. This story, too, was told to my mother by people whom it puzzled and distressed. The man had fire sticks, the people said—no man travels without his fire sticks—so why had he not built a fire and shaken a burning branch at the hyenas? His companions had assumed that he would be safe, they said. His group had misjudged his situation.

To take a straggler is entirely in keeping with the hunting methods of hyenas, who are always alert to weakness and may monitor any group of sizable nonhyenas that happens to be on the move, to see if one of them is lagging. Knowing this, people never intentionally left their close relatives behind, no matter what their condition. My brother knew a disabled woman who was carried around for years by her relatives. I knew an older woman who carried her very sick, almost unconscious adult daughter and her daughter's two children for the last part of a thirty-mile journey, following her group as they traveled. She arrived at the destination just before dark and many hours after the others, but she got there, and her family was safe, thanks to her. Why hadn't the others helped her? I can't answer that, but I assume that her daughter had started the journey on foot and may not have seemed to need help. Perhaps she was carrying one child, and her mother was carrying the other. Perhaps the daughter began to lag, because of her sickness. Her mother would have stayed with her and carried her when she could no longer walk. By then they would have been far behind the others, who would not have known of their condition. The mother did well to carry her daughter and the children—all of them would have been in considerable danger alone in the night. Perhaps they didn't have fire sticks, as men, not women, use them. The dictum of survival of the fittest includes the love that we feel for our families and our willingness to sacrifice for them, and today, thanks to their grandmother, those two little children are adults with children of their own, perpetuating their grandmother's ability to care for her family.

There were other examples of care, not always with sociobiological implications. The /Gautscha people knew of an old man who could not travel with his people when they had to go elsewhere after their waterhole dried. The old man had to stay behind, but his two sons stayed with him and remained with him until he died, then gave him a proper burial. Their own well-being was thus jeopardized, and with it, their future generations, but their concern for their father overrode that.

Virtually all of those who became the victims of hyenas were enfeebled, elderly people without caring relatives, and did not receive special protection either because they were so unpleasant and difficult that their groups considered them burdensome, or because they had outlived their circle of close kin. Such people, however few, might be left behind when the group moved camp, or allowed to fall far behind when the group was in transit. If these people were

conscious, as some certainly were, they would watch the sky darken and the stars come out, and then, alone in the black night, might hear hyenas whooping in the distance, and then, much later, might see a pair of green eyes shining dimly in the moonlight or starlight, or perhaps just hear the grass rustle and feel the brush of fur or a waft of warm breath.

Such a fate the Ju/wasi found disturbing, and no wonder. Lazy /Kwi was among those who gave these accounts to my mother. "Shaking his head and staring with unseeing eyes as he imagined the scenes," wrote my mother, "he said with a shudder that he hoped the old people were 'finished' before the hyenas came."[2]

Not all were, and their deaths were not to be imagined, as hyenas see no need to kill their victims before starting to eat.

The largest of the Nyae Nyae predators were, of course, the lions. In Nyae Nyae, as far as we could tell, they lived near waterholes, as did the people. At /Gautscha, a large pride of perhaps twenty lions seemed to camp in assorted places southeast of the water (diagonally opposite the den of the spotted hyenas but perhaps at about the same distance). We never saw them there, but if they were at all like lions elsewhere, they would have spent the entire day asleep. When the shade moved, they would feel hot, get up, trudge over to the new spot, and flop down again. There is something very personal and intimate about sleeping lions. Sometimes they dream, and their eyelids flutter. Sometimes they lie motionless for such long periods that an observer can mistake them for dead. If the patch of shade is small, they sometimes sleep all in a pile, even lying on top of one another, so that all will fit in the shadow. No other creatures of the savannah sleep as deeply or as soundly as lions, but after all, lions are the main reason for not sleeping soundly, so this is not surprising.

Lions can hunt anytime they please, day or night, but certainly in the dry season, especially in the hot time, the lions at /Gautscha hunted long after dark. Having no need whatever to conceal their presence except from an intended victim, they often roared spectacularly at night, calling and answering as if to keep track of one another. Aside from that, the main difference between their hunting style and that of the people was that the people hunted in the daytime. Otherwise, the two kinds of hunting styles were very much the same. A group of three or four individuals would set out together, then spread out to learn what might be available, then make a quiet stalk, and then, from about the same distance, make a charge (if the hunter was a lion) or shoot an arrow (if the hunter was a man) with the same kinds of animals, from springboks to giraffes, as victims. No need to determine which animal was the weakest. These hunters chose the nearest. Perhaps the most important difference in the two styles of hunting was that if a lion's charge was successful, she and her party could start eating immediately, whereas a successful bow shot was only the beginning of the arduous process of tracking, which even then did not guarantee a meal. The lions could have one successful hunt and go on to another before a group of Ju/wa hunters could reap the benefits of the first.

The Ju/wasi said that lions were better hunters than themselves. Perhaps that's true. When we were with the Ju/wasi, we did not do what a biologist would do, keep track of the number of hunts that were successful, which could then be compared to the hunting success of other creatures. It was not that we didn't know of every hunt, but the Ju/wa hunters tended to keep on hunting until they got something, and except for occasional failures in tracking, they seldom came back completely empty-handed, so if seen in that light and not in the light of how many man-hours were spent or how many animals were spooked or how many arrows missed their target, their success rate was almost 100 percent. But by that standard, so was the lions'.

We seldom saw lions in the daytime. Once, however, when my brother and I were walking through some heavy bush a few miles from /Gautscha, we noticed a lion standing almost beside us. He was fully mature but still young, very large, and in perfect physical condition, with a heavy golden mane. A leopard would have vanished in a heartbeat, but, calm and confident, the lion stood right where he was, looking us over with interest as we looked with awe at him. We should, I suppose, have observed the Ju/wa protocol and walked calmly away at an oblique angle, showing that we were minding our own business and meaning no harm. But faced with such a magnificent lion, John and I were spellbound and kept staring, open-mouthed. I had never seen anything so fascinating.

The lion might also have been intrigued. Although we were quite

. . . .

close, we evidently were not alarming, so he considered us for a while. He showed no fear, made no threats, and seemed not to view us as possible prey. Perhaps he expected us to leave. Anything else so close to a lion would have left in a hurry, as must have been his experience. When we didn't, he saw that it would be up to him to observe the protocol. So, in the most gentlemanly manner imaginable, he walked calmly away at an oblique angle. Clearly, such behavior was the Old Way.

If we rarely saw lions in the daytime, we certainly saw them at night. Or sometimes they came and we didn't see them. On several occasions when we moved camp and set up in a new place, the local lions would visit us, perhaps the same night, perhaps a night or two later. Cats are very interested in their surroundings, and lions are no exception. They would want to know what was going on in their area. Sometimes we would notice their big green eyes at the edge of camp, but sometimes we would be asleep and unaware of their visit. Once we returned to /Gautscha very late at night and were too tired to set up a camp, so we just lay down on the ground. That night the lions came and walked all around us, even standing right over us and looking down at our sleeping faces. We learned this from their tracks in the morning and were glad we had been asleep at the time, glad to have missed what would have been a dreadful experience.

On a number of other occasions, lions came at night to view the Ju/wasi. I remember one night in particular, when my mother was at the Ju/wa encampment, and I was in my parents' tent at our camp writing notes. I soon heard a man's strong voice in a stern, commanding tone telling someone to leave immediately. The Ju/wasi never took that tone with one another. I came out of the tent to see what was happening, and behind some of the shelters I saw four very large lions, each three times the size of a person, all standing very tall as if on tiptoe, stretching their necks, looking over the tops of the shelters at the people. The women and children were sitting perfectly still, but two of the men were on their feet, standing with knees and elbows bent, the partial crouch of someone confronted. The lions began to shift a little, as if they were uneasy. They had been seen. What might have started as a viewing session was turning into a confrontation. They didn't seem entirely comfortable with that.

The speaker was ≠Toma. Without taking his eyes off the lions, he repeated his command while reaching one hand back to grasp a flaming branch that someone behind him was handing to him. He slowly raised it shoulder-high and shook it. Sparks showered down around him. "Old lions," he was saying firmly and clearly, "you can't be here. If you come nearer we will hurt you. So go now! Go!"

He had the full attention of the lions. Perhaps they knew about burns. Also, like many other animals, they might have been impressed by the extra size the flaming branch had added to what at first might have seemed to be a little creature. Suddenly he became much bigger. The lions watched ≠Toma for a moment longer, then gracefully they turned and vanished into the night.

Not all lions were so obliging. Nor did all share the same motive for visiting. Once we camped on a hillside near a place called Cho//ana, a waterhole north of /Gautscha, where we had traveled with some of the /Gautscha people, and on the first night of our visit, a few hours after dark when my father and brother were away somewhere, a group of lions began to roar not thirty feet from our tent, right between our camp and that of the Ju/wasi. The roar of a lion will travel twenty miles, which puts it into the category of jet engines and major explosions. That night, I didn't doubt it. It was the loudest and most terrifying sound I had ever heard, as some of the lions would roar until almost breathless, whereupon the roar would be taken up by other lions to make one never-ending, horrid sound. The lions were so loud I couldn't think, so loud that my mother and I couldn't hear each other as we tried to discuss what best to do. I had a little flashlight with low batteries and was shining its weak beam out the door of the tent to try to see if the lions were doing anything besides roaring, when I heard my mother telling me that she would zip me between two sleeping bags, so that if the lions came into the tent I'd be hidden, or, at least, they couldn't bite me—my dear, brave mother, wanting to save me if not herself—but I couldn't let her sacrifice herself for me. Anyway, death before dishonor. I didn't want to be discovered zipped up between sleeping bags in the aftermath of what might happen next. So we sat down and waited. And after a while, as suddenly as it began, the roaring stopped. Dead silence. Again I shone the flashlight. The lions had left.

What had they been doing? At first, of course, we didn't know. But since then I've learned that lions roar this way to send a message to other, distant groups of lions, showing them with noise that they, and not the distant lions, are the owners of the area. I now believe that the Cho//ana lions saw us as intruders, as if we had been another group of lions, and they engaged in choral roaring to get us out of there. They were showing us that they were many and strong and that the place where we had parked ourselves belonged to them. They, not we, were the owners of that hillside near Cho//ana.

Something similar happened one night at /Gautscha, when only about fifteen Ju/wasi were living there and most of the men, including my father and brother, were again away on a trip. My mother was again visiting at the Ju/wa camp, and I was again in my parents' tent, writing notes. The night was very quiet, as were all nights in that endless veld, no sound but insect voices, when suddenly, as if a bomb went off, a lion roared right next to me. I was shocked, then terror-stricken. My mind went blank. I couldn't breathe. And, because I am a primate with the atavistic wish to seem bigger at a time like that, the hairs on my head and body rose. (Why we primates feel that this small gesture will somehow help is a great biological mystery.)

After what seemed like an eternity, the dreadful roar became a series of grunts, then stopped, and I heard someone drawing a deep breath. Then another roar started. I was afraid for my mother, sitting in the open in the Ju/wa camp. The roar was so deep and so loud that it had no direction. It seemed to be coming from anywhere, everywhere. With trembling hands, I lit a lantern and carried it outside the door of the tent so that anyone in the vicinity would know where the lion was (as if anyone would go walking around under the circumstances), and by its light I saw a young but fully adult lioness in admirable condition standing between the two camps. She had entered the area from the south and was about a quarter of the way though the clearing between the camps, looking at neither, facing straight ahead. Her toes were spread, and her four round feet were planted firmly. Her head was low, level with her shoulders, her ears were up and slightly turned, and her rigid tail was sweeping, sweeping. She was the very picture of angry agitation and she seemed to be roaring *at us*.

Beyond her, between the little trees (none big enough to climb), I could see the Ju/wa families at their tiny fires, all sitting motionless, hoping for the best. As has been said, most of the men were away, and obviously, nobody else was going to challenge this lioness, or shake a burning branch at her, or draw her attention in any way. Her demeanor was quite different from that of the lions who had come merely to view the people and who had seemed open to suggestion. This lioness was far from that.

The light of the lantern disturbed her not at all. She seemed not to notice it but continued her terrifying roars. Was she trying to scatter us into the dark so that she could catch us and kill us? At one time, lions were believed to do this, but scientific research has shown that they don't, which makes sense, really—why would she roar to make us run when she could kill us right where we were, and more easily if she kept quiet? We had no meat in either camp, so she wasn't trying to scare us away from a carcass, and we posed no threat to her or to any other lion. Nor, assuming that she was one of the resident lions, could our presence have surprised her as it had surprised the Cho//ana lions, because we had all been camped there for almost a year, clearly evident to every animal who drank from the waterhole. Why was she so upset with us?

At last, as suddenly as she began, she stopped. She stood still for a moment with her mouth partly open, as if she were wondering if she had roared enough or should keep going. Evidently she had roared enough. Eyes front, she strode off quickly, straight ahead, and vanished. Everyone waited a few minutes to be sure she was really gone, then began to move about slowly, talking in brief sentences and low voices, occasionally laughing softly and uncomfortably as one might laugh in the aftermath of a person's unmannerly display of anger. The Ju/wasi put more wood on their fires, which all then burned very bright, and my mother, a calm person and an animal lover, stood up and started back to our camp. I went to meet her with the lantern.

What had happened? We had been deafened by a lioness who evidently was trying to make us do something. What that was, no one knew. No one offered any explanation. It was a lion thing, unknowable. But if the four lions in the firelight had come to learn about us, this lioness had come to tell us something. How leonine it was of her just to stand there roaring, leaving it up to us to fathom what she meant!

We learned of encounters with lions that were considerably more frightening than those we experienced. My mother presents the following story, which she heard from the people of /Gautscha: "A little group of two families was making a long journey. They were en-camped in the night alone in the vast, flat space. A lion came and prowled around them. The moonlight was bright and the people could clearly see the lion circling. They were terrified. They took their children in their arms and stood, shifting around to keep the fire be-tween them and the lion, ready to throw burning brands at it. One of the men, Bo, cried out to the lion, 'You lazy beast. Why do you not go and kill an animal instead of coming after us? We are not equals.' The lion growled and did not go away. Toward morning, one sup-poses in response to the long-continued emotional stress, Bo fell into a trance. At sunrise the lion left, and the people said that Bo's spirit followed it and chased it far away, and they never saw it again. When Bo's spirit returned to his body, and he came out of the trance, his nose bled severely."[3]

Among the predators at Nyae Nyae, the lions with their visits and their roaring might have seemed the most dangerous to people. Yet, despite the abovementioned incidents, lions were the least danger-ous. The study made by my brother and Claire Ritchie, for all its ac-counts of leopards and hyenas, showed only one instance of a lion causing a death during the time of which I am speaking, when a paraplegic girl who moved by dragging herself was tragically killed by a lion. Because of her unusual locomotion, he probably misun-derstood what she was. A similar mistake could have been made by any other predator, including wild dogs and possibly even cheetahs. Otherwise, the lions never preyed upon the people, although in the events described above and in others not included, they could have done so. There we were, near their waterhole—a group of midsize primates with small teeth and little strength or speed. And there they were, right beside us, the world's most formidable predators, very much bigger and often more numerous than we. But the lions didn't hunt us or kill us, and only they knew why.

II

Lions

Although the Ju/wasi said they were afraid of lions (and surely they were), in daily life, this didn't show. The people who had listened to the lioness at /Gautscha, and the people who had caused the four visiting lions to leave the encampment, had not seemed frightened. They were concerned, of course, and they took all precautions, but they certainly were not panicked. That the encounter had been so benign is nevertheless mysterious. Why, when the lions could so easily have killed us if they chose, did they so easily give way? And why would four lions retreat from two determined-looking men and a burning branch? By no means would lions everywhere have been so cooperative.

We had a rifle but never thought of it as a weapon of self-defense and therefore never had it at hand at dicey moments. It was always in the back of a truck or under some boxes in a tent—who knew? And the bullets would not have been easily found, as they would have been stashed safely away in a cool, dry place by my father. Also we never would have wanted to shoot anything that we were not planning to eat. But aside from our own moralistic considerations— we were the guests of every creature in that country, occupying their place, not our own—we were taking our cue from the Ju/wasi, who

*The lions had the night, and the people had the day, so when the
predators were hunting, the people stayed in their camps.
My mother, brother, and father*

also did not deploy their weapons at times like that. We felt that they knew best, and with good reason. If we had decided that we knew best and had shot one of the lions, who knows what our action would have said to the other lions, and who knows how they would have treated us the next time they came? Besides, we respected animals. Just to kill lions for the sake of getting rid of them simply didn't cross our minds.

Our attitude probably served us well. ≠Toma later told us that where lions were hunted, they were dangerous to people, but where they were not hunted, they were not dangerous. He was referring to a place about fifty miles east of /Gautscha called Kai Kai, where, as at /Gam (the first place we visited), a group of Tswana pastoralists kept cattle. Of course, the lions tried to hunt the cattle and the people tried to hunt the lions. In broad daylight, these lions would stride boldly into the village and roar to chase the people into their houses. Some of the men had smoothbore muskets, which they loaded with gunpowder and nails, and would blast away at the lions. On one such occasion the village dogs challenged the lions, then, when the lions came after them, turned and ran behind the men, bringing the lions right on to the men. At Kai Kai, obviously, the dogs, the cattle, and the people had created a messy situation. But Kai Kai was post-Neolithic, the more so with the muskets.

Needless to say, the Ju/wasi did not hunt the lions. They did not hunt any of the large predators, not even the individual leopards and hyenas who occasionally took human victims. The weapons of the Ju/wasi were not made for combating dangerous animals but were designed for hunting ordinary game. Poison arrows are of course effective, but because the poison takes so long to work—perhaps three days or more for a three-hundred-pound lion—the lion can easily dispatch the hunter and other people, too, before it dies. Not even the Ju/wa spears are very effective against lions, as these spears are about the same length as a lion's reach. Jabbing a spear into an oncoming lion would be quite dangerous—the consequences can be seen by trying to poke a housecat in the chest with a pencil. A spear thrown from afar would be equally dangerous, as the hunter would have to drop the lion in its tracks, no easy matter, or else be confronted by an angry, wounded lion at close quarters. It is true that in East Africa, the Maasi men hunted lions with spears, but the Maasi used much longer, stronger spears, and not all Maasi men survived the experience. And because the Maasi were pastoralists with cattle who successfully competed for grazing with the game, the lions and the Maasi were rivals, and neither lived exactly in the Old Way.

≠Toma's observation that lions did not bother people who left them alone was surely accurate, but it cannot be the whole answer. The question is deep, and the answer probably has two parts to it, the people's part and the lions' part. Many non-Bushmen have guessed at answers—some say that people have an unpleasant taste, for instance, which of course is silly. (And how do they know?) Even if it's true, which allegedly it isn't—allegedly we taste like pork, according to the cannibals, hence the name "long pig"—the hungry predators are not gourmets and are not particularly concerned with taste. Another proffered explanation is that predators don't normally hunt one another, or at least not simply for food, and we are a kind of predator. Well, yes, but so are leopards and hyenas, and these animals hunt our species. Yet another theory was offered by an anthropologist who pointed out that *we* are the dangerous species, so surely the lions are afraid of people. He suggested that in the past, people probably had killed off the dangerous animals and would do so in modern times if animals were threatening them. He believed that this explained the relative safety, at least from lions, enjoyed by the Ju/wasi we knew.

I didn't think so. Killing the giant cats with any Stone Age weapon, let alone slow-acting poison, is too risky. And even if the problem lions were eliminated, other lions would eventually occupy the vacant territory, and the problem could reappear. I see the anthropologist's suggestion as a product of our own, post-Neolithic culture. To him, as to all post-Neolithic peoples, eliminating lions would seem the only way to be safe from them—it is the traditional method of agricultural and industrial humanity, whereby any inconvenient animal is killed. Most of the world has been post-Neolithic for twelve thousand years. We can imagine no other method.

Without question, we are an extremely dangerous species, and I would guess that if an individual man-eater had materialized, the Ju/wasi might have shot him. Yet if in any given place the lions were generally aggressive, I believe that the Ju/wasi and also the earlier savannah hunter-gatherers would have coped with the problem by leaving the area—not an option for sedentary farmers or other settled people who can't just pick up and go. We had no way to check this theory among the people we knew because lions were not troubling them sufficiently. When I asked what would happen if lions became truly dangerous, the people said vaguely that they would not live in such a place, suggesting that there was no set plan to deal with the specific problem. No one, however, suggested killing them.

Interestingly, many years later when I returned for a visit, the people of /Gautscha had acquired cattle. One year, when the cattle were grazing far from the encampment (by then, a permanent village), lions killed a bull and a cow. Some white people were also living at /Gautscha—members of an organization formed to help the Ju/wasi—including an arrogant and blindly stupid young American who imagined himself the master of any situation. Against all advice he organized a lion hunt. He then took some of the Ju/wa men in the back of his truck (although some of the Ju/wasi could drive by then, the young American wanted to be safely in the cab) and went to visit the scene. There, the young American instructed the Ju/wa men to shoot the lions with poison arrows when the lions returned to eat the rest of the carcasses.

Knowing nothing of vehicles, two lionesses came. The men in the back of the truck didn't shoot them. Through the almost-closed truck window, the young American demanded that they shoot, and quickly. One of the men then took a shot, but the arrow fell far short of the lionesses. Like any other Ju/wa hunter, he could easily have made the shot. Instead, he missed intentionally, which was not a bad idea, seeing that an idiot was driving the truck and he was standing in the back, exposed, if the lioness charged. I was in a nearby vehicle with other visitors, trying to put a stop to all this, and glanced over at the Ju/wa hunter. Our eyes met. He knew I knew he'd missed on purpose, thus avoiding the long-term presence of a wounded lion, and he seemed very serene about it. He had kept the Old Rules and had done the right thing. He had also obliged the young American. The lionesses left, the hunter went over and picked up his arrow, and the Ju/wa people present built a fire and cooked a quantity of the beef, which they ate before taking home the rest to share with the others. What else could one do? It was the Old Way.

. . . .

Killing lions did not seem to be an option anywhere that people lived in the Old Way. For what it's worth, while making a general search north of Nyae Nyae for other Bushmen groups, we encountered a group of people on the move. They wore tattered Western clothing, but they looked like Bushmen, and when asked who they were, they said they were Bakalahari (which simply means Kalahari people and is what others might have called them). When asked if Bushmen were living in the place they came from, they said that no one was living there, that lions had killed everyone. Those whom the lions had not killed had left the area, they said. And they were leaving, too. At the time, knowing only of the /Gautscha lions, I wasn't sure whether to believe these people, but looking back, their story seems not only possible but convincing. These people had livestock, including chickens and a donkey, which would have brought lions in their direction, but they seemed to have only spears and digging sticks for self-defense. (I didn't notice any bows or poison arrows among their possessions.) Man-eating by lions seems almost inevitable under such circumstances. But although this little group of travelers had not been living in the Old Way as completely as were the people of the Nyae Nyae interior about one hundred miles to the south, and may have put themselves in harm's way as a result, they were not so far from the Old Way that the old solutions were no longer useful.

Avoiding a problem is preferable to combat. At /Gautscha, for instance, the lions and hyenas seemed to visit the waterhole at different times of night so that they didn't encounter one another, thus avoiding possible conflict. And the people and the predators moved about the veld at different times, the predators taking sunset to sunrise, and the people taking the middle of the day, when the lions and most other predators were sleeping in the shade. These habits were extremely important for avoiding conflict. Moving away was a version of this arrangement and an excellent method for solving many kinds of problems. It's true that in the rather crowded game parks of East Africa, different species of predators battle one another—most of us have seen the nature films of lions making war on hyenas, and vice versa. But game parks are not entirely of the Old Way, and the losers of these battles might have moved if they could, if there were somewhere else to go that wasn't already occupied. Relocating could be difficult in the game parks. But in the past, relocating was not difficult in sparsely populated Nyae Nyae. One of the most important things that can be said about the Old Way at Nyae Nyae is that there was plenty of room.

When, for instance, a certain kind of biting maggot infested the shelters of one Ju/wa group, those people moved. They didn't go far, but they moved. When waterholes dried, the people at those waterholes moved. When an illness came to /Gautscha, where, at the time, many people were encamped, most people moved. When the food supply dwindled, or tempers flared and arguments started, people went to live in other places where they had relatives who would welcome them, just as they themselves had welcomed others who came to them when things went wrong. The entire cultural system of the Ju/wasi, about which more will be said later, was based upon the ability to relocate, and this was usually effective. Other solutions usually were not. "I live here. I'm staying on this spot come hell or high water. If you make that hard for me, I'll kill you" is a post-Neolithic concept. It is not a message from the Old Way.

Some responsibility for the lack of man-eating lay with the lions. For one thing, they usually prefer larger game, as did the Ju/wasi. Even house cats specialize, or many of them do, some choosing to hunt only birds, others only small mammals, others only snakes and frogs, and so forth. In the same spirit, a Ju/wa hunter might pass by many a rat or snake as he searched for an antelope because he wasn't out there looking for just anything—even though he and his people were hungry, they wanted an antelope to eat. The same seems to be true of lions, although they would of course eat whatever they could catch if they felt the need. But as far as their normal hunting practices are concerned, lions don't need to search for weak or disabled victims and therefore would not be particularly tempted by our seeming vulnerability. Lions can pull down African buffaloes and bull giraffes, or some of them can, so they would not be as interested as, say, hyenas, when they saw a line of traveling people with a straggler.

Then, too, lions are very intelligent, as are all cats, and also profoundly good observers, and can be open to suggestion, unless they are already excited with their minds made up. Thus, if they are thinking things over near a Ju/wa encampment and find that the occupants are challenging them with firebrands, they are easily able to revise their plans. That night in the Ju/wa camp when four lions came to view the people, the lions were merely doing research, but if the people had done nothing and seemed not to object to the lions' presence, the lions might have taken the next step, and the outcome might have been different.

And finally, like most other mammals, young lions do as their parents do, preying upon what their parents prey upon, learning techniques and patterns of behavior from their elders. Man-eating is a learned behavior, and if lions of the past didn't start it, their descendants would have a good chance not to be thinking about it and therefore not to pick it up. So if the lions of Nyae Nyae did not hunt people, perhaps it was because their parents hadn't done so.

And why was that? Even before we were tarsiers back in the Eocene, we must have been of interest to predators. Our closer relatives, the great apes, all climb in trees for safety and sleep in the trees, too—all but adult gorillas who, being so massive, seem safe enough on the ground. True, all cats including lions can climb trees (although some cats are more arboreal than others), and leopard-sized cats probably climbed trees in pursuit of our primate ancestors, perhaps hoping to grab a victim by the foot to tug him down. But trying to subdue a struggling animal while also clinging to a tree is much more difficult than simply catching prey on the ground by the normal methods favored by most cats. In the rain forests, our arboreal habits would have helped us.

When our ancestors lost the safety of the trees, large predators surely posed a new challenge. However, we lived in groups and were active by day, while the very large predators surely hunted at night. Not only were they so big that most savannah vegetation wouldn't hide them, so they needed the cover of dark, but also they got too hot if they exerted themselves in the daytime. The larger the predator, the greater the challenges of visibility and overheating. This meant that if we were watchful, we would have been relatively safe in the daytime, taking care not to disturb a sleeping predator, but not having to worry very much about being hunted. Still, we would have had to protect ourselves after dark. Here, something that helped us against nocturnal predators was surely the *tshu*, the little grass shelter that appears to have replaced the arboreal nest for those who lack forests. A flimsy *tshu* doesn't look like much when one imagines a big cat attacking, but as with so many aspects of the Old Way, it addresses part of the problem, perhaps the most important part, that a cat often attacks from behind and to the side. From this position, of course, his prey is less likely to see him coming and is also less able to put up a defense.

Horses can fend off an attack from behind by kicking, but most animals can't, or not as well, which of course is why cats prefer the rear approach, first studying the victim briefly, then taking him by surprise from a position of advantage. But normally the cat has just one chance to do this and must must see the victim clearly from the start. Hence to break through a *tshu* in hopes of catching something inside is not efficient—there you are with a mouthful of grass while your intended prey wriggles out of your paws and goes scuttling off, sounding an alarm and bringing its fellows swarming around you with flaming branches, stones, and noise. Your hunt is ruined. You are bruised and disappointed, you can't get the grass off your tongue, and worst of all, your potential victims now know that you are hunting them. You have no luck. You leave, to try elsewhere.

A little grass half-dome shelter may not seem like much, but, as many people know, man-eating tigers of the Sundarbans have been dissuaded by as flimsy an item as a mask that a forester wears on the back of his head. The tiger stalks the forester from behind, but instead of seeing the back of his head, he sees a face staring at him with wide open eyes. A man with two fronts and no back! Improbable as it seems, the tiger is foiled and sometimes even follows the forester, roaring in protest. (A trick of this kind is not quite the same as screening the entire person and didn't work as well, because the tigers eventually realized that the masks were not real faces and again began to take victims.)[1]

The screen effect explains why people sleeping in tents are relatively safe from lions, even where the lions are somewhat dangerous. Like the *tshu*, a tent partially screens its occupants even if they show through the fabric like shadow puppets, and while a tent as a safety measure is certainly less than perfect, it is far better than nothing. In the Old Way, in which improvements come in small increments, a partial solution can be significant. I have heard of several instances in which a lion took a sleeping person out of a tent, but in the only instance that I know anything about, the man's foot was sticking out and the lion, seeing a quiet, motionless foot, took hold of it. The man of course woke up and called for help, and was saved. So the screen was somewhat helpful in that case, if not completely, and the event suggests why a predator doesn't want his primate victim flailing around and shouting.

The next step to foster safety, if the sleeping habits of the Ju/wasi are any example, is to construct the shelters so that they face in different directions. The Ju/wasi of /Gautscha faced their shelters every which way, perhaps without predators in mind, as the basic reason for circling might have been long forgotten, but the encampment always formed a rough circle, and the result was that all directions were covered.

A further safety measure is that everyone sleeps lightly and not at the same time. In the Ju/wa camp at night, someone always seemed to be awake, getting warm by a fire or having a sip of water from an ostrich eggshell. At /Gautscha, our camp was right next to the camp of the Ju/wasi, and never did I wake up at night and not see at least one person awake and sitting by a fire. People took naps by day, so no one lost sleep because of this. It became my impression that whoever was awake at night would not lie down again to sleep unless someone else got up—an impression I cannot confirm because I myself was sleeping. Also, almost every creature who is subject to predators sleeps lightly (only lions appear to sleep deeply, their eyelids fluttering with dreams), and perhaps the people would not sleep well if they felt that no one was awake. The arrangement was very informal, not like a soldier's guard duty or a sailor's watch. It just seemed to happen, part of the normal way of life. But again, it was the Old Way.

The fires themselves were helpful, of course, but also detrimental—detrimental because the predators know perfectly well that campfires indicate the presence of creatures the size of small antelopes, but helpful because a fire provides burning branches. Then, too, if the animal is hunting for something bigger and knows that people can make problems for it, it can avoid stumbling upon the people's camp more easily than if it were relying on scent alone, as the scent of the people would be spread far and wide. Often at night in our quiet camps in Nyae Nyae, we would hear the faraway voice of some large creature approaching—a hyena, perhaps, or a leopard, or even a lion—and we would wait, listening, and then, after a time, would hear the voice beyond us, no matter which way the wind was blowing. Whoever it was had noted our presence and avoided us, not wanting an encounter. Surely the firelight provided a clue, or at least confirmed the suspicions of whoever was approaching.

Then, too, fire creates eye shine. The light of a little fire doesn't dispel darkness and would not reveal the body of a nocturnal predator until the animal was very close. But while the animal is still at a distance, his eyes shine. This is true of any predator. No matter how stealthy he is or how effective his camouflage, sooner or later he needs to focus his eyes on his victims, and when he does, he can't do much about his eye shine. Any camp of hunter-gatherers, human or otherwise, is on the lookout for two little green moons shining in the darkness and can take appropriate action.

Thus, as far as lions were concerned, we were too small to be highly desirable victims, and we took too many precautions to become easy victims. With burning branches, we might even have made ourselves appear to be somewhat dangerous to some predators—too dangerous, at least, for all but the most determined predators. If all this were so, man-eating by lions probably didn't get properly started. And in Nyae Nyae, while the Old Way pertained, the culture of the lions perpetuated the notion that people were not prey.

That there was a cultural aspect affecting the behavior of the lions is very clear and can be seen in the fact that different populations of lions behave very differently toward our species. When in later years I participated in a research effort in Namibia's Etosha National Park, about two hundred miles from /Gautscha, I noticed the difference. Thirty years earlier (accounting for very few generations of lions—not nearly enough to distribute a behavioral gene), Etosha was part of the original wilderness and the lions there belonged to the same population as the lions of Nyae Nyae. In the 1950s we once traveled near the area that was to become Etosha Park,[2] and when we camped at night, we were visited by a group of three lions, a young maneless male, a young but full-grown female, and (we believed) a mature male, who did not seem to want to harm us but merely to look at us, just as the lions of Nyae Nyae would have done.

But thirty years later, the Etosha lions had become so dangerous that they were credited with keeping SWAPO guerrilla soldiers from crossing into Namibia from the north. Visitors to the park were instructed never to leave their vehicles for any reason, and I could easily see why. The restrictions did not apply to people doing research there, so our research team went about on foot, and in consequence I was twice stalked by Etosha lions and charged by another, mainly because at first I assumed that the lions would be like those in Nyae Nyae in the 1950s. I had not taken into consideration the fact that conditions were no longer the same.

What had happened? In the past, the area of the park had been part of the pristine wilderness that we had entered from the east. Very much belonging to the Old Way, it included its own population of hunter-gatherers—not only Bushmen but also Khoikhoi—and the Old Rules pertained. But by the 1980s, the hunter-gatherers had been rounded up and evicted from the park, partly because the park authorities didn't seem to know where our species had evolved and held the naïve but prevalent view that human beings are everywhere a foreign element, that nothing about them is "natural," and partly because the hunter-gatherers killed the game that the tourists had come to behold. Besides that, every now and then a brown-skinned hunter in a loincloth would emerge from the bushes to approach a vehicle and beg for cigarettes. This the tourists found annoying. Just as they were viewing a rare bird or antelope with their binoculars, they would hear something tapping on the car window and look around to see a half-naked man smiling ingratiatingly and puffing on his finger, suggesting that they offer him a smoke. The park authorities intervened on behalf of the tourists, and the brown-skinned people appeared no more.

Thus tourists in vehicles were virtually the only human beings left in Etosha for lions to learn from, and the lesson was not the same. If young lions could not learn from their elders how to interact with hunter-gatherers who went about on foot, hunted the same game, drank from the same waterholes, and otherwise shared their territories, the lions remained naïve about our species and quickly reverted to their Pliocene ways. Their instincts told them we were easy prey. The cultural guidelines that had overruled their instincts were forgotten.

Cultural guidelines can be fragile, especially those of the Old Way. A cultural shift in birds called honeyguides is an example. In the past, these birds would locate a beehive, and then find someone to open it for them. Choosing someone who would want the honey, such as a person or a honey badger (also called ratel or African badger), the bird would flutter around in front of the helper to attract his attention, or perch on a branch and give a special call "like a small box of matches being shaken rapidly," as the biologist Richard Estes describes it.[3] Everyone, man and beast alike, knew about honeyguides in those days, so the helper would know what the bird had in mind and follow it to the hive. The bird would fly conspicuously from tree to tree, waiting for the helper to catch up before moving on. At the bee tree, the bird would wait while the honey hunter did the hard work, breaking open the hive, swatting bees, and getting stung. When the melee was over and broken bits of the hive lay scattered on the ground, the honeyguide would fly down and eat the larval bees, which was the whole purpose of the venture. The birds made no discrimination among people—anyone would do. I myself was once led by a honeyguide in Angola.

But honeyguides no longer try to lead people in places like Etosha. The hunter-gatherers are gone and the tourists in the cars don't understand what the birds want. Nor would they follow the bird or open the hive if they did. So the whole honey-hunting partnership has collapsed and vanished. The birds of today have no memory of the ancient partnership between their kind and ours. I hope, though, they still lead honey badgers. The ancient honey badger population has not been replaced by legions of ignorant, uncaring honey badgers. So the resident honey badgers would still understand.

Even though the lions of Nyae Nyae did not molest the Ju/wasi, the Ju/wasi respected them beyond all other animals, including the animals who did molest them. They respected lions for their power and also for their abilities. They respected lions for hunting cooperatively, whereas the people cooperated mainly during the tracking phase. Perhaps, as the Ju/wasi said, the lions were in fact better hunters. At any rate, lions secured their victims right away, but the people had to hunt for many days and over great distances.

. . . .

In contrast, the leopards and hyenas, while certainly dangerous, were not deeply respected, not considered awe-inspiring. Far from it. Hyenas could even be figures of fun—little boys imitated them and laughed at them, making games of their mating and quarreling. The people we knew had no special or formalized explanation for their feelings about lions except that to respect lions seemed obvious. Yet the very fact of the truce made lions different from the other animals, and because a truce implies that both sides honor it, it was as much the responsibility of the lions as it was of the people. More so, because the lions could have broken the truce whenever they pleased, with more to gain and fewer perceptible negative consequences, at least temporarily. What's more, if they broke it, no one would know why.

To the Ju/wasi, therefore, the lions were not unlike the gods, who also could kill a person for unknown reasons, and there was nothing that the people could do about it. Perhaps not surprisingly, therefore, the Ju/wasi treated the lions and the gods in somewhat the same way. For instance, they sometimes called lions "owners of the west,"[4] which is the home of the god associated with death. The word for lion is *n!hai*, but the Ju/wasi rarely said that word during the daytime, just as they rarely said the names of the gods. The gods and the lions rest in the shade when the sun is hot, and they don't like to hear people summoning them. If a person had to communicate something about a lion during the day, he might make a hand sign, the clenched fist held tensely at chest level to represent the round head of a lion.[5] If people came face-to-face with lions, they would always address them with the respectful term *n!a*, meaning "big" or "old"—a term that they also used when speaking of the gods. In addition to the respect term, according to Megan Biesele, the people had several avoidance terms for referring to lions, including "night" and even "moonless night," which obviously have more sinister implications than "old" and "big." No other animal had such an aura. Among the people we knew, only lions generated profound respect.

At night, on the rather rare occasions that the Ju/wasi held their great trance dances (about which more will be said later), when the trancing healers or shamans ran fearlessly out into the night to confront the spirits of the dead, they also confronted lions, cursing at both kinds of beings, commanding them to leave the people alone.

Whether real lions were actually present during these encounters, or just the spiritual aspect of lions, is hard to say. The trance dances took place near encampments, which meant that they were also near waterholes, and they lasted through the night, which meant that if lions came to drink, they might indeed be nearby while the dance was in progress, at least for a short while. Yet it was a spiritual aspect of lions that the healers were cursing, not the actual lions who lived nearby and more or less left people alone.

There was more. The power of the healers was such, said the Ju/wasi, that some of them—very few, and none among the people we knew—did not want to work for the common good and instead would secretly shape-change into lions. The verb for doing this is *jum* (pronounced *zhum*) as the word for the big cats is *jumhmi*. These supernaturals would cross the savannah at night in great mile-long bounds, a concept that may have come from the way that lions sometimes move across the veld, not one behind the other as is the way of those who must keep watch for predators, but in a row and widely spaced, staying in touch by roaring. One lion roars, the next answers, then the next, and the next, as if the roar itself, or one of the lions, were leaping across the veld. Although the survey made by John Marshall and Claire Ritchie showed only one person killed by a lion in the population of Nyae Nyae—the paralyzed girl—it was nevertheless well-known that elsewhere lions mauled or killed people, and these lions, said the Ju/wasi, might be malevolent shamans in lion form.

≠Toma's wife, !U, had encountered such a lion. One day she was walking in the veld with her little son, Tsamko, when a lion jumped out of a tree. "!U knew it was a man in the form of a lion," wrote my mother, "because it acted in such a strange way. !U told me that the lion came down as though from a branch of the tree, but it was not actually on the tree. It came down toward them, then went up again, but it did not seem to be climbing; it passed them as though flying. !U thought the flying lion was a man named /Gaishay !Khoa, who, she believed, had the power to *jum*. She and Tsamko were terrified. At the encampment, the people stayed awake and made noises all night to keep him away."[6]

According to Megan Biesele, an additional avoidance term used by the Ju/wasi for the lions was "jealousy." Jealousy was surely the primary cause of discord among the Ju/wasi, yet the term does not suggest that lions caused the people to feel jealousy. No, it was something else, and an attempt to explain it presents a cultural dilemma in the purest form. I cannot say why the emotion of jealousy is similar to the existence of lions. Yet I think that perhaps I can feel the reason, and for an example, I turn again to /Gaishay !Khoa, who was a real person. Although he had died before we came—probably to the great relief of others—he had lived at Kai Kai, which had been a hunter-gatherer encampment long before the Tswana people and their cattle took it over, and he had been involved in some important quarrels. These, as most Ju/wa quarrels, stemmed from jealousy, and because of them, /Gaishay !Khoa had killed two people. His first victim was a man who had seduced and then married /Gaishay !Khoa's son's wife. /Gaishay !Khoa killed this man supernaturally, with chest pains. But before the man died, another man had tried to cure him. /Gaishay !Khoa resented this, and when the helpful man later took a drink of water, he felt something hard and sharp go down his throat. He immediately knew that /Gaishay !Khoa had done something to him. Three days later, he also died.

People such as /Gaishay !Khoa were very dangerous. Most of the time they might seem open and forthcoming like other people, but there was something reserved about them caused by their jealous secrets enhanced by their tremendous supernatural powers to harm, so these people were not what they seemed to be, and no one really knew what they were thinking. In the meantime they lived right among other people, who had to take care not to displease them. There was no way to tell when such a person might suddenly do something terrible to you—you just had to act normally, going about your daily business and hoping for the best. Most of the time, everything would be all right. But the jealous person was embedded in your group, always a presence. At his pleasure, things could go well, but also, without your knowledge, things could go wrong, quickly and dramatically. And because he was supernaturally stronger than you, if you were just an ordinary person, the first you would learn of his malevolence would be to find yourself at death's door.

Except for the supernatural element, all of this could be a metaphor for lions—out there in the dark not far away from you, able to kill you whenever they felt like it, refraining from killing you for reasons you were not equipped to determine. You hoped that they wouldn't kill you, but you could never be sure.

At first I wondered if the concept of healer-shamans who became lions was truly a Ju/wa concept, as it coincided in certain ways with the worldview of the neighboring Bantu-speaking pastoralists, a worldview rich in the supernatural where witches and were-animals abound. The Ju/wa worldview seemed to have less of the supernatural, as I saw it (although here again, my personal perspective is at work—I knew something about the worldview of the Ju/wasi but not about the worldview of the Bantu-speaking people, hence the former seemed familiar and the latter seemed exotic). Even so, my mother agreed that the belief in healer-shamans who became lions was in ways uncharacteristic of the Ju/wasi we knew. She wrote, "The belief seemed not to be integrated with the current concept of healers." However, she suggested that the belief might be from "a different, perhaps older, stratum of concepts of the supernatural."

I now feel sure that she was right, that the belief could indeed have come from an older stratum of concepts. Of the two Ju/wa gods (about whom more will be said later), one is believed by anthropologists to be considerably older than the other, a figure from an earlier time. Like eland music for the menarchal rite, the concept of this older god is scattered far and wide among many disparate groups of people, not just the groups of Ju/wasi but also among the other language groups of Bushmen as well as among the Khoikhoi, suggesting that his image comes from a time when all these related people were one people with a single set of religious beliefs. This could make the concept very old indeed. The older god is associated with death.

And here, I think, is the connection with the deep, mixed feelings that the people had for lions, the natural animals who were supernatural, and also, perhaps, a connection to the feelings that our distant ancestors surely had for the very large cats who preceded the lions—the saber-toothed *homotheriums* or the giant, jaguarlike *dinofelids* who lived on the savannah. These great cats were nearly twice as big as lions. If the roar of a lion can travel twenty miles, what must the roars of these cats have sounded like? We would have to go back millions of years before we could find a time when those of our lineage were not in danger from cats or their ancestors, and, considering the relative size of their ancestors compared to ours, probably not even then.

Who could not respect lions? Whether they kill us or not, they certainly can, and much more quickly and efficiently than, in the past, we could kill them. And as for predation, although several animals preyed upon us, no one preyed upon lions. They are very much like us in their living arrangements, living in groups, sharing child care, owning territories from which others are excluded if possible, hunting cooperatively for the large antelopes but not refusing smaller animals, often hunting as a team with each participant having a special role, much like the people who also hunted cooperatively, also, sometimes, with special roles. Both the lions and the people concealed themselves only when actually stalking a victim and walked around in plain sight the rest of the time.

The lions had the night. The people had the day, which we think is the preferred time, but in reality, for life in general, the savannah by day is less desirable. The people of the savannah share the daylight mainly with insects and birds, while everything else favors the night and is well equipped to use it. For any species that hunts large animals, night is certainly the best time, which, of course, is why the predators are mostly nocturnal. Thus it was the lions, not ourselves, who roamed the savannah at the preferred time. Humankind had second best.

Lions often make their camps in shade not too far from water, where they sleep all day, all but comatose, in plain sight and in perfect safety. Certainly, no one is going to disturb them. If other species choose to live nearby, they do so at their own risk and at the lions' pleasure. Lions are at least three times as big as we are and their eye-teeth are as long as our fingers. Their eyes at night shine like green fire. And their roars, surely like the roars of the sabertooths before them, are by far the loudest sounds ever heard on the savannah except for overhead thunder.

Not even thunder awes a lion, or so it would seem. In fact, the lions of /Gautscha sometimes answered thunder. As if God were roaring at them from the sky, a lion might roar right back. Did he think that God didn't know where he was? If so, God soon found out from the terrible roars down below in a thicket—a reason to stay in the sky.

We say we fear God. In this spirit the Ju/wasi say they fear lions. But just as we don't spend our days worrying that God will kill us, the Ju/wasi don't spend their days feeling frightened of lions. Even so, lions are death. Their fearsome predecessors, the *homotheriums* and the *dinofelids*, also were death. Who would not fear the power of such large, dangerous, invincible, unknowable creatures?

12

Men and Women

Sometimes there seemed to be two worlds for the Ju/wasi, the world of women and the world of men. The differences seemed to appear in early life, in the games that children played. The boys played rough-and-tumble games and also hunting games with toy bows and thorn arrows, stalking a passing scarab or a melon rind on knees and elbows, filling the victim full of thorns. The girls played dance games and games of agility that left quite beautiful designs in the dust, made by the girls' tracks. The girls made ornaments of flowers. The boys made replicas of our vehicles, complete with axles and wheels that turned. I was deeply impressed by these little vehicles. Nobody had showed the boys how to make them—the boys figured out the main mechanisms of a vehicle all by themselves. They then attached long sticks to the toys so that they could run while pushing the little *auto-si* or *dosi*, as they came to be called.

Children of both sexes played with babies, mostly with the boy babies. Baby girls were less likely to leave their mothers to play with other children. But baby boys, as soon they could toddle away from their mothers, found a host of older playmates ready to amuse them. The girls might carry them around, playing "mother," and the boys might sit them down on a cape and run around the encampment, pulling the cape behind them while the babies laughed with pleasure.

Of course, in later life, gender differences also appeared in the kinds of activities performed by adults, although not nearly as conspicuously as such differences in many other cultures. People of both sexes gathered foods, not only the local plant foods that were the daily fare but also the important foods gathered in large quantities from distant places, the mangetti and marula nuts from certain groves, and the ground-growing beans known as *tsi*, all of which were carried back to the encampments in heavy bags. By and large, however, women provided the foods that sustained the people, which they did by normal gathering, and men provided the food that people liked the best and valued most highly, the meat of the important antelopes.

In most ways, women were the equals of men, fully as respected, fully as important in decision making, fully as free to choose a spouse or get divorced or own a *n!ore*. Most men, after all, lived for at least part of their lives on the *n!oresi* of their wives, in service to their wives' families. Men also were the equals of women, fully as tender toward their children, fully as ready to take part in daily tasks such as getting water or firewood. Yet there was a great dividing line between men and women that the Ju/wasi did not cross. For all their equality, they did not do as we do in industrialized societies— the Ju/wasi did not, for instance, have the equivalent of woman soldiers or male nurses—and the division had a biological element that, considering that the people lived in the Old Way, is no surprise. The division came down to childbearing and hunting. Matters of birth were only for women, and matters of hunting were only for men.

Interestingly, it was the biological role of women that created this division. The act of lifegiving had so much power that men needed protection from it. Women never took part in hunts and would not touch hunting equipment. To do so would harm the hunt and the hunter, not the woman. For the same reason a man would not have sex with his wife before a hunt. Menstruation was more dangerous still, so that a menstruating woman would shroud herself with a cape and stay apart from others, not for her protection but for the protection of others from the enormous power that clung to her at that time. After giving birth, she would bury all birth matter very carefully and mark the place with a tuft of grass so that men could avoid it. We tend to think of such prohibitions as an indication of the inferiority of women. And in some societies today that may be true. However, it was not true of the Ju/wasi. The power of men was fragile and required direction and development. The power of women was strong and exuded from them naturally, from the day they reached the menarche. I find considerable realism in this concept. No skill is required to menstruate or ovulate, and if one is pregnant, one gives birth with or without past experience. Hunting, in contrast, requires much skill and knowledge, much experience and hard work, with no guarantee of success.

Perhaps the passive power of women was the stronger of the two, but the active power of men was more apparent. It was the men, not the women, who confronted visiting lions, shaking burning branches at them and telling them to leave, and it was the men who came forward to meet us and our noisy, terrifying vehicles when we first appeared beside the baobab trees at /Gautscha. Men always accompanied women on any trip that required an overnight stay, but only to protect them, not to supervise them.

Then, too, the Ju/wa men had an inherent, almost natural bravery that everyone took entirely for granted. They hunted the world's most dangerous game with quarter-ounce arrows, they stood off lions and dealt with strangers, all without a shred of the bravado or machismo that so characterizes the men of other societies, including ours. The Ju/wa men simply did what men do without making anything of it, and didn't even think of themselves as brave. The Ju/wa women, in contrast, could be fearful, or so they seemed when alarming events occurred. One day at /Gautscha, a foot-long millipede ran through the encampment. Millipedes are not dangerous or poisonous, and this one posed no threat to anyone, not even mythologically. Yet the women freaked. Some screamed, others got up and ran. The few men present looked over at the women to see what was wrong, but then more or less ignored the millipede and did not make fun of the women for their fear.

I stumbled upon something very interesting when I was with the Ju/wasi in the 1950s. I happened to offer the people something called the Porteus Maze Test. This and the Rorschach Test were given to me by a professor of psychology at Harvard. I no longer remember

A young man on the day of his wedding,
showing reluctance, as was expected of him

why he asked me to administer these tests to the Bushmen. All I know is that it was to further his research, not mine. Nevertheless, I agreed to oblige him. The Rorschach Test went poorly. The women declined to try it. A few of the men gave it a go, all finding meanings that in those early days of psychological testing would have branded them as schizophrenic, or so I had been told. "Normal" people were supposed to see each ink blot as a unit, but the Ju/wa men saw them as composites, finding one little thing here and another little thing there. But this, of course, is the best way to view the environment, not as scenery, as landscape, as we view it, but as a series of small, very distinct messages—a freshly broken twig, flattened grass without dew where an animal was resting, the footprints of a certain kind of beetle that begins to move about after the day has reached a certain temperature, each tiny item an important clue as to what has taken place in the vicinity. The tiny items produce the whole picture, and these men were hardly schizophrenic. They were accomplished hunters and trackers, and the test was not cross-cultural.

The Porteus Maze Test was more revealing. This test involves a series of mazes of increasing complexity, from the first maze, which is essentially a straight run, to the last, which even the most capable of us would take a while to fathom. At the beginning of each maze is a drawing of a rat, seen from above. The person taking the test is supposed to show how the rat would get through the maze, which needless to say is not a problem of consequence to hunter-gatherers, none of whom had ever seen a graphic representation of any kind before, and until we came, had not even seen a piece of paper. Even so, after puzzling over the problem for a few minutes, every man and boy but one solved all the mazes as quickly and successfully as any American would have done. They rather enjoyed the challenge. The boy who didn't solve the mazes was a youngster of about fifteen who did well enough at first, then lost confidence and stopped trying. Needless to say, I didn't press him.

But the mazes stymied the women. Not one of the women or girls could solve even the first maze, the almost straight run. The women seemed uneasy and confused and stared down at the pages blankly, as if they flatly believed that whatever I was asking of them was impossible. Surely something very important was at work, a profound psychological difference, yet what it meant, I couldn't say. When I got home I gave the mazes and my notes to the professor, but what he made of them I never learned. Recent research by others has shown that men in general navigate by orienteering, while women navigate by using landmarks,[1] which is probably an insight into the implications of the cognitive abilities needed for long-range hunting (or to put it differently, for no fewer than thirty-five thousand years of long-range hunting) versus the abilities required to successfully complete a short-range gathering trip, knowing where the necessary plants are growing, spotting them in their settings, and getting back before dark. Such abilities may have pertained to the maze test. Or perhaps when confronted with something so strange and foreign, the women simply stepped back. In Ju/wa life, it was the men who dealt with difficult situations.

Whatever inequalities may have existed between Ju/wa men and women, these did not apply to marriage, or not strongly. Polygamy was allowed, although few people practiced it. A woman could have more than one husband if she pleased, or so it was said. We knew of no such marriage, although we once heard of a Ju/wa woman with two husbands. We never met these people, however. A man could also have more than one wife, and this was much more common. Of the eighty-eight men we knew best, nine had two wives, and we heard of a man with three wives and another man with four wives.

Men liked the idea of polygamous marriage. Some women were less enthusiastic, although there were certain advantages—if both wives lived in the same encampment, they might share a *tshu*, and the older wife might help the younger. Some women pointed out that a man with two wives usually preferred the younger woman, who virtually always was the second wife. Sometimes, the younger, second wife received more from her husband than the first wife. I remember a woman, a first wife, showing me the lacelike holes in her leather cape. She told me that she badly needed a new cape, but her husband had given the skin of an antelope he had recently killed to her younger co-wife, and nothing to her, although her need was greater. One older wife expressed the hope that her husband would not abandon her for the younger woman, would not reject and humiliate her by going to live with the younger woman while she stayed behind with relatives.

. . . .

As a rule, most men with two wives treated both of them fairly, but even then, co-wives did not always get along. In one case, the older wife was so unpleasant to the younger wife that the younger wife left the husband, never to return. The husband was greatly saddened but could do nothing to bring his younger wife back. In his sorrow, he would sit in front of his grass shelter and sing sad songs about her.

Two of the men at /Gautscha had two wives—a man named /Ti/kay whose wives were sisters and got along beautifully, and the man named Gao Feet, whose younger wife, Di!ai (the woman I was named for), got along with her co-wife so poorly that the two women could not live for long in the same encampment. When the first wife, Khwo//o, came to /Gautscha with her group for a visit, she made her *tshu* on the far side of the encampment, as far from Di!ai as she could get. Gao Feet would divide his time between his two wives as long as Khwo//o was at /Gautscha, but when her group moved on, he stayed with Di!ai. After all, he was still doing bride service for Da!ai. When their third child, as yet unborn, could walk, that would end his bride service—but that event seemed so far in the future that no one had contemplated what would happen when the time came.

In contrast to the wives of Gao Feet, /Ti/kay's two wives shared a *tshu*, which they had built together. They even shared a bed at night, lying on either side of their husband on the cape belonging to one wife, all three covered by the cape of the other wife. The wives were sisters. The Ju/wasi generally agreed that co-wives got along better if the women were sisters. Also, by marrying sisters, the husband could conduct his bride service in one place, so that both women would be with their husband and their family.

However, divorce was easily achieved and available to everyone, accomplished merely by making an announcement, so no woman had to remain in an unhappy marriage. Di!ai had not done so—Gao Feet was her second husband. Her first husband, Gumtsa, had lived at /Gautscha for a time, also doing bride service. The girl N!ai was his daughter. But after the divorce he had remarried, and when we knew him, he was living with his second wife at a place fifty miles away called Kubi.

Gumtsa and Di!ai had been married in the most traditional method, betrothed by their parents when he was a young teenager and she was a small child, and married when she was about twelve and he was about twenty. I don't know what caused the divorce, but Gumtsa, who was somewhat volatile, was a very different kind of person than Gao Feet, who was unfailingly calm and gracious and had the rather rare distinction of being an excellent hunter and also an important healer. Most men were one or the other, seldom both, because no Ju/wa person wants to stand out above the rest or have more of anything than anyone else, including ability. Thus a man such as Gao Feet was in a difficult position. His people needed both his talents. Any group would. Hence to forsake one talent for the other would have been selfish, depriving his people of a service in order not to arouse jealousy. Yet Gao Feet had such a low-key manner and was so modest and unassuming that people did not hold his talents against him. That was how he managed his excellence. Thus it is hard to imagine anyone being unable to get along with a man such as Gao Feet.

Gumtsa seemed quite different, although in fairness, we met him under circumstances that were difficult for him, when he came to /Gautscha in response to the engagement of his daughter, N!ai, who was about eight years old. When he learned of her betrothal to a young man named /Gunda, a betrothal arranged by Di!ai and Gao Feet, Gumtsa left his home at Kubi in a state of distress and, with a group of other people, walked fifty miles to /Gautscha to put a stop to it. It seemed that he had also arranged a marriage for N!ai with a man from Kubi. When Gumtsa reached /Gautscha, he complained that he had not been consulted and demanded that N!ai return with him to Kubi. I can remember that day very clearly. I remember hearing raised voices and wondering what was happening. My mother also heard, and together we went to find out. My mother described the scene in her book *The !Kung of Nyae Nyae*. "Tension rose," she wrote. "N!ai cried and looked very frightened. People from two groups were present at /Gautscha and although theoretically they had no authority in the matter, all expressed themselves and poured torrents of talk over the affair. Mostly they were supporting N!ai's mother, Di!ai, saying that N!ai's father had not fed N!ai, had not so much as sent her a gift, and should not now come and interfere in her betrothal. After four days of this, Gumtsa gave up and went home."[2]

Little N!ai was deeply relieved. She would not be required to leave her mother and her family and go to live among people whom she barely knew in a place that was not her own, married to a virtual stranger rather than to a boy from the neighboring encampment. Entering marriage at the age of eight is difficult enough. Her mother, her aunt !U, her stepfather Gao Feet, her uncle ≠Toma, and many other people had saved her from these difficulties.

N!ai and /Gunda were married in May 1953. She was about nine years old by then, and he was about sixteen. Even so, he had proved himself as a hunter. His victim had been only a duiker, but a duiker is plenty big enough to qualify a boy for marriage. Because the marriage was, needless to say, the first for both of these very young people, it involved a celebration of sorts, the only such celebration that either of them would ever experience, as among the Ju/wasi, no marriage is celebrated except the first.

But then, the Ju/wa concept of marriage is not the same as ours. We see a marriage ceremony as the joining of two people. The concept is so strong with us that we can scarcely imagine any other. Yet the Ju/wasi saw the marriage ceremony as a rite of passage that moved the young people into a new state of being. (Western custom may show a shadow of this concept, with white weddings, wedding gifts, and major celebrations for the first marriage, and semiprivate, toned-down weddings thereafter.) Once in the married state, the Ju/wasi remained there, if not always with the original partner, until they reached an age at which most people are no longer reproductive. Thus when people found new partners, no further ceremony was necessary because both people were already in the appropriate state. The absence of a ceremony when taking a new partner in no way implied that the couple was not joined—far from it. Ju/wa couples were fully as joined as the people in Western marriages, or more so. The couple knew it, the society knew it, and the relationships with others showed it. A woman who divorced one man and married another, for example, assumed the entire spectrum of in-law relationships with her new husband's people, just as she had done with her first husband's relatives.

Not surprisingly, the married state seemed to last throughout a person's reproductive years, as almost everyone of reproductive age was married and would remarry if divorced or widowed. Most older people who were widowed did not remarry, however, as if they had passed through the married state and were on the far side of it.

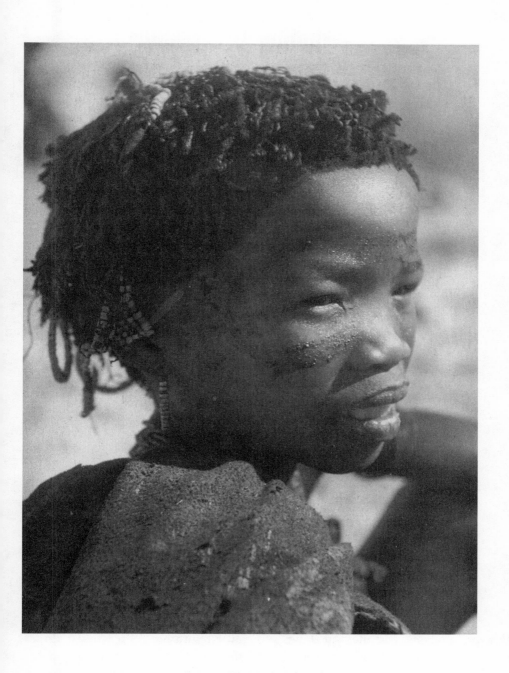

N!ai on her wedding day,
her face anointed with ochre powder

Among the Ju/wasi, so few people other than the elderly remained unmarried, whether by choice or by necessity, that the culture didn't address that feature. We knew only two such people in the entire population of Nyae Nyae. One of them was a man who had never hunted and therefore could not marry. He lived with a group of people that included his married sister. The other person was a childless widow who chose not to remarry. Her name was !Ungka, and she was the elder sister of //Kushe, who had come with us from /Gam. She was thus one of the owners of /Gautscha. She could have married Lazy /Kwi, her sister's husband, for example, as she lived with him and her sister. But she chose to remain single.

Early one morning, we observed the mothers of N!ai and /Gunda building a new, extra-large *tshu* between the two encampments. Obviously, something was going on. We were surprised to hear that N!ai and /Gunda were getting married that day. When I asked when the wedding would take place, Di!ai stretched her arm toward the west, showing that the sun would be below the horizon.

Di!ai then covered N!ai completely with a large leather cape. Under it, the girl made a little mound, sitting by her grandmother's fire. The Ju/wasi do not conduct their rites of passage in broad daylight under the burning, death-giving sun. N!ai was hidden from the sun as it cleared the horizon, and she stayed hidden all day until it set, at which point, still covered by the cape, she got up and walked alone to another fire, trailing the cape, to sit down opposite one of her kinsmen, an older man who had been alone at the fire and who paid no special attention to her. They didn't speak. He soon got up and left. N!ai stayed there all alone, and not until the sun was below the horizon did she uncover her head.

Ju/wa weddings are for children, and only for children. No adults may attend the ceremony, especially not the parents of the young couple. In the safety of the dusk, when it was time for N!ai to go to her husband, two young girls came to her. They were her cousins, and they sat down and chatted with her for a while, then got up, giggling, and took her by the arms. Young people are supposed not to want to get married and are expected to make a show of being forced. N!ai resisted, as was expected of her. One of the cousins then pulled N!ai over her shoulder, hiking her up so that her feet were off the ground, and carried her to the wedding *tshu*. She put N!ai down on the left of the entrance, the woman's side, and the girls sat down beside her.

At the other camp, perhaps twenty yards off, a group of boys had gathered around the young man, /Gunda. The boys were his cousins and stepbrothers, all about his age or younger. He, too, was expected to show resistance, and the boys made a show of catching him as if he were trying to escape. Then they formed a hand-holding chain with him at the end and led him to the new shelter. All these boys together then sat down on the right side of the entrance, the man's side. Soon other children began to arrive, all of them younger than /Gunda. The youngest of all was N!ai's youngest half brother, who arrived alone and sat on his little heels, enjoying himself. One of the boys had brought a small stringed musical instrument called a //gwashi, a hollow gourd with long pegs to which strings were attached, an ancestral guitar. On it he played several songs, not important or ceremonial songs, just songs that one might play for pleasure.

There was no food at the party except for four nuts that one of the boys brought and ate himself, but weddings are not occasions for feasting, and anyway, there was almost no food in the encampments. The children sang for a while, all except the bridal couple, who were not supposed to enjoy the event. Then they all talked and laughed until after midnight, at which point the little party disintegrated and all the young guests went back to the fires where they slept. These little people had conducted the wedding exactly right. With their help, N!ai and /Gunda had entered the married state together.

Just after sunrise the next morning N!ai's mother went to the wedding shelter. The fire had burned to embers. /Gunda had gone off to join a hunting party that was preparing to depart, but N!ai stood shivering beside the shelter, stripped of the big leather cape, dressed only in her little front apron and a scrap of a back apron that came up in front between her legs. Her mother brought a small bit of eland fat—the antithesis of hunger—and rubbed some of it over N!ai's body, then mixed the rest with red earth powder and drew circles on N!ai's face. Thus N!ai began her life as a married person. The ceremony was concluded. A routine gathering trip was planned for later in the day.

I must say, at first I had my doubts about /Gunda. He was an agreeable boy but seemed shy and repressed, lacking in drive and self-confidence. In fact, it was he who had been reluctant to finish the Porteus mazes. In contrast, his new wife was daring and self-assertive like her mother, Di!ai, and joyous too, which Di!ai was not. And both of these young people came from divorced families. It would be a question of time, I thought, before N!ai found someone she liked better, or before someone more prepossessing than /Gunda found her. I thought that this marriage might not last forever.

Wrong again. The wedding took place in 1953 and, at the time of this writing has lasted for fifty-three years and counting. It was strong when I visited the Ju/wasi in the 1980s, and strong when last I had news of them in 2006. Over the past half century, with all the difficulties and terrible sorrows that have come upon their people, these two found strength in each other, and their marriage has been their support.

Marriage was a connection, an important fiber of the social fabric, a means of expanding relationships. The marriage sanctions of the Ju/wasi spoke strongly to this. People did not marry within their immediate families, of course, including step-relatives and most primary in-laws, but also did not marry first, second, or third cousins, which means that their marriage sanctions were stricter than ours. Also the sanctions that applied to an individual extended to the individual's namesake, although these sanctions, while very rarely broken, were not quite as strong.

Such sanctions have been called incest taboos, but they were much more than that. The Ju/wa sanctions reached far beyond blood relatives and therefore had no incest implications. The Ju/wa patterns seem more clear if we think of what marriage is supposed to accomplish in that culture. Surely it was less desirable to marry someone to whom you were already tied. Better to tie yourself to someone else, thus gaining additional relationships that could be helpful. Better to expand your social network, gaining new allies and new places where, in hard times, you would be welcome. To expand and strengthen the social network was always a goal, and marriage presented an important opportunity to reach that goal, an opportunity never to be ignored.

!U's husband, ≠Toma, was an example of the benefit of expanding social ties. He came to /Gautscha from /Gam as a youngster, an orphan, after the death of his father, who had told him to go there because of the excellence of the place, with its permanent water. There, he met !U, then about eleven years old and already engaged to someone else. Unlike her sister, Di!ai, who was willing to marry her fiancé, Gumtsa, !U decided against her betrothed, largely because she liked ≠Toma better. He had few living relatives and no close ones, and thus could offer her no in-laws who could help her if the need arose, but he was an excellent hunter. This would appeal to any girl. So !U nagged her parents until they consented to the marriage. Thus, rather than living at /Gam as an unconnected orphan, ≠Toma joined the community at /Gautscha, where he became one of its most important, most honored members and lived happily with !U until his death in the 1990s.

Very few people broke the sanctions. We heard of a man who had married his stepdaughter, so that he was married to a mother and also to her daughter. He was said to be mentally ill, which explained this aberration, and he and his stepdaughter lived alone by choice, the only people we knew of who lived alone. We also heard of a third-cousin marriage. No harm came to any of these people, no punishments, no ostracism, except that others made fun of them and called their marriages *chi dole*, which means "a bad thing."

We learned little about the sexual behavior of the Ju/wasi. My mother, talking in extreme privacy with some Ju/wa women, was able to elicit the fact that they enjoyed sex and experienced orgasm, but that was about all. Sex with youngsters was of course prohibited, but this went without saying, as it didn't happen and would be mentioned only in the context of a young couple's marriage, as the couple would not have sex until the girl had passed the menarche. Young people might sometimes go out to the bush and fool around, but because most girls were married by the time they reached the menarche, there were no single mothers.

The Ju/wasi held a dim view of adultery, which was virtually unknown and seldom necessary, as divorce and remarriage were easily achieved. Women were supposed to act reassuringly in this regard, so they did not go moving around the encampment or visit at other people's fires at night. Men went visiting every evening, but if a woman wanted to say something to someone in the distance, she would stay where she was and shout.

Interestingly, the Ju/wasi took no position on homosexuality, which seemed unknown. Researchers of other hunter-gatherer societies have also found an absence of homosexuality. Perhaps the Old Way, with its arduous lifestyle, does not transmit this quality. We knew of no paternity issues, no one who questioned that he had fathered his wife's children. Rape also was unknown, although men liked the idea of marriage by capture and claimed that it was one of the ways to get a wife. We asked how this would be accomplished. "You go to the woman's encampment, and you grab her and carry her off," was the answer. This seemed not to be well thought out. What would you do next? She could walk home if she felt like it. And what about her relatives? Would they just sit there and watch? Or would you go back to her encampment and do bride service for her? We explored the issue carefully but found no example of it and concluded that it was a male fantasy that women more or less ignored. My mother wrote, "We are convinced that wives are not acquired by this means at present."[3]

The Ju/wasi also had a custom called /kamheri, which my mother discovered through interviews but not through occurrence. In this, two men could exchange wives for a time if everyone agreed. As one man said to my mother, "If you want to sleep with someone's wife, you get him to sleep with yours, then neither of you goes after the other with poisoned arrows."[4] Better to arrange a peaceful exchange and avoid problems. /Kamheri was permitted, but allegedly it was seldom practiced, as all four participants had to want it. A gossip told my mother that a man at /Gam had lent his first wife to an unmarried friend, but the husband was in love with his second wife and no longer wanted his first wife. This was not exactly /kamheri.

All in all, with the exception of sexual elements in some of the folklore and a few sexual jokes, sex did not seem of great concern to the Ju/wasi. It certainly did not obsess them as it does us. In fact, discreet sexual intercourse between a man and a woman, usually a man and his wife, was about the only important sexual activity practiced by these people.

It is interesting to note that while other hunter-gatherer cultures have similar attitudes about sex, only about 5 percent of all the cultures in the world prohibit sex outside marriage. Ours does, at least on paper, in that we have no formal or generally sanctioned alternatives. (In a different culture, for example, a man would be permitted to have sex with, say, his wife's sister, or would be expected to lend his wife to an overnight guest.) In this, the Ju/wa culture seemed quite close to ours. The big difference, as I saw it, was that they obeyed the rules and we don't. But then, the Ju/wasi in their open camps, with their ability to read tracks, had almost no privacy, and we do. And of course, there were always the poison arrows.

If we learned relatively little about sexual practices, we learned more about marriages. Divorce, although entirely acceptable, was quite rare—in a sample of about one hundred couples, we learned of just nine divorces. Both Di!ai and !U had long, very successful marriages, both resulting from choice. So did N!ai and /Gunda, although theirs was an arranged marriage, but arranged between two very young people who already knew each other. Perhaps theirs, too, was from choice, whether or not their parents realized this. Di!ai's husband, Gao Feet, died during the 1970s (I don't know from what), but !U and ≠Toma were together, warm and close, when I visited in the 1980s. We knew of marriages that were not so successful, evidently because the girl or woman had not chosen the man to whom she found herself married and would not have chosen him if choice had been an option. One of the nine above-mentioned divorces was instigated by a stunningly beautiful teenage girl who was somehow coerced into marriage with a much older man. Their group was visiting at /Gautscha when we met them, and the girl was always leaving her husband and returning to her grandmother's *tshu*, usually at night. Her family would persuade her to go back to her husband in the morning, but she wouldn't stay. Evidently, she didn't want to have sex, or not with him. One night he tried to force her, obviously not very strongly, and she made such a scene that the entire encampment got involved. The husband was quietly but deeply ashamed, and the girl was blazing with anger. She stayed with her grandmother after that, loudly saying bad things about her husband whenever he went by, referring not to the incident but to his appearance. He was ugly, she told the world. She didn't want a man like him. Not very long after that the marriage dissolved, the two went their own ways, and both of them remarried later.

We knew another very young woman (under twenty if not younger, I'd say) who also wanted a divorce from her much older husband, although he was very good to her, giving her many gifts, including hair ornaments. He was her second husband, and because of her youth, her parents had arranged the marriage as they had arranged the first. The first had failed because she didn't like the man, but she didn't like the second husband, either. In fact, she disliked him so much that when he gave her the hair ornaments, she cut off all her hair and rolled in ashes to make herself filthy. Her parents patiently arranged yet a third marriage for her.

We knew of a marriage that was badly shaken but not broken during the 1970s after a group of Ju/wasi tried to escape from a white man's farm and return to their n!ore, as ≠Toma's people had done some years before. In this case, a posse of white people on horseback, two men and a woman, rode after the escaping people, shot at them to scatter them, then grabbed some of the screaming children and carried them back to the farm. It was a melee. Not every Ju/wa person saw all that was happening or knew where the other Ju/wasi were. The parents who saw their children disappearing followed them and were rounded up and recaptured by the farmer. Other members of the escaping group, who were fleeing or hiding, regrouped and continued on their way, not knowing what had happened to the others but expecting that they would join them eventually. During the assault, a young married couple was separated. The wife had seen her only child captured, and ended up on the farm. The husband had not seen this, and ended up in his homeland. Two years passed before the authorities learned of this outrage and forced the whites to release the captured Ju/wasi, fining the whites in the process. During those two years, however, the wife took up with another man and had a son by him. When at last she was free to return home, she went back to her husband, who was shocked to see her with a baby that obviously could not be his. But after much soul-searching and anguish, and after some pressure from his people, who pointed out that his wife was hardly to blame for what had happened, he took her back and the baby also. The people felt that if he raised and fed the boy, the boy would be his son, but that the biological father should also do something good for the boy—perhaps make him an important gift when he was older. Even in the face of such terrible difficulties and after such appalling experiences, even after actions that those involved must have seen as betrayals—she because he did not return to the farm with her, and he because she had a child with another man—their marriage seemed to hold firmly.

Perhaps firm marriage belongs to the Old Way. It certainly was the way of the Ju/wasi. My mother wrote, "Divorce is untoward, disruptive; it can cause trouble. Anything other than peace and harmony in human relations makes the Ju/wasi uneasy. The instances of strife (that we observed) were breaks in their predominantly peaceful, well-adjusted human relations."[5]

13

The Life Cycle

N!ai reached the menarche when she was about seventeen years old, in 1959. At this time an important ceremony was held for her with eland music and dancing—a much more important ceremony than her wedding. But she and /Gunda had no child for three years, not until 1962, when she was almost twenty. This was a very normal age for a Ju/wa woman's first pregnancy—19.5 years was the average age.[1] During the next ten years, N!ai and /Gunda had four more children. In Nyae Nyae in the 1950s, most couples had from one to four living children, rarely more. Nine live births was the highest number on record for any Bushman woman, which is much lower than any other human population that does not use contraception.

How did this happen, considering that the people had no mechanical or pharmaceutical methods of birth control? In the Old Way, the human population, like most other populations who live in the Old Way, had its own regulation. The strenuous work and absence of body fat prevented hunter-gatherer women from menstruating at an early age, and after the burden of lactation was added to their bodies, they did not menstruate nearly as often as do the women of agricultural and industrial societies. They certainly did not menstruate monthly. It became my impression that many women, after menarche, didn't menstruate at all. We were able to note the absence of menstrual periods because the rules for later periods were the same as for the first—the woman covered herself with a cape, sat apart, and avoided men—and over the years we saw this only two or three times. At that, the women were young and had not yet had children. Even so, the twenty-eight-day cycle was understood by the Ju/wasi, as menstruation was associated with the moon, just as it is with us. According to Megan Biesele, menstruation was called "see the moon" or "go to the moon." A woman with menstrual cramps might say, "The moon torments me."[2]

After a woman had her first period, she would probably become pregnant as soon as her body could manage it. This, however, might not happen for several years. After giving birth, the woman would be lactating for about four years, which would inhibit future menstruation. All this contributed to the low birthrate.

Infant mortality was also an issue. We knew many women who had lost one or more children. Some died of infant diarrhea, which tragically is a primary cause of infant death in many populations. But among the Ju/wasi we knew, the majority of infant deaths involved children between one and three, a bit beyond the age most vulnerable to infant diarrhea. The women had great difficulty talking of such things and we didn't press them, so the cause of some of these deaths was not really known except in one terrible instance when a toddler fell into a fire and died of the burns. We were told of this tragedy but did not see it. I later learned that this particular kind of accident had happened more than once, which is understandable. I think of my own children and grandchildren as infants, wanting to walk but not yet proficient. I can imagine myself in the same situation as a Ju/wa woman, close to a fire on a cold night, with a little one between me and the fire, about to try a few steps, and I can easily see how this happens. There is nowhere else, really, for the baby to stand, except between oneself and the fire.

We were also told of a year when the rains hardly came at all and there was generalized hunger, at which time some women lost their milk, and although people tried to feed those babies anyway by chewing whatever food they had and putting it into the babies' mouths, this wasn't the same as breast milk, and some of the babies died, probably of starvation and dehydration. Sadly, this explained most

of the deaths and also accounted for the fact that several of the babies who lost their lives were over the age of one and therefore would have needed more food than the youngest babies. Also, certain groups of Ju/wasi seemed to have age gaps. A group might have knee children and babies, but then no other children younger than their teens. This, too, could suggest a time of hunger, when the children who would have filled that gap had died of starvation as babies.

Surely long-term nursing prevented many deaths from infant diarrhea, as virtually every small child we knew or saw, more than one hundred of them, was fit and in good health, thanks to pure, clean breast milk, with all its nutrition and immunities. We saw no babies showing any signs of any notable malnutrition. On the contrary, unlike most people in Nyae Nyae, the nursing children had visible body fat—just a little, but they had it. They were small and light compared to American children (just as their parents are small and light compared to us, of course), and after they were weaned they became quite skinny because they were active and played all day, but their good health continued. We knew very few children who got sick, and the few who did recovered completely.

This should not be surprising. The people were living in the Old Way, which is to say, they were living in the ecological niche that our species had evolved to fit. Old Way populations experience starvation and sometimes plagues as well, but as a rule, all Old Way participants, human and otherwise, are eating what they have evolved to eat, and all else being equal, this saves them from nutritional deficiencies. Such deficiencies and their complications are for those who live in agricultural societies—us and our animal slaves.

A Ju/wa woman produced enough milk to feed one baby at a time. She might feed a second baby also (as Di!ai was doing with her two small boys), but only after the first was eating solid food, with breast milk as a supplement. A woman could not produce enough milk to fully sustain two babies. (Some women in developed countries have been known to nurse two babies at once, but these women don't live mainly on roots that they dig themselves and they don't walk fifteen hundred miles a year.) If Ju/wa children of the Old Way were less than three or four years apart, both children would be undernourished and both could die.

Better to prevent this. Better to bring the first child to healthy independence at the relatively safe age of three or four. However, this could not always be achieved. Although lactation, strenuous work, and a low-fat diet almost always prevented conception, on very rare occasions a woman conceived anyway, even though she had a nursing baby under the age of three or four, and when this happened she might have to dispose of the new baby at birth.

A Ju/wa woman in labor would wait in the encampment, probably saying nothing, until she clearly was soon to deliver, at which time she would leave camp and go to a place in the nearby veld that she might have prepared in advance. The women gave birth alone, away from the encampment where no one saw them, unless the birth was the woman's first, in which case her mother would go with her. But a child who could not be kept would not be a woman's first child, so the woman would inevitably be alone. She would have a small grave waiting, the hole that any woman digs to bury the placenta and other birth matter, and would place the newborn in the grave and bury it before it drew breath. When people spoke of this, they spoke with deep sadness and the reason given for doing it was always the same—the mother already had a nursing child. She could nurse one baby to self-sufficiency, but she couldn't nurse two. Unless another woman had recently lost a child but was still lactating, no one else would be able to nurse the new baby either. The mother's choice would be to lose just the new baby or both babies. There was never a suggestion that baby girls were less welcome than baby boys, as children of both sexes were equally welcome, so it was always the spacing of children, not their gender, that determined their fate.

The act was called //kao, which means "throw down," "hurt," or "go from." The anthropologist Nancy Howell, who studied this question in detail, found a very low instance of infanticide—six infanticides in five hundred births. It was hard to be sure. Women were not forthcoming about infanticide, and if a woman had to do this she might return to the encampment and tell others that the child was stillborn. Some babies, of course, were stillborn. Because

a baby born too soon was doomed to malnutrition and an early death, stillbirth and unavoidable infanticide were almost the same thing.

We knew no one who had ever "gone from" a baby. We also knew no one who had twins, although it is not impossible that over the years twins had been born. But the thought of "going from" a baby was too painful for speech. If a woman had twins, she would have to "go from" one of them and would never need to tell anyone what she had done. Everyone was better off to think that a child was born dead than that its mother had "gone from" it. Even so, although everyone knew that infanticide sometimes took place, every shred of evidence that any fieldworker has learned about it shows that it was exceedingly rare.

The Ju/wasi were unfailingly good to their children. An infant would be nursed on demand and stay close to its mother, safe in the pouch of her cape, warm in cold weather, shaded in hot weather, complete with a wad of soft grass for a diaper. Ju/wa children very rarely cried, probably because they had little to cry about. No child was ever yelled at or slapped or physically punished, and few were even scolded. Most never heard a discouraging word until they were approaching adolescence, and even then the reprimand, if it really was a reprimand, was delivered in a soft voice. At least the tone was soft, even if the words weren't always.[3]

"The !Kung never seem to tire of their babies," wrote my mother. "They dandle them, kiss them, dance with them, and sing to them. The older children make playthings of the babies. The girls carry them around, not as a task set them by their parents (though they might carry babies around for that reason also), but because they play 'mother.' The boys also carry the babies around, give them rides, drag them on leather capes (a favorite game). If the babies utter a whimper, they are carried back to their mothers. When people are sitting at leisure, they spend time teaching the babies. They help them to stand or to take their first steps between outstretched arms of the adults and they play little games with them."[4]

We are sometimes told that children who are treated so kindly become spoiled, but this is because those who hold that opinion have no idea how successful such measures can be. Free from frustration or anxiety, sunny and cooperative, and usually without close siblings as competitors, the Ju/wa children were every parent's dream. No culture can ever have raised better, more intelligent, more likable, more confident children.

One day I heard grass moving, a tiny swishing sound, and saw a little shadow coming toward us. It was a child, all alone, coming for a visit. What competence! He was somewhere between two and three years old, and the grass was slightly taller than he was so he couldn't see where he was going, yet he navigated perfectly, without fear or hesitation. He was expecting to meet us, and when he saw me he held up his arms. I picked him up. He was soft and warm, and he held on to me with his arms and legs, strongly but gently, and then he looked right into my eyes and informed me of something quite frankly. At the time, I didn't know enough !Kung to understand, so he patiently told me again, carefully delivering his few words in an open, honest manner. That was the way of the Ju/wa children, open, agreeable, and charming, confident of their welcome. But who would not welcome a child like that? We were moving our trucks around so I carried him back to his mother lest we lose track of him, but he was determined to visit, and three more times that morning I noticed his little shadow advancing alone through the grass.

Only one child, the little two-year-old son of Lazy /Kwi and //Kushe, sometimes cried or had an occasional little tantrum—nothing compared to an American child's tantrum, but a tantrum nevertheless. One day, for instance, he cried when he saw Lazy /Kwi with his bow and arrow and hunting bag, and realized that his father was about to go hunting. The little boy didn't want his father to leave him. His father held him and spoke gently to him, but the other hunters were departing and Lazy /Kwi had to go with them, so he gave the baby to //Kushe. The baby arched his back and screamed. //Kushe then sat down on her heels to hold him and tried to distract him by offering him her breast, which he refused. She then bounced him gently up and down, but he was not to be comforted. //Kushe was at a loss and looked up at the other people as if for suggestions. Her unspoken question was met by somewhat puzzled stares— everyone seemed slightly baffled. Most people then pretended it wasn't happening and went on with what they were doing as if nothing was wrong. Nevertheless, it seemed to me that they were radiating a certain restrained displeasure. Both the boy's parents seemed unsure and embarrassed. Evidently, a tantrum was surprising. In the years that I was there, this was the only tantrum I ever saw.

Unless in extremis, as //Kushe's little boy had been, children were respectful of their parents. They had only to learn what the adults wanted of them, and they'd willingly, unquestioningly do it. Most of the time, the tension between adults and children that often characterizes American families did not exist there. Most of the time, but not always. One day, both of Di!ai's boys were nursing at the same time, each unhappy with the other's presence, and once again they started to push each other surreptitiously. Di!ai put a hand between them but also mentioned to her older son that he might be old enough to stop nursing. He didn't think so. Instead, he took his mouth from her nipple, looked her in the eye, and cursed her, calling upon a //gaua, a spirit of the dead, to choke her for saying such a thing.

If lightning had struck, the surrounding people could not have been more startled. The Ju/wasi didn't curse one another (although where did the little boy learn this if they never did?), and nobody loudly called upon the spirits of the dead in broad daylight. To hear such words from a child's mouth! To hear such words from anybody's mouth! A shocked silence fell. The younger brother froze and stopped sucking. Di!ai, however, was quite serene and looked down coolly at her older boy. He had taken her nipple back in his mouth. Their eyes locked. She told him, somewhat scornfully, that words from someone as small as himself could never cause her harm.

We often wondered about people's ages, how old they had been when life-changing events happened to them. We ourselves, belonging as we did to a Western culture, were accustomed to reckoning age almost daily. But the Ju/wasi didn't do the same. They didn't count years. They didn't, for that matter, recognize years as such, or not particularly, because the time-related events that concerned them were the passages of the seasons. So they did not, as we in Western societies sometimes imagine them doing, mark people's births and thus their ages by events. No one was said to have been born "in the year of the great drought" or "when the elephants came to /Gautscha." The people of course would know of the events, but if you haven't been counting the years since the elephants came, what difference does it make when it happened? Events were remembered for their relationship to the seasons, when the rains were not good, when the rains didn't come, when a waterhole dried, when a fire swept the encampment. In a similar spirt, the Ju/wasi measured their lives by stages of their development.

People's numerical ages were nevertheless of interest to us, if only to refute the unfounded but prevalent notion that hunter-gatherers die of old age at forty. We knew that one man was in his seventies when we met him because as a young adult (meaning age fifteen to twenty) he had seen the Boer voortrekkers as they came through Nyae Nyae on their way to Angola. The voortrekkers had passed through in 1903. This man then became a benchmark for us. People might not have reckoned their age in years, but everyone knew who was younger or older than everyone else, and thus we could determine the number of other people who were close to his age and also those who were older.

To reckon life's progress in terms of human development is probably more realistic than our assiduous counting of months and years, which have little to do with our development, physically, emotionally, or intellectually. The Ju/wasi used developmental stages as measures. A newborn was a "little young child." When its fontanel closed and it began to smile, it reached a new stage of development, another when it sat up alone, and another when its teeth came in. This, it later seemed to me when I had children, was a good way of looking at child development, in contrast to the other young mothers in our apartment building who were competitive about their babies. They knew the exact age, almost in hours, of every other baby in the building, and held their own babies to the prevailing standard, to triumph if their baby was ahead of the game, to call the pediatrician if it wasn't. In contrast, if a Ju/wa baby wasn't an early talker, nobody worried—the baby was so charming that such things didn't matter, and anyway, it would talk eventually. (Interestingly, when babies first talked, they didn't use the clicks. That also was developmental and came later, first with just one click, which some babies seemed to substitute for all the clicks.) When an infant began to toddle, it reached another stage, and another when it walked with skill. It then became a "knee child," moving on to become a "young child," then an "old child," a young teenager. An older teenager who had reached puberty was a young adult.

If you asked a woman how old her child had been at any given time, she would hold up a fist to represent its head, showing how tall it had been then. When someone reached full growth, people would say that he or she had reached the "head's place." For a while after that, development was reckoned by the number of children a person might have. Someone might be old enough to have had two children, whether or not these two children were actually born. (A woman at this point might be in her mid-twenties, statistically speaking, having had her first child at about twenty and her next child perhaps four years later.) When a couple had had three children who could walk, or were old enough to have had this many children, the man's bride service was completed and the couple could move away from the bride's parents' group, if for some overriding reason they had not done so already.

Menopause was not the issue with the Ju/wasi that it is with us, because women did not menstruate regularly. However, a woman's reproductive ability was nevertheless considered, and when it faded, perhaps at the age of about forty-five, she joined the most honored people in the population, the old people. When she verged on becoming one of the seniors, at about the age of fifity-five or sixty, she might be given the extra name of N!a. My mother's name was Di!khao N!a, for instance—Big or Old Di!khao. Someday I hope to return to Nyae Nyae, bringing copies of this book to the people who are in these pages or to their children, and when I do, I hope I will be called Di!ai N!a.

In our culture, of course, we dislike old age and do our best to mask it. But to the Ju/wasi, old age was good. Old people were not burdensome, as the older people continued their activity for as long as possible, so that some of the oldest women went gathering with the rest, sharing what they brought with their families as they had always done. But eventually, as at /Gautscha, where three of the oldest women did not gather, others gathered for them. Four of the oldest men did not hunt, not feeling up to the arduous traveling and the days without food or water. They, too, were given food by others. Even so, they were valued, as factors other than their labor made them valuable. They were valued for what they knew.

This was not surprising. That we are here at all is attributable, in large measure, to the fact that a number of our ancestors lived to old age. No group of hunter-gatherers has many old people as members, but the more of them there are, and the older they are, the better. They are the ones who hold the largest amount of important information.

To us today in Western societies, the facts held in the memories of the old people seem like unimportant lore. But the Ju/wasi felt differently, for a very good reason. The older someone is, the more that person remembers about what happened before the rest of the group was born, events that, without written records, would be lost if someone couldn't describe them. In the event of a fifty-year drought, for instance, it would be those in their sixties and seventies who might remember a way of getting water, or of getting by without water, something that their own grandparents had shown them the last time this occurred.

Among certain groups in Nyae Nyae, it was the old people who knew what a white man was. One or two white men had appeared in the distant past, perhaps hunting ostriches for their valuable feathers. White people didn't reappear for many years, and when they did, only the old people knew what they were. The seventy-year-old man at /Gautscha would have recognized white people, as he had seen the voortrekkers on their way to Angola. He also remembered a herd of elephants that once had come to /Gautscha. Perhaps the people had tried to hunt these elephants. Perhaps they had simply gone too near them. At any rate, the elephants had been disturbed, and one of them had killed a man. Years later, if elephants were to reappear, those who saw the killing could have described it for others, warning them of the danger.

An old man at /Gautscha, a man who knew I liked to climb the baobab tree, warned me against climbing the ladder of pegs that ran up its side to the top. Many years earlier, he had seen a man fall to his death from the ladder. Perhaps a peg had come loose, perhaps the man had lost his grip, or perhaps bees had stung him, said the old man, who had seen the climber suddenly come off the tree and plummet to his death, one hundred feet below. I hadn't realized the danger, but I heard what the old man told me and didn't climb the ladder.

Another old man who had been on a farm told me why it was dangerous to throw bullets in a fire. I had no intention of doing that and also had no bullets—the old man was simply cautioning me. On the farm, he had seen one of the farmer's children throw bullets in a fire, and they went off, barely missing some of the spectators. Best not to do that, he said.

If this had happened recently, everyone would have been talking about it. But it had happened in the distant past, and only the old man had been there to see it. Nor were the Ju/wasi familiar with bullets, or at least, no one except the old man. Most people knew what bullets were, of course, having learned about them from us and our rifle, but no one would necessarily have known that bullets would shoot off if thrown in a fire. So this was a useful bit of information and those who heard it would remember it. I remember it, after all these years, and here I am now, passing it on. If you, the reader, should refrain from throwing bullets in a fire and thus save your life and those of others, you can thank word-of-mouth information about an event that took place on an African farm probably in the 1940s and was imparted by an experienced old man at /Gautscha, now no longer living, but who gave the information to me. I am now about the age that he was then, and here I am, keeping the information going. He also, of course, told his own people, and perhaps they, too, are advancing it.

Thus, with the help of the old people, the collective memory of a group can go back sixty, seventy, or eighty years, or long enough to contain the kinds of events that happen only rarely. Not too many perilous events happen at intervals greater than that, or at least not the kinds of events that people can do anything about, and any group fortunate enough to have old people in their midst would have these challenges covered.

We are not the only species that depends for information upon its oldest members. Far from it. The same elephants who came to /Gautscha, for instance, may have visited because of something re-membered by the oldest member of the group—their leader. Perhaps she remembered the shallow lake with browsing opportunities and no ivory hunters. Elephants resemble us in that they live in groups and care for their children to maturity and beyond. Like us, elephants also depend heavily on the knowledge of their oldest member, always their leader, always a female. Many other mammals, such as horses, have been proved to have long memories. So have many kinds of birds, including parrots and ravens. So have crocodiles and alligators, if anecdotally. Probably the dinosaurs had long memories, too, to help them through their long lives. Few attributes could be as useful as a long memory, or contribute as much to survival.

For a group to avail itself of the memory of its elders, however, the elders must be respected. If not, the younger people won't take them seriously, just as we tend to discount information offered by small children, often to our sorrow. Various populations of animals know this and use their eldest members as their leaders. Sometimes this doesn't work, as it doesn't, for instance, for the whales or porpoises who strand themselves by following their leader onto the beach, but it works in the long run, as the species with long memories gain more good than harm from following the leadership of their elders.

Among the Ju/wasi, the elders—those who were, say, over fifty or sixty—were greatly respected. They were at the pinnacle of their society. The anthropologist Richard Lee found a fascinating factor in the kinship system whereby the elder of two people gets to choose how the younger person will relate to him. Will the younger person assume the identity of the person he or she was named for in the all-important Ju/wa name relationship, or will the name relationship be bypassed, and the biological relationship pertain? The oldest person in a group will have made that determination for all who are still living, and thus, in a sense, has shaped the group to his liking. In !Kung society, whereby equality is the favored condition, only the elderly have this kind of rank.[5]

As has been said, the older people had the term of respect N!a as part of their names and were well known to be the repository of important information, received either through personal experience or from their own elders, in a chain of memory going back through time, a chain in which they themselves were an important link for transmitting information into the future. If we asked the Ju/wasi how they knew something, a very common answer would be, "The old people told us." If they didn't know, they might say, "The old people

The older people were well known to be the repository of important information, and were greatly respected for it.

didn't tell us." Sometimes in the course of our work we would ask questions of younger people, who then would refer us to the old people for answers. And indeed, the old people very often found answers learned long ago from their group's collective memory. Or if they didn't know, they, too, would explain by saying that when they were young, their old people hadn't told them.

Megan Biesele speaks of this cultural feature, pointing out that within these egalitarian groups of Ju/wasi, the oldest person acts "as a focus for collective decision making." She adds, "Women take an active part in decision making. The respect given to women's opinions is linked to their importance in providing over half the edible food by weight and their intimate knowledge of the whereabouts of plant food and resources."[6] Many times, I sat with the /Gautscha women while they talked such things over, and often it was Di!ai and !Ungka, the two older sisters of the two groups of owners, who had the most to say. Freely expressing herself, however, was Di!ai's mother, N/aoka N!a, who was perhaps about seventy and sometimes did not go gathering with the others if their destination was far. Nevertheless, her thoughts were valued. She didn't speak as often as her daughters, but when she did, others would listen with real interest. If she introduced a new destination as a possibility, one that had not yet been discussed, the others would turn the discussion to the place suggested by N/aoka N!a.

In addition to valuable factual information, cultural concepts were also passed to new generations by the elders, who accomplished this with stories. Among the Ju/wasi, the older women told most of the stories, although every adult knew them. An older Ju/wa woman said to Megan Biesele, "The old person who does not tell stories just does not exist."

Literal facts are not necessarily communicated by stories, but concepts are. The concept of confidence, for instance, is exemplified by the sleek python. The concept that nervousness and shrillness are signs of trouble is exemplified by the jackal. Good things happen to the python, and bad things happen to the jackal. Better to be sleek and serene than nervous and anxious. Better to seem confident than insecure. Megan Biesele, in discussing the folklore of the Ju/wasi (she spells this Ju/'hoansi), refers to the work of the anthropologist John Pfeiffer. "Though speech does not fossilize," she writes, "it is clear that oral tradition consistently preserves enough material to be recognizable over time as 'the same tradition' while processing and incorporating new material." Tales of today represent, in Pfeiffer's words, "part of a 'vast untapped linguistic archaeology' reflecting no single point in time but an accumulation of realizations out of the past mixed with an attempt to encompass new realities. Seen this way, contemporary Ju/'hoan tales can be understood as a combination of conservative elements from the deep hunting-gathering past with elements introduced by recent changes and pressures." The telling of stories among the Ju/wasi, says Biesele, "is no watered-down nursery pastime but a substantial adult pleasure. . . . Young Ju/'hoan people, when asked for stories, often protest that they 'have not grown old enough to have learned the things that old people know.'" She adds that storytelling "may be part of a general practical stratification of knowledge in Ju/'hoan society."

When the old people told stories, the young people listened, and because many stories are funny, they would laugh. The small children also listened, but often, at the parts of the story that the adult audience might consider the funniest, the small children did not laugh. No, they sat in awe around the edges of the gathering, listening carefully, their eyes wide and their mouths open. Storytelling was not aimed at children, as it is in our culture. Yet it was the children who absorbed the meaning.

What happens to the very old? In the case of elephants, they starve to death. An elephant eats rough food and has several sets of teeth to cope with it. As one set wears down, another set erupts to take its place. In time, all sets wear out and that's it. The elephant gradually starves and weakens. But her followers do not abandon her. If she collapses, they may try to help her to her feet. If they can't, they may stay beside her. They may come back to visit her body later. They appear to mourn. And indeed, they have lost something of value—they have lost not only their matriarch and their leader but also the information that she carried in her head.

It was much the same with aging people, although factors other than starvation might cause their collapse. (Although here the parallel with elephants is not entirely far-fetched, as aging hunter-gatherers also lose teeth. If they cannot chew the rough foods of the veld as well as they could when younger, they become malnourished and weakened.) And whereas they had certainly been valued for their knowledge and memory, they were equally valued because the people around them were their relatives, their group, and they were its focal members. That mattered to the Ju/wasi.

In the past, it was said that the Bushmen abandoned old people who could no longer support themselves. Not so. Almost all old people had relatives who would care for them until their deaths, sharing food, bringing them water, digging their graves, and burying them with care at the end. Their bodies would face toward their birthplaces and their few possessions would be broken over their graves. Then their people would leave and not return to that encampment. Only then would these old people be left behind for a god to find and bring to his home in the west.

14

The Social Fabric

"The [Ju/wasi] are extremely dependent emotionally on the sense of belonging and companionship," wrote my mother. "Separation and loneliness are unendurable to them. I believe their wanting to belong and be near is actually visible in the way families cluster together in an encampment and in the way they sit huddled together, often touching someone, shoulder against shoulder, ankle across ankle. Security and comfort for them lie in their belonging to their group free from the threat of rejection and hostility."[1]

I believe that the importance of the group showed clearly in the way that the people made decisions. Women were as much a part of this as men. The people would talk together, for days if necessary, until every point of view had been considered. Our notions of secret ballots and majority rule would have seemed unpleasant to them—they preferred consensus, with everyone knowing the thoughts and feelings of everyone else, and everyone pleased with the decision. Our notions of individuality would also have seemed inappropriate to the Ju/wasi—they expected to function as group members.

This became obvious in the instances of service offered by some people to others. I remember one day in 1951 when five men and four women set out for a mangetti grove about thirty miles distant.

One of the women put on an extra cape before she left, a cape given to her by someone else, tying the second over the first, to be used as a bag on the return journey. The owner of the cape would own the nuts brought home in it by the harvester, who was planning to walk sixty miles, carrying perhaps eighty pounds on the return journey, at the end of which she would be empty-handed, as the nuts would belong to someone else.

Each woman took two or three ostrich eggshells, putting them into the pouch of her cape. Some of the people took leather bags, and others took nets made of grass fiber, which they would line with leather capes. Then they left, each person with a walking stick. They stopped at the waterhole, where they sat on their heels, drank from their cupped hands, and filled the ostrich eggshells. They then stood up, readied themselves, and set off in single file toward the northwest. As they were leaving, I was fixing a puncture in the inner tube of a truck tire, but after a while I looked up from my work to check on their progress and just barely made out their little procession far away. They were moving slowly and steadily through the low acacia bush, tiny figures in a vast landscape on a journey to bring food to their people. I recall no other scene that better illustrated the Ju/wa population density—one person for every ten square miles. And I recall no other scene that better illustrates the Ju/wa sense of community and cooperation. Soon the bush swallowed these committed individuals, and they vanished from our sight.

As the sun set, I thought of these nine people far away in the enormous veld, camped beside a small fire as the world of night opened around them. I wondered if they had reached the grove. They had waited until midmorning before leaving and would have camped while the sun was still in the sky—perhaps by night they had not finished their journey.

Several days later someone noticed them returning. Again we watched their small procession, now coming toward us, all together, no one far ahead of the others, no one lagging behind, all carrying enormous bundles bulging with mangetti nuts, balancing the bundles with their walking sticks. On they came, getting closer each time we checked on their progress, until at last they walked into the encampment and put down their loads. All were tired, yet all seemed glad to be home after their successful journey and happy with the

pleasure that was blossoming around them. Soon, the bundles had been opened, the bounty had been shared and shared again, and everyone was roasting and eating mangettis. These nine strong men and women had brought important food to sixteen other people, including the children, two elderly men and three elderly women, one very pregnant woman, and the other able-bodied adults who had stayed home to take care of the encampment. Eaten sparingly and supplemented with other foods, the harvest of nuts would feed all the people for almost a month. Never has there been a better example of a well-functioning group.

An elderly woman, the mother of one of the women who made the trip, said later to my mother, "It is bad to die, because when you die you are alone." Thus even death did not seem as bad as isolation, although death of course is isolation, because not until you die are you left alone. You are buried, your group leaves your gravesite, and for the first time ever, the line of your people, their backs turned to you, deliberately moves away. I suspect that this image has crossed the minds of many Ju/wasi who left loved ones behind in their graves.

We knew of no one who lived alone. There seemed to be no such thing as an unattached person. Even the insane man who married his stepdaughter lived with her when he wasn't with his people. We did, however, know one man who was marginal, who had no firm place in any group. He was the man who had never married because, for some unknown reason, he had never successfully hunted, and no family would give a daughter to a man like that. Nor would a divorced or widowed woman ally herself with such a person, to join him in his precarious state. Therefore, this man had no real tie to anyone except his widowed sister. She alone took care of him, sharing the foods she gathered. By the time we met her brother, he was too frail and elderly to make long-distance trips to the mangetti groves and had no leather cape to lend to those who could, a cape that would have made him the owner and distributor of the nuts that the gatherer would bundle inside it. Perhaps he could have made a poison arrow to give to a hunter who would bring meat home on his behalf, but perhaps the hunters would not welcome his arrow. We never heard of him trying to give an arrow. Perhaps he feared rejection more than hunger.

He was a sad, depressed person, almost but not quite an outcast, who lived in the shadows, seldom speaking and always at the outskirts of any gathering. I remember the first time I saw him, when his sister's group came to /Gautscha before the rains. As their long line of people with their bundles made its way toward us through the grass, I noticed that one man was trailing behind, carrying nothing, quite a distance from the next to last person in the line. When I saw him straggling far behind the others, the image that came to me was that of a dog.

The people had come for a visit and made camp on the opposite side of the pan about a mile away from the main encampment. Other groups had also come from other directions, one of these from the Tswana cattle camp at Kai Kai, about fifty miles to the east, and these people brought a flu virus. Many people became extremely ill, but no one died except the unmarried man's sister. A few weeks later, when we were returning to /Gautscha from a visit elsewhere, traveling in a vehicle in the middle of nowhere on the enormous veld, we noticed her brother lying on the ground not far from our track. He was alone, at least three or four miles from any other people, just lying there without food or water. Why? Sooner or later, night-hunting predators would come upon him. As has been said, the predators of Nyae Nyae seldom bothered the Ju/wasi, but their respect for our species would not apply to someone lying on the ground out on the veld alone at night. What would happen then?

How he came to be there, we never knew. He was slightly disoriented and didn't answer our questions. Our ethic was not to interfere with the people's affairs except to try to understand them, their lifestyle being considerably older and more successful than ours, although we offered medical help whenever we could (and had done so during the flu epidemic). A lonely old man lying on the ground far from any encampment, apparently of his own free will, was obviously a Ju/wa thing and not really our business, but we couldn't leave him there. He got up rather shakily and let us help him into the truck, although he seemed bewildered and showed no relief at being rescued. We took him back to his group and also gave him food. Other people asked him to share it.

Very soon, that group left /Gautscha, perhaps because of the sister's death. The people had only been visiting and had no reason to inform us of their departure, and the unmarried man evidently went with them, or we think he did. Without a wife, without family or others who were socially or emotionally connected to him, and very much alone without his sister, he was a heavy burden on his group's slim resources, which meant, of course, that his life was essentially finished. The rules of sharing were driven by the social ties, especially those of kinship, and he had no such advantages. And the Very Old Rule also applied—gathered foods were shared at the discretion of the person who found them, and if such foods were scarce, as they were at that time because many groups were visiting at /Gautscha, perhaps no one felt the urge to share hard-won foods with him. Perhaps he had been on his own solitary gathering trip when we came upon him. Or perhaps, with his sister gone, he had felt so alone and so marginalized that he had gone off by himself, to meet his death on his own terms, to lie down and wait.

It was the Old Way, the dark side of the Old Way. We were not sure what happened to this man, but we didn't see him again. Better to marry, because your partner will help you. Better to connect to your partner's people, because they will help you. Better to connect to the next generation by having children and grandchildren, because they will help you, and their partners will help you, and their partners' people will help you. Better to be part of the social fabric. That, too, was the Old Way.

Sharing was perhaps the most important element of the social fabric. Fear that others would not share was the constant preoccupation of many people. I remember a woman talking about sharing. "I am sick," said the woman as if speaking to herself although in fact she was speaking to my mother, who was nearby. "That is why I don't go out for plant foods. I want my mother [meaning Lorna] to give me some and she does not give me any. I am lying down sick. I am starving. If my mother [meaning her own mother] were here, she would give me some plant foods. She is not here. So I am starving. [Lorna] does not favor me. She does not give me food. Why does she not give me some fat? My ankle is sore. If she gave me fat, my ankle would be better and I could go out for plant foods. I could not go to the mangetti trees. I did not think I would be able. That place is far. This is what I say. The people who stay there are not people who favor others. Not sympathetic. They do not give food. When they see people from a far place coming to their place, their hearts do not feel good. I do not want to go to see those people."[2]

Continuous sharing reassured the people of their membership in the social fabric, and failures of sharing, or perceived failures of sharing, suggested the fear that people felt of marginalization and exclusion, the deathlike state of being all alone. My mother reported numerous events in which people felt excluded from sharing. "In an extreme instance," wrote my mother, "we saw a woman visitor go into a sort of trance and say over and over for perhaps an hour in ≠Toma's presence that he had not given her as much meat as was her due. It was not said like an accusation. It was said as though he were not there. I had the eerie feeling that I was present in someone else's dream. ≠Toma did not oppose her. He continued doing whatever he was doing and let her go on."[3]

These two women were not marginal. The woman who complained to my mother was one of the owners of the /Gautscha *n!ore*, and the woman who complained to ≠Toma was a core member of a visiting group. Yet the fear of exclusion was in every person's heart, although women, not men, were more likely to express it.

However, the people who were truly marginal did not express fear of exclusion. The unmarried man, who was already as good as excluded, had done his best to mask the signs suggesting this. *Hide your weakness* was among the oldest of the Old Rules. This, the Ju/wasi could do with amazing ability. I think of a Ju/wa girl who was caught in a trap set by a biologist for a hyena. The biologist was with us for a time on one of our expeditions and was making a study of the wildlife. The trap was set far from the encampment, but somehow the girl, who was out by herself, stepped on it and its teeth went through her foot. She couldn't sit down because the trap was anchored and wouldn't yield to motion, so she stood on the other foot and waited. Hours later, her uncle, who was hunting, saw her from afar, wondered what was wrong, and went to see. He couldn't open the trap, but he gave the girl his spear to lean on while he went for help.

I will always remember her calmness as we brought her to the encampment and dressed the wound. She had been alone, helpless, and in pain for many hours in a place frequented by hyenas, yet she acted as if nothing had happened, nothing at all. Instead, she chatted with other people about this and that in an offhand manner. To me, such composure in these circumstances did not seem possible, and I remember wondering if the nervous systems of the Ju/wasi were not superior to ours. But of course, their nervous systems were the same as ours. It was their self-control that was superior. You can say that things are wrong, but you cannot show it. Your body language must suggest that everything is fine.

The value of this is firmly from the Old Way. Nothing would be more attractive to a predator than a weeping, struggling creature, alone and unable to run away. This concept carried into the social fabric, too, because, as with other human and nonhuman populations, need and weakness tend to be punished. Hungry people did not show that they were hungry. A person could certainly talk about hunger and complain about it, too. And a person could show pleasure when important foods came into camp—when hunters brought meat, for instance, or harvesters returned from distant places with nuts. But if, for instance, a group was sitting around a fire passing and eating portions of cooked food, a newcomer joining the group was expected to conceal his hunger and sit down far away from the person who was eating, as if the food did not interest him. I remember a hungry man who failed to do this but instead sat down beside the person who was eating, expecting that when that person passed the food, he would be the next to eat. His manner was jovial—although he was jumping the line, so to speak, he was pretending that he thought he would be welcomed. But the man he sat next to passed the food around him to the person who was rightfully expecting it, and the meal did not go twice around the circle. Thus the newcomer was given no food and was deeply hurt. Hungry as he was, he had been deliberately excluded from the sharing. He later composed a song about the experience, just music, no words, as people sometimes did to express lingering sadness, and he called the song "Pass on By."

Such restraint promoted group cohesion, as people did not openly express their negative feelings. People who were angry would mope rather than let fly their anger. People who were critical of others

. . . .

might whisper their feelings to their most intimate confidants but would not criticize openly and at most would express their criticism with jokes. The criticized person was not supposed to take offense at the jokes and would be sure to laugh along with the others. On the very rare occasions when self-control broke down, such as happened when two women could not stop quarreling, other people made a song about them and sang it when the arguments started. Hearing the song, the two women felt shamed and fell silent. Thus the community prevailed without mentioning the problem directly.

No one wanted disapproval. No one wanted to make others jealous, or even mildly envious. No one wanted more influence or more possessions than anyone else. What good would it do to have many possessions if others were jealous and excluded you? The goodwill of the group was one's most valuable asset. Such respect for the social fabric eliminated many of the ills that plague our society. Theft, for example, was unknown. Surely it is significant that, at least in those days, the !Kung language had no specific word for theft. !Kung speakers could discuss the deed, of course, but unlike ourselves, with our massive lexicon ranging from *pilfer* to *larceny*, covering every nuance of this cultural feature, the Ju/wasi did not seem to have named it at all. Theft was not even mentioned as a perceived wrongdoing, unlike fighting, failure to share, failure to observe the marriage sanctions. Those things could happen. Theft essentially could not. We heard of only one instance of theft in living memory, when a man took honey from a beehive found by another man who was planning to return for it. The man who found the hive killed the man who took the honey.

This episode was so far in the past that it had a mythlike quality about it, so that the part about the killing was not explained or justified but merely mentioned, like a killing in a story. Probably the man who found the hive was too shocked to think of any other action. He might have felt that his very existence was invisible to the thief. He might have felt himself disappearing. The social fabric had been so deeply rendered by the theft that the owner of the hive had no choice but to do what he did. And perhaps as an unplanned consequence, an antisocial person was eliminated.

In contrast was an episode that occurred when we were leaving the encampment at /Gautscha, with our trucks packed full of our things. As we pulled away, a man came running after us with a nail that we had left behind. The nail might have been very useful to him, but this didn't seem to have crossed his mind. Obviously, with our vehicles and rifle and loads of equipment, even an inexperienced person could see that we could easily afford the loss of a nail. Yet this man ran after us with it. Otherwise we would have left without it. It was our nail. As I recall, my father thanked him very much and gave him the nail, which surprised him a little. He had no such expectation.

But then, the Ju/wasi would have had difficulty surviving in that forbidding country without perfect integrity. On another occasion, a man led us for miles to show us a certain kind of root that we wanted to identify botanically. He once had noticed such a root in its vine-producing state and was planning to harvest it later when it became edible, knowing that no one else would have taken it because he had found it, which made it his. And yes, there it was, out in the middle of nowhere, still waiting for him. Another time when we were with some of the Ju/wasi several miles away from the /Gautscha encampment, we came upon a broken ostrich eggshell. The Ju/wasi took a look at it but on second thought didn't pick it up because someone remembered that someone else had mentioned it and would probably come for it one day. What if it was gone, and that person had counted upon finding it?

Considerate behavior and respect for others came at a cost. A man who could not express anger might hide it, but he experienced it nevertheless, often deeply. A woman who thought that others were not sharing properly could whine a bit and make generalized accusations but could not take matters into her own hands and help herself to what she wanted. A person who wanted something that belonged to someone else might ask for it but, if denied, would be forced to see it with its owner every day and feel the bitter pain of envy and rejection.

To push down one's negative feelings was a lifelong commitment, worth the discomfort for the sake of belonging, but not accomplished easily. Everyone knew that everyone else was bottling such feelings, but everyone also knew that if the negative feelings flared, harm would come, and a fight might start or the group might disintegrate. I sometimes wondered if this was why the Ju/wasi feared the spirits of the dead and were so quick to leave a fresh grave. The person's spirit had been set free, and with it, all the bad feelings of a lifetime, no longer contained, but loose in the air.

Perhaps to counter the very serious problem of suppressed negativity, the Ju/wasi had developed something called *xaro*. This was the practice of giving gifts, which the Ju/wasi did most earnestly. With the possible exception of certain articles of clothing (the Ju/wasi did not have spare clothes), almost every object in Nyae Nyae was subject to *xaro*, received as a gift from someone else, to be given as a gift to another person later. The extreme importance of the practice could often be seen during a social upset, at which time people might begin to cite the failures of *xaro* as they cited failures of sharing. When N!ai's father came to /Gautscha from Kubi, for instance, wanting to break her engagement to /Gunda so that she could marry the man he had selected for her, a great commotion arose surrounding gifts.

"Some of N!ai's relatives began to express objection to her betrothal," wrote my mother, "not because they wanted her to go with her father, but because they were angry with the mother of the bridegroom. Possibly, older stresses underlay the episode, but what brought them to light was an affair about a knife. N!ai's stepfather, Gao Feet, had given a present of beads to one of his relatives. He was expecting a return gift to be made in due time, and it had seemed that there was a knife making its way to him in the ever-flowing currents of gift-giving. However, his wife, Di!ai, and her sister, !U, claimed that the bridegroom's mother had got possession of the knife and had given it instead to one of her relatives. Feelings flared up and a talk ensued. !U began it, declaring in a voice that could be heard across the encampment that the bridegroom's mother was a grasping, stingy woman whose second husband loved her so much that he spoiled her and let her have power over his belongings. !U disapproved of N!ai's marriage to the son of such a woman, but said that she would reconsider her position if the knife that had been diverted were now given to Gao Feet, as had been expected.

"It never was, but gifts of ostrich eggshell beads and a blanket were given and Gao Feet declared himself satisfied. His wife, Di!ai, wanted the marriage so much that she was ready to overlook the matter of the knife, and they all started again in peace."[4]

. . . .

. . .

Almost every person had a set of partners with whom he or she exchanged gifts, thus *xaro* was one of the most powerful bonds within the social fabric, because a *xaro* partnership could last for life. One person would give a gift to a partner, time would pass, and the partner would give a gift in return. More time would pass, the first partner would give another gift, and the process would continue. Meanwhile, the two partners would think of each other with affection and would prepare their return gifts with pleasure, anticipating the good feelings that would result. A gift could be almost any item, and would most likely be made of things from the savannah. But since the resources of the savannah were available to everyone, such items as digging sticks and intact ostrich eggshells were not often given as gifts, although they could be. More commonly, items obtained in trade, such as metal knives, and special items that people made, such as bead belts, headbands, and hair decorations, were given. These were small items, yes, but much effort and skill had gone into their making, and when worn by the recipient they became the visible icons of the important bonds.

We have this too, a little. When we wear a grandmother's ring or a father's watch, we are reminded that we belong with the people who gave us these objects that symbolize our ties. In a similar manner, if not necessarily by sentiment, the necklaces on a Ju/wa woman, received as gifts and later to be given, tie her reassuringly to those within the social fabric with whom she belongs.

There were rules involved, of course. You could never refuse a gift, although it obligated you, and you had to make a gift in return, but not immediately. A return gift made too soon would seem like a trade, not like a gift made from the heart, and thus would not strengthen the social bond, which was its purpose. This concept was so strong that the Ju/wasi never traded with one another. Trading was acceptable, but only with different people. The Bantu pastoralists at the edges of the Kalahari were suitable trading partners, for instance, but other Ju/wasi were not. Trading was too likely to stir up bad feelings. Perhaps this concept came from trading with the Bantu pastoralists, who in any trade unfailingly got the better of the Ju/wasi. At any rate, among themselves, the Ju/wasi avoided the practice.

. . . .

We ourselves were not included in the gift exchanges, although we gave many gifts to people, and sometimes were given gifts as well, but, despite our Ju/wa names and the implied relationships, we were not an integral part of the social fabric and no one felt the urge to include us, as indeed, we did not belong. This showed, I think, the purity of the practice, as no one tried to "buy" us, no matter how many possessions we had. Certain individuals would ask us tirelessly for our things, but this was because they thought we should be sharing our obvious wealth, not because they envisioned us as *xaro* partners. More important, the gift exchange was not about buying, and we could not have entered it by giving gifts. Membership in the social fabric could not be sold.

Nevertheless, we learned about the gift exchange because of a certain gift of our own that we made to some of the /Gautscha people, a gift of cowrie shells. Before we ventured out to find the Ju/wasi, we had tried to imagine what gifts we might bring that would please them and decided upon cowrie shells from the Pacific Ocean because of their general, cross-cultural popularity. These shells had found their way to many parts of Africa, but news of them had not reached the Ju/wasi. When we arrived, we found not a single cowrie shell in all of Nyae Nyae, although there were a few ordinary, store-bought beads gotten in trade. Then one day we made a present to each of the /Gautscha women of twenty small white cowrie shells and one large brown cowrie shell, or enough for a nice necklace. Yet when we returned to /Gautscha a year later, not one person there had a cowrie shell in her possession. The shells had been given as gifts to other people, and they appeared not as necklaces but singly or in pairs in people's ornaments all the way through Nyae Nyae to the edges of the area. In other words, they had immediately entered the *xaro* system. Because they were exotic objects, introduced by us on a specific date, we could trace their wide distribution and the speed of their progress.

The anthropologist Polly Wiessner, who has since studied this interesting practice, says that the average man or woman had fifteen *xaro* partners, many of whom lived more than one hundred miles away, and some even farther. Wiessner found that many Ju/wasi spent three or four months a year visiting these partners. She also found that the exchange of gifts was the primary reason for groups to come together—that, and the exchange of news and the opportunity for visiting. Of course, in the dry season, groups of people would converge at sources of permanent water, but gift giving became the focus when these groups met. Thus the word *owned* seemed misapplied to objects, especially the objects that were received from *xaro* partners. Virtually every one of them would eventually be passed on.[5]

Much was gained by this custom. Most important, it provided all groups with access to a widespread food supply as people visited one another. It was also a method of transmitting information. Sooner or later, but within a year, if the experience with the cowrie shells says anything, any important information could be spread throughout Nyae Nyae. It also gave respite to groups that were forced to spend too much time together, wearing on one another's nerves. A group experiencing stress could visit *xaro* partners elsewhere, bringing gifts, anticipating friendship and goodwill. And finally, to give or to receive a gift spread happiness and decreased jealousy and ill will. Everyone welcomed a *xaro* gift. Thus *xaro* strengthened the social fabric by holding far-flung groups together and reaffirming bonds. Even the homeless family of Lame !Kham, the man who walked by swinging himself between two sticks, benefited from *xaro*. We did not know if he himself had *xaro* partners, but he was welcomed, however briefly, at the encampments of others because he transported *xaro* gifts for other people.

Thus the social fabric of the Ju/wasi was preserved and strengthened by many different methods, through their method of making decisions, through the social mores, through the name relationship, through the kinship system and the marriage customs, and through unfailing sharing and the preservation of equality. But perhaps the strongest fibers in the social fabric were the *xaro* bonds.

Some might feel that with so many methods for gaining social cohesion, the Ju/wasi might find at least a few methods redundant. Yet redundancy is a hallmark of the Old Way, in which survival is tenuous at best, in which there is no such thing as overprotection. With so many options, no person need suffer from want of life-giving food or water unless all groups suffered. And virtually no individual who could follow the rules would become isolated and alone. But then, nobody wants to be isolated and alone, not even those of us in the industrialized societies. We have certainly gone downhill from the social excellence of the Ju/wasi, but perhaps we still know in our hearts how it would feel to be left behind on the quiet savannah, with hundreds of miles of empty veld around us, just grass and bushes, and night coming.

. . . .

15

Peacekeeping

Referring to the Kalahari of the Old Way, the anthropologist Richard Lee has said that the Ju/wasi had a murder rate equal to that of Detroit.[1] He found that during a fifty-year period in his study area, twenty-two murders were committed, giving the Ju/wasi a homicide rate of 29.3 per million, which (I'll take his word for it) makes eastern Nyae Nyae the equal of Detroit. Sociobiologists and others picked up on the image—I even caught some flak from it because in my first account of the Ju/wasi I had called them the "harmless" people.

Although "harmless" was an interpretation of their name for themselves (as the book mentioned), the title nevertheless was taken to mean that I thought that the people were wimpy or that I viewed them through rose-colored glasses. After Lee made his announcement, I was very surprised to find myself criticized, however mildly, because of my claims that the people were nonviolent. A famous sociobiologist whom I won't name was impressed with Lee's assessment. The sociobiologist also knew, of course, that violence is inherent in people as well as in chimpanzees. Few people could argue with that! Yet he was faced with our body of work, with our claims of a nonviolent hunter-gatherer society, and he resolved the apparent contra-

diction by assuming in print, believe it or not, that during the time our expeditions were in the limitless reaches of the unexplored Kalahari, the Ju/wasi were prevented from fighting and killing by the South West African police. If not for the police, he implied, the people would have been at odds with one another, just like the rest of humanity, and we said differently only because we had received a false impression.

Is it necessary to say that there were no policemen in the Kalahari? Perhaps the sociobiologist got his impressions from descriptions of how, in all southern African countries, Bushmen frequently came into conflict with white and Bantu people, and were brutally oppressed. They were taken as slaves, hunted down like animals, and, wherever possible, forced from their land. Of course they fought back with poison arrows and also with rifles if they could get them. Numerous accounts of this fighting appear in court documents and government reports, and were comprehensively reported by the anthropologist Robert Gordon and others.

However, the Bushmen were seldom on the offensive and did not try to enslave other people or take other people's land, although they sometimes took livestock, if only because domestic animals were displacing the local game. Rather, the Bushmen fought because they had no choice but to defend themselves. Often they were unsuccessful, but they were brave, tried hard, and sometimes succeeded. No one has ever said that they were pacifists. One Ju/wa man blandly admitted to killing a Herero man who was trying to take his wife. The Ju/wa man, who was newly married at the time, shot his rival with a poison arrow and seemed to have no regrets about it. But this kind of fighting did not take place in the enormous, remote areas that we visited, the places where the whites and Bantu peoples did not go, the places where the Bushmen managed their lives according to their own standards. As my mother wrote, "The !Kung are strongly set against violence, and accord it no honor. To have to fight is to have failed to find a solution by wiser means. As one man remarked, 'Fighting is dangerous—someone might get killed.'"[2]

Thus the practices that contained violence were not imposed on the Ju/wasi by outsiders and most certainly not, as the aforementioned sociobiologist suggested, by the apartheid-driven brutality of the South West African police. The practices that contained violence were set by the Ju/wasi themselves. Naturally, the Ju/wasi had violence in them. We all do. We had it with us when we lost the rain forest, and we keep it to this day.

What the Ju/wasi had that we seem to lack was a successful method of containing it.

Sometimes the Bushmen did kill one another, of course, and not always by mystical means, as had the sorcerer-shaman /Gaishay !Khoa. ≠Toma's father, for instance, was killed with a poison arrow in a dispute over territory when ≠Toma was a boy. There were a number of other instances as well. I was told the following account. In a camp of about fifteen people who were sitting around their evening fires, a man shot his wife with a poison arrow. He then ran off into the night. The horrified people pulled out the arrow and tried to suck out the poison, at which point the husband rushed out of the darkness and shot two more arrows, one into his wife's brother and one into another man. The people also tried their best to help these two men, but by morning all three of the killer's victims were dying from the poison. The account did not offer a reason for these shootings. One reason for dissent in Ju/wa society is rivalry for women. Possibly these killings resulted from jealousy over the killer's wife. But perhaps not. Perhaps the killer just lost control of himself over something much less. Anyway, at dawn, some of the other men armed themselves, tracked down the attacker, and killed him.

They had no choice. They had no way to imprison a dangerous person and nowhere to go that they could escape from him. They were just there, their bodies unprotected even by much clothing, out in the open, lit by firelight at night, completely at the killer's mercy as long as he was on the loose with poison arrows. They might have disarmed him temporarily, but he was perfectly capable of making himself another bow and more poison arrows. The people were not safe while he was living and they took the only course open to them.

The Ju/wasi were, I think, understandably disturbed by signs of mental illness, which accounts for another killing that I learned of. A man went off alone into the veld and crawled into an aardvark burrow. Obviously, he was not entirely sane. When people passed by, he would burst out of the burrow and shout at them. The passersby were very startled, of course, which others later said was the disturbed man's intent—he wanted only to scare them away, not to hurt them. Nevertheless, the people pondered what to do about this man in his burrow and eventually decided that he was too dangerous. So a few of the men sought him out and killed him.

It was a safety measure. The people's experience with mental illness confirmed that a disturbed person could be very dangerous. I should add that in the years we were there we met people from a very wide range of personality types, but not one of the people could be described as disturbed or mentally ill.

These two episodes account for five killings in a population of about 550, in which an unknown number of other killings might also have occurred but went unrecorded. Yet it doesn't seem useful to compare a large American city with a hunter-gatherer population. We all agree that people are violent, and that those who cannot control their anger, or those with disturbed minds, can be dangerous. More useful, I believe, is to consider the acts of Ju/wa violence in context, including the choices that were open to the people confronted with the man who shot his wife and two men. That man's eventual execution should not be called a murder—it was a move for public safety, as was the execution of the man in the aardvark burrow.

Thus as I see it, if my minuscule sample counts for anything, two of the five known killings were safety measures, conducted out of necessity, not as the result of anger or loss of control. Part of my work while we were in the Kalahari was to make a specific search for instances of killings, which I did through interviews, and by 1955, when I left our family project, I had found very few. I make no claim to have found them all, but I know there were not many.

One of the fatalities that our culture would have called a killing was seen by the Ju/wasi as a form of accident. A very young boy witnessed his father having an argument with another man. Distressed, he took his father's bow and bone arrow and shot the other man. The man pulled out the arrow as soon as it struck, and everyone tried to help by sucking the wound, but the poison was too deadly. They couldn't help. The man died. His death was considered a tragic event, just as we would consider a fatality resulting from a gun discharging accidentally, and it served to enhance the people's dislike of arguments.

The self-control of children grows with time, and very young children cannot be expected to have it, or not fully. One of my most vivid memories also involves a boy, Little /Guyshe, the youngest son of Di!ai. One of my tasks in our research effort was to determine as best I could the development of the little children, and the best way to do this was to look into their mouths (with their parents' permission) and note their baby teeth. Most children just obligingly opened wide, but not Little /Guyshe. He was sitting in the archway of his parents' *tshu* when I asked if I could see his teeth, and he pressed his lips together. That was certainly a no, but I didn't take him very seriously and gently squeezed his cheeks to open his jaws. He reached for his father's quiver and pulled out a poison arrow. His father had been planning to go hunting, and his quiver, uncharacteristically, had been temporarily leaning against the archway, not up in a bush or tree. I ran!

Thus the point to make about the Ju/wasi and their murder rate is not that they didn't have one, not that they were peaceful by nature, and not that our species isn't violent or hasn't always been violent since we parted from our sometimes violent relatives, the chimpanzees. The point is that the Ju/wasi knew only too well what the human animal is capable of doing. The point is that they knew how to suppress anger and aggressive impulses, and placed a very high priority on doing so. Their extraordinary success at social cohesion could not have been achieved without this priority.

The importance of their control cannot be overstated and came to be illustrated in a most dramatic and tragic way. Although the Ju/wasi dealt with anger and violence very successfully as long as they lived in the Old Way, their mechanisms for doing this broke down after the 1970s, when change came and Western civilization overtook Nyae Nyae. Then, when there really were police and government officials, when the Ju/wa population became concentrated at a government post where they lost their ancient lifestyle, when hunger, alcohol, drugs, disease, and poverty overtook them, they began killing one another like madmen. Quite literally, every family that we knew lost at least one member to a killing, and many families lost more. To my infinite sorrow, Di!ai's two beloved little boys—Little /Guyshe and his brother, both of whom I came to love as if they were my own and who were young men by that time—were killed in fights. So was //Kushe's boy, the baby who had a little tantrum, the baby who was wearing a bead and riding on his father's shoulder on the day we first came to /Gautscha. And Short /Kwi, the superior hunter who in his prime had provided hundreds of pounds of meat each year for up to forty people, the man who could run elands down, was murdered by his son-in-law, a soldier. The young soldier was drunk and had not the slightest knowledge of the event until the following day when he wondered where Short /Kwi was and others told him. This was the son-in-law who in earlier times would have hunted for Short /Kwi, as Short /Kwi had hunted for his wife's parents, as his father had hunted for his mother's parents. The young man had not wanted to murder Short /Kwi. He just did it, and he never got over it. Things too terrible to say happened to these people.

Yes, they had violence in them. But for as long as possible, they curbed it. No matter how provoked, they rarely acted out their discomfort, nor did they vent it on one another as long as their ancient culture served them. Not for nothing did they call themselves the Harmless People, the Pure People, when the harm and impurities were jealousy, violence, and anger.

In this book, I am trying to reexamine some of our experiences in the light of all that was learned since our first visits. One of the most important questions to revisit is the lack of violence. When I first met the Ju/wasi, I took their lack of fighting for granted as I had taken their phenomenal self-control. Of course they didn't fight. At home, our friends and family didn't fight either. Only criminals killed people, and we weren't criminals, and neither were the Ju/wasi. A sociobiologist I wasn't, and it didn't occur to me to wonder how, in small, tightly knit groups under the very real stress of daily living, violence almost never occurred.

It would have been better, perhaps, to ask if the peacekeeping was typical. We might have asked ourselves if we were just lucky to have met some very nice people, while other, more violent people whom we didn't know, lurked elsewhere. We might also have asked if the lack of in-group violence was traditional, or if we had just happened to appear on the scene at a time of peace.

But if we had asked these specific questions, we might not have gotten answers. The people lived as they lived. It was their custom. Just as we don't always have specific, well-understood reasons for acting as we act, neither did the Ju/wasi. However, I believe that these questions can be answered at least in part by looking at the tools used by the Ju/wasi. They had no weapons meant for fighting, not one. The deadliness of the poison served as a deterrent rather than a weapon. If someone lost control and loosed an arrow, somebody else would almost certainly die. In communities as small as those of the Ju/wasi, the loss of even one person was a disaster, as would be the unleashing of violence following a killing, promising the loss of more people by more killings. The only path to safety was to avoid pushing things to a point where somebody got his arrows.

There's more. Although poison can certainly be called an ultimate weapon, it takes so long to work that it is almost worthless in a fight. Before a person shot with an arrow even feels the poison, he can do enormous damage with arrows of his own. This is not to say that sharp arrows are not dangerous in and of themselves, even if they don't carry poison. They are, of course, and a well-placed arrow in the heart or throat at reasonably short range would be lethal immediately. But the arrows were lightweight, intended as darts to inject poison, not to inflict flesh-tearing wounds. Only a perfect shot to the heart or throat would do the job immediately. No one would go into combat armed only with slow-acting poison unless to do so was absolutely necessary—if invading people tried to take one's land, for example. Nor would anyone go into combat armed with a spear unless he had no poison arrows. For one thing, once you have thrown the spear it's gone, and your hands are empty. Your adversary then picks up your spear and throws it back at you. You would need dozens of spears to equal the weaponry of a quiver full of arrows, even if the arrows were not poisoned. To enter a combat situation with a spear while intentionally leaving poison arrows at home is the kind of thing that bow hunters just don't do. So the Bushmen took their arrows. In conflicts involving Bushmen and settlers, the settlers reported being shot at with arrows, usually from ambush, as if they were being hunted by the Bushmen. They did not report going against Bushmen who fought with spears.

Yet perhaps the most telling feature of the Bushmen's tool collection was that they had no shields. They had nothing remotely like a shield, nothing that could even serve as a shield if the need arose. What's more, the poison arrows are so light and delicate that to shield oneself against them would be easy. And this, I think, is the most important example of the people's inclinations. If violence was a recurring problem, if people were inclined to fight with poison arrows or even with unpoisoned arrows or spears, they probably would have made some kind of shields, even while giving lip service to peaceful inclinations. They would have been deficient if they hadn't. And to make a shield would have been easy. An excellent shield can be made from a simple piece of hardened leather, especially from an animal with thick hide such as a giraffe, and the Bushmen could get plenty of that. Even the giraffes themselves could have shown people the use of shields, or they could if the giraffes of old were like the giraffes of the 1950s, who would protect themselves from human hunters by standing behind small trees when they saw people on foot. (The bushy parts of most savannah trees were about chest-high to a giraffe.) A bullet would cut through the feathery branches without a problem and hit the giraffe in the chest, but those giraffes knew nothing of bullets. They knew only that a little, featherweight arrow, powered by the twenty-five-pound pull of a small bow, could be deflected by the twigs. If giraffes can shield themselves, then so could the Bushmen. But they didn't. They didn't make shields because they didn't think they needed them.

Thus that their weapons were designed for hunting and for nothing else seems inescapable, especially when comparing the weapons of the Ju/wasi to those of other people. Six years after I left the Kalahari, I spent some time among a pastoral people in northern Uganda, and there I saw what was indeed a violent population. The people, who were brave and capable, had clubs, knobkerries, and nine-foot spears with razor-sharp blades that could fly great distances (a spear like this can do as much damage as a bullet—sometimes more, because the resulting wound is even worse). They had large assortments of knives, and they had two different kinds of long shields to protect their bodies when in battle, the shield of choice depending on the kind of fight they planned. They didn't do much hunting—they only confronted animals who attacked their cattle. No, they used these weapons on one another and in frequent cattle raids against the neighboring pastoral peoples, who also raided them.

The people were violent in other ways as well. Front teeth were considered undesirable, and these were removed from the mouths of young people by strong adults who pried them out with knives and sticks, complete with squirting blood, horrible cracking sounds, and screaming. The culture did not have a high regard for women—men sometimes beat women violently. I knew of two instances of rape and heard of others, all of them occasioned by the woman declining to have sex with the man. Sometimes the rapist was assisted by his friends, who held the woman in place while her assailant penetrated her.

Solving problems in a peaceful manner, while often attempted, did not meet with regular success because violence was always at hand, an acceptable option. Not everyone wanted to risk his life every time a problem arose, but because violence was so important as a problem solver, it had popular support, to which end the people bestowed honorary names and body scarification upon men who had killed other people, even if the victims were children. Some of those who held these honorary insignia expressed contempt for those who did not. One important warrior asked me if I had ever killed anyone, and when I said I hadn't, he insultingly called me a woman. ("But Lokapelemoe, I *am* a woman," I told him. Not in his eyes, I wasn't. I was an androgynous biped who didn't have the balls to kill a person. He had the balls and then some. He looked down at me disdainfully.)

Interestingly, many people in that culture didn't like the violence. Some men who had killed others didn't want the body scarification that, the next time they went into battle, would announce to the enemy that they were responsible for the enemy's recent losses. This of course would make them more vulnerable to attack. If they did accept the scarification, they might wait for the wounds to heal completely before going into battle so at least the scars would not look fresh. Some men were slow to rally when they heard an alarm call indicating that a raid against them was in progress, and some didn't rally at all.

Often the men held meetings at which these failures of aggression would be brought forward in an effort to persuade the reluctant people to take a more active part in the battles. These rallies didn't do much good, however. The reluctant people remained reluctant. Surely, many members of this pastoral culture would have preferred to see less violence. But violence was everywhere. The genie was long gone from the bottle, and the people couldn't put it back.

In later years, these people replaced their spears, knives, clubs, and knobkerries with automatic weapons. When Idi Amin's troops vacated northern Uganda, they left behind a large tin building containing thousands of automatic weapons and millions of rounds of ammunition. Needless to say, the pastoralists immediately broke in and helped themselves. Since then, other weapons have become readily available. An anthropologist who has visited there recently told me that every man and boy in northern Uganda now carries at least one, often two, AK-47s and a full belt of ammunition on his person wherever he goes.

That's what a violent population looks like. It looks something like ours. With the possible exceptions of prying out teeth without anesthetic and such an array of visible weaponry, those pastoralists didn't do anything that we in Western cultures do not do. In short, the people of northern Uganda are very much like us, whether we see that or not.

The Bushmen were different.

When we first met the Ju/wasi, they had no experience with alcohol. Unlike virtually everybody else, they didn't make it. It is hard to say why. If asked to guess, I'd say it was because the hard-won foods that would produce alcohol are better used for nutrition. After all, nothing that truly lives in the Old Way makes alcohol (although several species other than our own sometimes partake of fermenting matter if it happens to be available—moose and elephants sometimes get drunk on such items as fermenting apples, for instance, and, like us, they seem to enjoy the experience). Nor did the Ju/wasi use mind-altering drugs except tobacco and marijuana, which they occasionally got in trade from the distant pastoralists. But tobacco and marijuana don't inflame people, and alcohol does, and to people who devoted much effort to keeping the peace, whose entire culture was focused on keeping the peace, the sudden release of all their carefully controlled feelings under the influence of alcohol was devastating.

And this, however tragic, was also significant, because it demonstrated the amount of violence that the Ju/wasi knew perfectly well was boiling around inside our species, a violence that, while they were alert and functional, they had been able to control very well. But their culture gave them no practice in exhibiting the violence that lies within us all. The sudden release of their violent feeling took them by surprise. After a few drinks, many of the Ju/wasi went straight from calmness to murder—all or nothing, no middle ground. And this, too, indicates the success of their earlier efforts to control violence, showing how different they were from people like ourselves or the people of northern Uganda, we who expect violence. We are trained in it, and we plan our moves with it in mind. If a northern Ugandan pastoralist planned to fight a relative, for instance, or someone from the household next door, he would take a big, strong stick and a wicker shield designed to absorb blows from the stick wielded by his adversary. His intent would be to batter but not to kill. However, if he planned to raid one of the other pastoral peoples, a people not his own, he would take two or three nine-foot spears and a hardened leather shield designed to stop a spear, intending to kill two or three of the enemy, or even more if he could capture some of their spears. (In these battles, each side counted upon capturing some of the enemy spears and throwing them back.)

Our Western culture, of course, provides everything from boxing gloves to nuclear bombs, depending on our intentions, and as children we gain experience in using some of these things. Many childhood games are, of course, pretend violence, with the result that by the time we are adults, even with alcohol in our bodies, most of us have learned how to steer our violence, at least to some extent. You can fight but not kill, our culture seems to tell us. Well, maybe you can kill sometimes, under certain provocations. We have fines, prisons, and electric chairs to punish those who mismanage their violence. Yet as we all know, while these punitive measures certainly satisfy our desires for revenge, and sometimes keep some of the worst of us away from of the rest of us, they don't deter us, or not much.

The Ju/wasi didn't need punishments or deterrents. They didn't even have rules against murder. No god appeared to them to say, "Thou shalt not kill." No god needed to. The Ju/wasi fully understood the disaster that resulted from killing and took care of that themselves without reference to a commandment. The boy who shot his father's adversary was not punished, unlike a boy in a similar situation in our culture, who, if he lived in a state such as Texas, might have been tried as an adult and even executed. Little /Guyshe, who might have stabbed me with an arrow, also was not punished. In the case of the boy who shot his father's adversary, the event was so far removed from the boy that when a nickname was given to commemorate the killing, it was given to the deceased, not to the boy. The deceased, whose name was Tsamko, became known as Tsamko Bone Arrow, and when people spoke of the event, they mentioned that Tsamko had raised his voice to the boy's father. The boy remained as closely linked to all his people, including the victim's kin, as he had been before the killing.

And finally, the murder of the woman, her brother, and the other man on that long-ago night when their little band was camped in the veld was also seen as a tragedy, not as a crime. Nor was the execution of the murderer seen as punishment or revenge, although surely the relatives of his victims were deeply upset. However, punishment was not seen as a social tool. People were assumed to know how they should behave, without the clumsy efforts of society to educate them. Those who killed others did not fit into society and should not be there at all. The people intended to permanently remove the killer, not to punish him.

How did the Ju/wasi achieve their magnificent nonviolence? Part of their success can be attributed to child rearing. As has been said, a Ju/wa child was any parent's dream. And these serene, pleasant childhoods, filled with plenty of happy attention, free of hurt and punishment, helped to explain the absence of helpless anger and frustration that many people of our culture carry throughout life. A Ju/wa person arriving at adulthood was well prepared to control behavior that could lead to violence.

In addition, children were never without adult supervision, and childish acts of violence were immediately interrupted. Since babies and small children virtually never witnessed adult violence, and since their own attempted acts of aggression were always squelched, often by older children, they were very well socialized by the time they were six or seven, or even earlier. At the time that Little /Guyshe was preparing to stab me with a poison arrow, an older child knocked the arrow out of his hand and several adults instantly materialized to put the arrow in its quiver and the quiver in a tree. But after that, although the social electricity was almost palpable, there was no flurry of excitement. Far otherwise. Most people's facial expressions were all but blank. The child seemed suddenly alone, almost isolated, the object of silent if undirected disapproval. Without moving his head, he looked around with cautious anxiety, as if he suddenly knew he had done an unspeakable thing.

To find a similar example in our culture is difficult. Unfortunately, I can think of none except public farting, unlikely as such a comparison may seem. As a culture, we seem to agree that the activity is undesirable (as do the Ju/wasi, incidentally), yet we never debate how best to discourage it. We don't need to. Instead, we commonly greet its occurrence with blank faces, as if *nothing happened*, but if it had happened, it would have embarrassed everyone. We assume that the culprit agrees. Our demeanor is not meant to punish the culprit, or to discourage him from doing it again, because our culture assumes that no sane person would voluntarily do it at all. Our demeanor is meant to shield the culprit from his own disgrace. Very few American children beyond kindergarten age are under the impression that public farting is culturally acceptable. They know it isn't. What they do with that knowledge varies widely, but the knowledge itself has been implanted very firmly. And that, to me, was what a small child's threat of dangerous aggression seemed to be like to the Ju/wasi.

One of the few instances that we saw of anticipated violence among adults involved a man whose wife had gone off with another man. Before she left, she told other people that she intended to divorce her husband and remarry. When her husband learned of this, perhaps an hour after his wife and her new partner had departed, he was beside himself. He talked of getting his weapons and following them. Many of the other men then sat down with him and talked to him for a long time. Nothing would be gained by his following the departing couple with his weapons, they told him. Instead, some of the men, including ≠Toma and his brother-in-law, Gao Feet, offered to go after them and point out some of the difficulties that the two were about to start. The husband eventually saw the merit of this plan, and the mediators then went off to persuade the woman to return to him. They succeeded. She accompanied them back to /Gautscha, and her lover went on to his destination alone. The husband was deeply relieved and deeply happy. A terrible situation had been turned around with the help of the community, and nothing bad happened.

Violence was the greatest threat to the all-important social fabric, and sharing and gift giving were its greatest strengths. Not surprisingly, therefore, it was issues surrounding gifts, not outbreaks of violence, that displayed the inner stresses of the Ju/wasi—the issues that gave lions the avoidance name of "jealousy." On the rare occasions when a bad, very important event took place, the feelings engendered by the terrible event boiled over in the form of problems with the all-important gift exchange.

We witnessed such an event. It came about through a tragic accident that happened to Short /Kwi, the excellent hunter. One day while hunting, Short /Kwi failed to see a puff adder and he stepped on it or near it. It struck the back of his right leg a few inches below the knee.

We had been away from camp on the day this happened and returned a few days later after dark. At once, the people told us about Short /Kwi, who was sitting in his own camp nearby, alone except for his wife and little daughter, and very depressed. He also would have come to see us, but he couldn't walk. We went at once to see him. After the snakebite, everyone had tried to help, sucking the fang marks, which he could not have done himself, of course, because of the location of the bite. The people had also tied fiber string above the bite to contain the poison, tying more fiber string later to contain the gangrene, but the gangrene had eaten across his leg and through his shin bone.

This was almost the worst thing that could happen to anyone, and the people did not at first accept the tragedy. They had hoped that the leg might get better. Short /Kwi had also been hopeful and told others that he thought he was improving. But during our arrival when the others came to meet us, as we all milled about in the truck's headlights hearing this terrible news, Short /Kwi picked up his leg to change its position, and the shin and foot came off in his hands. He then put his leg back together, but in his heart he knew this would do no good. In the heavy dark, by one mere ember of a fire, he and his wife were silently weeping. When the rest of us went to visit him and he showed us what had happened, we wept too.

In a social fabric as tight and thick as that of the Ju/wasi, what happens to one happens to all. Gone was the life-giving meat that Short /Kwi's hunting had provided. Gone was the health of one of the most valued people, he who unfailingly gave to others. Surely the spirits of the dead were all around us, looking for us in the night to do more evil. They had caused this accident. They had led Short /Kwi to the snake and distracted his attention so he didn't see it. Perhaps they had tried but failed to kill him. Perhaps they would try again later. Perhaps they would kill us all.

One by one, the people went to their shelters to sleep if they could, but nobody could, and neither could we, as we were making plans for the morning. My father would take Short /Kwi to the nearest hospital, which was four hundred miles away in Windhoek, and where, since those were the days of apartheid, my father would stay to make sure that the doctors took care of him even if he wasn't a white man. His wife and baby daughter, who was still nursing, would also go with him. We would need to prepare these people so that they would not be partly naked, dressed only in skins, among all the townspeople. Before dawn we began to gather clothing for them, choosing the clothing that we had been saving to wear home to America, my brother's khaki shirt and pants for Short /Kwi, my striped blouse and green skirt for his wife, so they could meet the Western world in Western dress.

In the dawn, the people saw what we were doing. Because of the distance and difficulty of travel, we were in a hurry to get an early start, so we didn't take time to explain. The people watched us in dismay when they saw the clothing. Surely we were not going to give so much to just two people. But that was exactly what we were doing. While ≠Toma and others carried the leg into the veld to bury in a grave as they would bury a person, we helped Short /Kwi and his wife into the clothing. I even reached through the sleeve of the blouse to take his wife's wrist and pull her hand through. The structure of the blouse had confused her. In that terrible hour, devastated by what had happened to her husband, not knowing where my father planned to take them except that it would be far from her people, not sure why my mother and I were stripping off her leather clothes and bundling her into our clothes, or why in such a hurry, she couldn't find her way into the blouse by herself. Then the skirt was too big and fell down around her hips. My mother and I found needles and thread and quickly sewed it to fit.

I can still remember the reaction of Di!ai's sister, !U, as all this was happening. I was showering Short /Kwi's wife with clothes and services, and giving nothing to her. In the past, the people of our expeditions had tried to give gifts equally and explain everything. Suddenly, at the worst possible time, we had ceased to do that. The expression on !U's face was one of frightened despair. She immediately asked for a similar gift. I just looked at her and shrugged. I didn't have one. She went pale and seemed aghast, dumfounded. Gift giving was life. Selfishness and favoritism were death. And I was powerful, in possession of clothes and other things that people find useful. That morning, with death and danger all around us, would have been the time to strongly reaffirm that I wanted to be helpful, to reassure those in this terrible situation that I would exclude no one, that I was there for all. But that morning I excluded !U from my possessions and gave an important gift to someone else.

We then heard raised voices at Short /Kwi's camp. The other people were erupting. The grief that all had felt turned to jealousy and anger when we gave so much to these people and nothing to anyone else. We went there and found all the people sitting together in a thick circle, recounting in impassioned voices all the slights and stinginess that anyone had ever shown to them or anyone else. *He was supposed to give me a knife. She was going to give the knife to Gao. Where is the blanket you promised my brother? When I gave her a necklace, she should give a gift in return. She never did. The necklace went to her sister. That was wrong. I have nothing. I am empty-handed. They should have controlled that necklace. Others have it now. Those people are selfish. They don't want to give. They won't give the necklace. People don't think of what they should be doing. They are stingy. All this is wrong.*

Surely some of these grievances had been festering for years. In the middle of the circle was Short /Kwi in his starchy khaki shirt and trousers. Not only was he badly damaged by the loss of his leg and therefore in serious need of his people's goodwill for the future, but we were heaping him with gifts that would cause others to envy him for years to come. Already he was trying to give the clothes to other people.

I continue to remember that event with sorrow, and can still see, in my mind's eye, the striped blouse and green skirt. I had thought I understood the gift-giving process, and perhaps I did to some small degree, at least as far as some of its simpler aspects were concerned. But knowing facts is not the same as empathizing, and I unhesitatingly reverted to my own ways in a time of crisis. Since then, because of a bandanna I was wearing that day to keep my hair out of my eyes, I have learned enough to feel the process more deeply.

I was reminded of the bandanna by my brother. After I left for home and got married, not to return to Nyae Nyae for many years, he remained in constant contact with the /Gautscha people, and almost twenty years later in the 1970s, after the terrible difficulties of transition had come upon the Ju/wasi, he met a woman who told him that she often thought of me. It was my bandanna she remembered, she said. In her mind's eye, she saw me wearing the bandanna in my home, where I was safe, with food and family. I had become her dream of security, when she herself had none.

When I heard that, I realized that this woman would have liked to have the bandanna. Probably she had asked for it that day. If so, I obviously had refused. Perhaps she still wanted it. Perhaps it would have joined her to the person who wore it, in her vision of security. If she were joined to that person, she could picture herself *with* that person in a place of safety. It would be *as if* she could go to that safe place she imagined, to be welcomed by me if she went there, joined by the bandanna to my safety as gifts among her people joined them to life and food.

I then thought of the blouse and skirt and saw how much I must have hurt !U, this good person. To have caused her anxiety and sorrow is one of my great regrets.

. . .

Fortunately, the difficulties of /Gautscha were smoothed over eventually, although some of the people left and went somewhere else. The stress had been too great and the accusations too terrible. Relocating was always preferable to conflict. In a few weeks, Short /Kwi and his wife came back from Windhoek with my father. The doctors had done a good job, saving his life and removing as little of the leg as possible. They had also given Short /Kwi an artificial leg, which he didn't like. Back at /Gautscha, he asked for tools, which we gave him, and with them he whittled a comfortable if simple peg leg from the branch of a tree. With this, he resumed his former life, continuing to hunt, if not as successfully. No journey was too long for him. He made journeys of any length on foot whenever necessary. In short, throughout the twenty-odd years that remained of his life, he adapted.

The clothing that we gave to Short /Kwi and his wife soon entered the network of gift giving and vanished from /Gautscha. I never saw the skirt or blouse again, but my brother thought he might have seen the blouse on a woman in Kai Kai in 1960, seven years later and fifty miles away.

!U felt better later and forgave me. She forgave me so much that when I returned for a visit in the 1980s, she gave me a necklace. I gave her a soft blanket. The necklace is made of many tiny, store-bought beads, white and red, and is among my most treasured possessions, with my mother's silver ring and a photograph of my father. Unlike !U, I can't seek support from an extensive network of kin and affines, which is not the same as having friends, so one day I will give the necklace to one of my granddaughters, just as my mother gave her silver ring to me, just as, after her death, I gave her gold ring to my daughter, her diamond ring to my brother's daughter, and her wedding ring to my son's wife. If these women feel a chain of affection in the necklace and the jewelry, if they feel that they and I belong together as all of us belonged with my mother, then surely in my hour of need, if I have one, they will offer help.

16

Knowledge

Too often we assume that nonliterate people are superstitious, in awe and fear of the world about them, comfortable only when the natural phenomena are explained, and creating fantastic theories to explain them, no matter how unlikely. For instance, to the makers of the popular film about a Bushman and a Coke bottle, *The Gods Must Be Crazy*, it seemed reasonable to say that the Bushmen believe that thunder is god's stomach rumbling, a concept originated by the filmmakers themselves, as it exists nowhere in Bushman mythology. The filmmakers would not expect to get away with claiming that a university professor thought that thunder was god's stomach rumbling, but it seemed acceptable to say that about the Bushmen. The real Bushmen, of course, believed no such thing. Perhaps they didn't know what actually produces the sound (as most of us don't), but they considered thunder an entity in and of itself (as most of us do). What is thunder? It's thunder, just as a rock is a rock or a tree is a tree. There were kinds of thunder, to be sure, just as there are kinds of rocks and trees. But no superstitious construct was needed to explain these familiar phenomena.

As for fantastic explanations, how's this? When asked where the stars went in the daytime, ≠Toma said, "They stay where they are. We just can't see them in the daytime because the sun is too bright."

Some natural phenomena have causes that cannot be observed, however, such as the sun crossing the sky every day to set in the west, yet coming up in the east the next morning, raising the question of how it got back there during the night. For this, the Ju/wasi had a story. The sun is an elephant, which mythological people, the People With No Knees, kill and eat at night, then throw the clavicle back to the east, where a new sun grows to rise in the morning.

As for the phases of the moon, these resulted from a quarrel that the moon had with the hare, who said that the dead should remain dead and be buried, otherwise they would smell. The moon disagreed and thought that the dead should be resurrected. The hare and the moon fought and the moon won, which is why the moon is resurrected after it dies, and why all other creatures die forever, like the hare.

While most Ju/wa stories had considerable cultural significance, they were not intended as factual explanations (a point that non-Bushmen such as the producers of *The Gods Must Be Crazy* unfailingly overlook). After saying why stars can't be seen in the daytime, ≠Toma later told us that stars were ant-lions who in the evening went up to the sky and returned to their sandy traps at dawn. He had, in other words, an observable explanation and also a story, perhaps more than one.

Therefore it seemed to me that the Ju/wasi respected both the observable and the mythological explanations but never confused the function of the two. Many stories that served as explanations had several versions, often contradictory. This might bother the people in our culture, but it bothered the Ju/wasi not at all, as factuality was not at issue. Always, the little snatches of stories, such as the one about the stars being ant-lions, were offered lightly. Perhaps one cannot observe the whereabouts of the sun at night, but one can observe the whereabouts of an ant-lion, thus the ant-lion story resembled ours of a similar nature. We say, for example, that if the woolly bear caterpillar's black bands are wide, we'll have a hard winter. Most woolly bear forecasters would not stake their reputations on this story if for no other reason than that caterpillars lack the wherewithal to furnish a long-term forecast. (Please don't point out that the color black absorbs heat, so that large black bands would help to warm a small creature. Woolly bears freeze solid like ice cubes. You can ring a bell with one of them. Their ability to live although frozen, not to avoid being frozen, is their survival strategy.) Still, we like the woolly bear story and we revive it every year in the fall, but if we really want a forecast, we turn on the weather channel. And an anthropologist trying to understand our culture would do well to take the woolly bear theory in the spirit in which it is offered and turn to the meteorologists to understand the kind of knowledge that we value and respect.

True, there are plenty of superstitious people in the world, but they live in agricultural and industrial societies, removed from the natural world and afraid of it. In contrast, the hunter-gatherers of the Old Way belonged to the natural world in which phenomena such as the sunrise were an integral part. They accepted the natural world as it was, and their stories about it, while important to the culture, did not carry the weight of dogma. This meant that stories such as the hare and the moon (with, perhaps, its implications for human aggression—see what happened to the hare who picked a fight) were more like our story of the man in the moon and were not intended to be taken at face value, as some of us take, for instance, the creation myth or "intelligent design." The savannah hunter-gatherers could not afford to stake their lives on any theory or belief that did not yield to further information.

As a consequence, the Ju/wasi of the 1950s were exceedingly well informed. Perhaps they didn't understand the galaxies, but then, neither does the average American, and meanwhile the Ju/wasi knew more about every observable aspect of the savannah than anyone else alive. (The same is true, incidentally, of many animals.) The poison hidden in the *Diamphidia* grubs was merely one example. A mammalogist, the late Charles Handley, who was to become the curator of mammals at the Smithsonian Institution, accompanied one of our expeditions, and from discussions with Short /Kwi he learned that the Ju/wasi recognized almost exactly the same species as the Western taxonomists, including insects and spiders, not to mention birds and mammals. Short /Kwi was only about the age of a college freshman, and therefore was not considered by his own people to be an expert,

A young woman plays a //gwashi, *a stringed instrument.*

nor was he unusual in this respect, but he knew as much or more about the fauna of his country as a Smithsonian scientist with a Ph.D. Even so, during the discussions he continually reminded Charlie that he was still young, and that the old people would be able to answer more fully.

A /Gwi man named Ukwane once dissected a springbok for us, naming its various parts, including its internal organs, and accurately describing their functions, pointing out that the blood was moved around the body by the heart and that the lungs were for taking in breath. He knew what the testicles were, of course, and that the semen they contained would create infant springboks. But he didn't confuse the antelope body with the human body, as he understood the different functions of the stomach and the rumen. Perhaps not every reader of this book can say the same.

Among the Ju/wasi, their biological information included the role of urine in ridding the body of toxins. As has been said, one of their few customs involving magic was to stick an arrow point-down into the damp spot of urine left on the ground by an antelope whom they had shot and were tracking. The purpose of the arrow was to prevent the antelope from urinating again, thus diminishing the poison in its body and prolonging the time of its collapse. The gesture might have been magic, but the concept certainly wasn't.

More difficult to appreciate was the botanical knowledge of the Ju/wasi, which could not be evaluated by the outside world. While many Kalahari plants had been named by Western botanists, the Ju/wasi seemed to have named all of them, and while the properties of most plants were not understood by Western science, the properties of hundreds of plants were entirely familiar to the Ju/wasi.

Most Bushmen knew that a certain plant stopped hunger, for instance. For years, the few Western people who knew of this took it to be wishful thinking—a hungry people's dream. But recently, Western entrepreneurs have learned that the plant does indeed stop hunger, just as the Bushmen had said. At the time of this writing, the entrepreneurs are figuring out how best to exploit and commercialize this plant, which recently was touted in the media as the diet aid of the future. How much the Bushmen themselves will benefit from their age-old knowledge is not clear.

Most difficult of all to evaluate was the people's knowledge of animal behavior because, until fairly recently, Western science did not see animal behavior as a field of study. Instead, the anecdotal information that one gathers by observing wild animals seemed unimportant, and only the carefully controlled studies of animals conducted in laboratories were believed to be worthwhile. When considering the Bushmen, therefore, the people of our culture had an inadequate body of knowledge to use as a measure. This meant, of course, that much of the lore accumulated by the Bushmen about animals was assumed to be superstition. For example, an American visitor to Bushmanland mentioned to me an alleged superstition about weaverbirds who make a nest with two openings, the upper one leading to the eggs or fledglings, the lower one leading to an empty chamber that, according to the Bushmen, was "for the snake." A superstition if ever there was one, assumed the visitor. No bird would make something for a snake, certainly not as part of its nest. Yet an ornithologist went on to discover that when a snake climbs on the nest, the snake's weight pulls open the lower chamber even as it closes the upper one, thus hiding the eggs or fledglings. The snake enters the lower chamber, finds nothing, and leaves. Wasn't the lower chamber for the snake?

Did the ornithologist make this discovery? Or did he merely confirm a discovery that had been made by others long ago? I remember my disappointment upon learning of a professor of zoology who visited the Ju/wasi briefly as a guest/consultant of the Harvard Group. While there, he evidently quizzed the people about the natural world and then returned to tell his fellow academics that the Ju/wasi "knew almost as much we do" about the plants and the animals. What seemed disappointing was that the professor missed the fact that when it came to matters of their own environment, the Ju/wasi knew considerably more than we do. Unlike Western scientists, who had scarcely begun to study the Kalahari ecosystem, savannah hunter-gatherers had been studying it for 150,000 years.

However, in the minds of many, the knowledge of nonliterate people is not only assumed to be inaccurate, it is often deemed not to be knowledge at all. Our cultural contribution to this intellectual fiasco was that a person whom our culture ranks highly (in this case

. . . .

the professor) felt he could say what was and wasn't knowledge as understood by persons whom our culture ranks less highly (in this case the Ju/wasi). Our culture considers the professor well within his rights to determine how the Ju/wasi measured up to his standard, never dreaming that they, not he, should be setting the standard. No Westerner could even ask the questions that would reveal the true depth of the people's knowledge because, of course, Western science had not replicated their discoveries (and hasn't to this day). For instance, the professor couldn't have asked about the double nest of the weaverbird unless he knew of its existence. And spending a few days in the Kalahari wouldn't help him. More than twenty years would pass between the time that he made his patronizing announcement and the time that the news about the weaverbirds, their nests, and the snake found its way into the literature. And that is merely one example. Virtually any plant or animal in the Kalahari might provide an equally compelling example. Our disregard of Old Way knowledge persists, however, whether for people or for other species, no matter how often our noses get rubbed in our ignorance.

Sad to say, the depth of the Bushmen's knowledge may never be fully appreciated. The generation of people we knew in the 1950s was essentially the last generation to live entirely in the Old Way, the last to have practical, hands-on access to the full array of a hunter-gatherer education. After that, as their way of life became modified, their young people received increasingly less exposure to the old knowledge—a situation that almost guarantees its disappearance. Transmitting a body of knowledge through the generations with nothing but word of mouth and hands-on experience is no easy matter. Without hands-on experience, it's almost impossible. Hence the Old Way knowledge is fading fast, at least in our species.

To appreciate the loss, we might think about mammoths. Long ago, the Paleolithic hunters knew about mammoths. They would have observed their behavior, recognized them as individuals from their appearance, their footprints, and their voices, understood their habits, known their favorite foods, plotted their migration routes, taken advantage of their breeding seasons (if any), and guessed at the likely meaning of their calls. Now nothing is left of mammoths but their bones. As for all the knowledge that people had accumulated about mammoths, not a whisper remains, although the descendants of the people who knew them are everywhere, one of them writing this book and others reading it.

As the knowledge of the Bushmen belonged to the Old Way, so did the method of acquiring the knowledge. The process was essentially the same for every person and started early in life, not by sitting at the feet of some elder who imparts bits of wisdom by telling stories (the reconstructionist's version of the caveman's classroom) but by accompanying adults, watching what they did, overhearing their talk, and participating when possible. Witness Di!ai's youngest boy on the day of the gathering trip, watching his mother dig out a root while she showed him its stalk and told him its name. As he was holding his mother's hand, she was holding her mother's hand, on back to what seems like infinity. By these methods, young people absorbed a body of knowledge that their ancestors had been accumulating since the rain forests withered, the knowledge that would help each generation reach reproductive age in good condition, ready to educate the next generation. Thus, over the millennia, inaccuracies were filtered out, leaving the oldest and purest scientific product— solid, accurate information that had often been put to the test.

We happened to be present at /Gautscha during an eclipse of the moon and were mildly surprised when the Ju/wasi made almost nothing of it. (In fiction, they would have fallen to their knees in terror, beseeching the white people to save them.) "Don't worry," they said, scarcely bothering to look up at the spectacle. "The moon will come right back." One man said that the moon had gone behind clouds. But later, when I pressed him for more, he told me that the eclipse was caused by a lion covering the moon with his paw to give himself darkness for better hunting. Yet even this explanation had strong roots in reality. In places such as /Gautscha at the end of the dry season, when most of the grass is short and sparse, the lions prefer to hunt during the dark of the moon because the darkness hides them when the short grass won't. (Not for nothing do the Ju/wasi call a lion "moonless night.") Still, the story was not meant to be taken as fact in the way that, say, the Book of Genesis is sometimes taken. It was a story, and it showed, among other things, the profound awareness that the people had of lions.

In short, the Ju/wasi knew almost everything that was observable, and knew so well how to manage themselves that there was nothing about the natural world that seemed disturbing enough to require lengthy, tortuous constructs. If, for instance, you asked about a line of footprints, the Ju/wasi could tell you the species, sex, age, physical condition, state of mind, direction of travel, and short-term plans of the animal who made them. If a scat was included, the Ju/wasi could virtually tell you the story of the animal's life. But if you asked about lightning, the people might simply say that it was a death thing, god's fire. They did not expect to understand everything. "We don't know" was a perfectly acceptable statement. "The old people didn't tell us."

17

Religion

To live in the Old Way is to live with the sky. On the flat savannah, the sky is the spectacle, always with you, telling you where you are heading, how much more darkness or daylight you can expect, and what will happen next in terms of heat or cold, wind or rain. All living things are alert for its signals. If the Ju/wasi knew the things of the earth for their qualities and their details, they knew the things of the sky for their power, their mystery, and their enormity and, as was true of the rest of their knowledge, they had known these things for a very long time.

My mother studied the stars, and an old man, Old Gau, was her teacher. From him she learned that the Ju/wasi see Orion as a constellation just as we do. To them, the stars of Orion's belt are an arrow and the stars of his sword are three zebras walking down the sky in single file, a mare in the lead, then a stallion, then another mare, as if on a game trail. Long ago, a god shot at them with the arrow. It fell short and still lies there, pointing at them. The god then sent the zebras down to earth for the Bushmen to hunt. And every night they come. In May, you can see this. As the constellation slowly touches the horizon, the three zebras step onto the earth, first the leading mare, then the stallion, then the other mare. This constellation is recognized by all groups of Bushmen and also the Khoikhoi, and thus perhaps is like eland music, an echo from a much earlier time when these now-disparate groups were one people. No zebras lived in Nyae Nyae in the 1950s, as they, like buffalo, need accessible, year-round water, so the story perhaps was very old, coming from a time when buffalo lived at /Gautscha, the Place of Buffalo, when the omarambas were rivers, when the Kalahari had more water.

Not all the Ju/wa constellations were the same as ours, however. One, the most important, was so vast that all its stars could not be seen together except for a short time once a year. This constellation is called Tshxum and includes the Pleiades and two other, very distant stars. What does Tshxum mean? Nobody knew. Tshxum was the name of a huge, horned thing that could not be identified. My guess is that it was a buffalo. The Pleiades, which rises first, was at its center and may have been its face. Its right horn was Canopus, bright and conspicuous in the southeastern sky. But its left horn, called the Green Leaf Horn, was more elusive. Try as she would, my mother could not locate it. For many months, Old Gau tried to show her where to look, but it never appeared. Then, before dawn one morning in September, Old Gau hurried to my mother's tent and woke her, telling her that at last, the Green Leaf Horn was visible. She got up quickly and went to see, and yes, just above the northeastern horizon was the star Old Gau had been trying to describe. It was Capella, on the other side of the world from Canopus, and about to fade into the dawn.

My mother saw the Green Leaf Horn for the first time on September 17, 1953. On that day, at long last, the entire constellation was visible, and then only between predawn and daylight. The rains had not come, but the plants were preparing themselves for growth. A few little green triangles, the first shoots of lilies, were rising up among the long, dry grasses near the pan. Seven days later, the first rains came, and soon after that, the pan became a shining lake. Frogs appeared, lilies and other flowers bloomed, and leaves unfolded among the thorns on every little tree.

My mother wrote of seeing the Green Leaf Horn as one of her great experiences: "For a moment of breathtaking beauty, in a seeming arc soaring over the sunrise glow, Capella and Canopus were paired, matched in brilliance and color, marking the north and the south. An arc drawn between them would bracket the earth. With the Pleiades they formed a great embracing triangle."[1] She also pointed out that the Pleiades, Canopus, and Capella were seen by other ancient cultures (none, it would seem, as ancient as Ju/wa culture) as marking the beginning of the year. However, only the Bushmen saw the entire Tshxum in its enormity. And it wasn't the year that began at that time, but *Bara*, the rainy season, and the life-giving force of rain. The concept of a year had little meaning. The rain was everything.

The sky has shifted slightly since the Paleolithic; back then, the entire Tshxum may have been more readily perceived. An astronomer could make that calculation. But the Ju/wasi held it in their collective memory. After the Old Way is lost to humankind, probably only migrating birds will look at the sky with a similar comprehension, noting a relationship between stars on opposite horizons, foreseeing their relationship with stars yet to rise, and knowing that all this means something.

Perhaps only people and migrating birds would note a constellation as seemingly abstract as the Tshxum, but everything of the Old Way looked at the sky. Ju/wa religion came from the sky and indirectly had much to do with the sun. The religion might even reflect some of the thinking of other species, as many animals react to the sun as it rises and sets and do surprising things to mark the moment. In the rainy season when the pan at /Gautscha was a big, shallow lake, the flocks of ducks, geese, and other waterbirds who swam there would wait for the last red flare of the sun to vanish below the horizon, and at exactly that moment they would all fly off as if at a gunshot, all together, in a rush of wings. On cloudy days, when the sun could not be seen, they flew off more or less as dusk gathered, one flock at a time. To me, it was awesome to think that on clear evenings, the hundreds if not thousands of waterbirds on the pan were all keeping their eyes on the sun, readying themselves for its signal.

Equally impressive were two captive wolves whom I met years later in the United States (and about whom I have written elsewhere but mention again here because their behavior is both compelling and pertinent) who would crowd together at a window and wait for the sun to rise, and as soon as its first bright ray came into view, they would howl together, each voice singing a different part in a breath-taking song that set on end the hair of all who heard it. But, like the birds, if the wolves didn't actually see the sun itself, they took no special action. On cloudy mornings, they just paced around below the window without howling. It clearly seemed to be the sun itself, not the daylight, that they were saluting. They did this every morning until someone fed them poisoned meat and killed them.

As a third example of an animal responding to the sun, I offer the observation of a lion in Etosha Park in Namibia whom I watched one evening (an observation I have also discussed elsewhere). When we first saw the lion, he was all alone on an open plain near a natural spring, lying propped on his elbows with his head raised, apparently watching the sun set. At least, he was facing the sun, which was sinking toward the horizon. He seemed patient but alert, as if he were waiting for something. As the sun touched the horizon, he began to roar. He continued to roar as the sun sank out of sight, and fell silent the moment it vanished. His mission seemingly accomplished, he then stood up, turned his rump to the gorgeous western sky, and slowly walked east across the plain. A mile away was a distant woodland and into this, his tiny, lonely figure vanished from sight.

Can any of this have meaning? Well, sunrise and sunset have meaning, because, of course, dawn and dusk are the times when many animals either retire to their resting places or leave them and become active. As for the wolves, the elder of the two was a buffalo wolf, born in the Canadian wild. There, he would have lived with his parents and would have learned that the rising sun meant that the cold night was ending, that the warmer day was coming, and that one of his parents might return to the den. If he was born above the Arctic Circle where night and day are measured in months, not in hours, the appearance of the sun might even have signaled spring, the birth of caribou calves, and an end of hunger. To the lion, in contrast, the blazing, daytime sun was something to avoid. In its presence, savannah animals seek the shade, saving the water in their bodies, waiting for night. What sunrise might mean to an Arctic wolf, sunset might mean to a lion.

It would be difficult for any Old Way religion to ignore the sun, and the Ju/wasi certainly were no exception. But they did not view the sun as we do. The religions with which we are most familiar celebrate the sun as life giving. We focus on the solstices, celebrating the sun's return with Christmas candles, bonfires, and the like. Not so the Ju/wasi. On the African savannah at 20° south of the equator, there was so little seasonal movement of the sun that, believe it or not, the Ju/wasi hadn't noticed it! They were slightly taken aback when asked about it. But without permanent camps as points of reference, and because the sun's lateral motion covered such a short distance, perhaps it is no wonder.

Anyway, the Ju/wasi thought very little of the sun and by no means paid it the honors that we do. On the contrary, where to us the sun is life, to the Ju/wasi it was death. When the sun was up in the sky, hot and dangerous, no act of passage such as a marriage could take place. The people in transition were protected from sunlight, covered with capes, if necessary. These ceremonies took place after the sun had gone. Nor could the names of dangerous beings such as gods and lions be mentioned when the sun was present. The gods and the lions sat under trees to escape the blazing sun, and didn't want to leave the shade for any reason, but they might feel they had to if they heard people talking about them. This seemed particularly interesting to me because the people, in contrast, were thoroughly diurnal and rarely if ever went about at dawn and dusk. In this respect, therefore, the gods were more like lions than like people.

The two gods of the Ju/wasi lived in the sky and in anthropological terms have been called sky gods, but unlike the true sky gods of pastoralists and farmers, gods such as Zeus or Allah or Jehovah, the Ju/wa gods didn't live right overhead. Any god might want to keep out of the zenith above the Kalahari, where the daytime sky is a scorching void that none would enter except the morning star, which, to the Ju/wasi, is an unfortunate being. This star finds itself alone in the sky at sunrise, and all by itself it starts on its dangerous day-long journey like a lonely person starting across an enormous salt flat while the death-giving sun burns down. People can cut branches to shade themselves if they must do this, say the Ju/wasi, but the star can find no branches in the sky.

Yet although the sun itself was dangerous and death giving, its path was the axis of the world. In our culture, north is the primary direction, governing the way we think about the world, the way we orient ourselves, build roads and houses, make maps, and navigate. For the Ju/wasi, however, east and west were by far the most significant directions. And as we have good reasons for our concept, so do they. Few who live in the Old Way know the actual shape of the world—only migrating birds and the great whales could have much sense of it. But everything with eyes or merely with eyespots must be aware of the path of the sun. Even plants track the path of the sun.

The two gods lived at the ends of that path, one in the east and the other in the west. Yes, they lived in the sky, sort of, in that they didn't inhabit rocks or trees, but when we asked where one might actually find these gods, people would point just above the horizon to the places where the sun rises and sets, when the beings of the savannah go about their business in the dawn and twilight. So I can't see the Ju/wa gods as sky gods. No, they were horizon gods. Like the living things of the savannah, not wanting to be disturbed by day, not even present by day most of the time, they were crepuscular. They were gods of the Old Way and they belonged entirely to the savannah.

We knew some people who had actually seen the gods. Once, the eastern god had appeared to Gao Feet as a small humanlike apparition, about eight inches tall. On another occasion, the western god appeared to a man named Demi as a small, almost mouselike figure covered with hair. Yet another man saw the eastern god as a white man on horseback, wearing a hat. White people should not get too puffed up about this, however, as the god was presenting himself as a ghastly apparition.

These surprising forms taken by the gods were temporary, what they had chosen to be at the time. Otherwise, the gods were said to look like human beings of normal, human size. They hunted, just as people did, and had wives and children and lived in camps with fires and grass shelters, just as people did, according to the stories that were told about them. As our gods allegedly made man in their image, so, allegedly, did the gods of the Ju/wasi.

Quite unlike the gods of some religions, the Ju/wa gods did not worry about human shortcomings or concern themselves with human behavior. Nor did the Ju/wasi look to the gods for moral leadership, probably because a camp full of people who can read tracks is a more powerful deterrent to antisocial actions than a god could ever be. Hence the gods didn't punish moral wrongdoing or reward moral virtue. Neither did anything else that lived on the savannah. Again, it was the Old Way.

Perhaps the gods didn't mete out punishments, but they hurt people who did things they didn't like, even though the few human acts that brought on divine harm were accidental. This also is in keeping with the ways of the savannah. If you step on a poisonous snake, it doesn't take into account that you are a good person or that you stepped on it by accident. It bites. The bite is punishment, yes, but in the manner of the Old Way. You won't live long enough to step on that snake again, but it is hoped that before you die you will communicate its species to some of your fellows. That way, they won't be stepping on that sort of snake if they can help it. The snake has done himself and his species a service.

As for the gods, at least one of them, the eastern god, disapproved of killing bees, which people never did intentionally and only when gathering honey. But before reaching into the hive for the honeycombs, honey hunters would first stun the bees with smoke and sometimes would use too much smoke, which killed some of the bees. One of the names of the wife of the eastern god is Mother of Bees, so he has an interest in them, and if honey hunters should harm the bees, this god might then harm the honey hunters, taking the form of a honeycomb that the careless honey hunters would eat. Once the god was inside their stomachs, he would kill them. Then, too, if a god happened to be in the form of a gemsbok or some other antelope, and if hunters accidentally shot him, not realizing who he was, he might punish them even though they were merely hunting in a normal, innocent manner, not meaning any harm. In the manner of a snake that bites those who step on him, the god might punish the hunters, and, in the form of the meat of the gemsbok, he would burn in the stomachs of those who ate him until they, too, were dead.

Otherwise, the gods interacted with people by sending good or bad luck, not to punish vice or to reward virtue, but because they felt like it. People of Western cultures might consider it sacrilegious to say that God was zapping them for no special reason, even though that hypothesis certainly seems to describe the human experience, but the Ju/wasi had no trouble with the idea. The gods harmed people because they wanted people to be afraid of them. "I am unknown and unknowable," says the eastern god, according to the Ju/wasi. "I am *tchi dole*."

The words *tchi dole* ring in the mind—*tchi* means "thing" and *dole* means "bad." Clumsily translated, this ominous phrase could mean, "I am your worst nightmare."

We ourselves use the phrase "fear God" without much reflection, but why would a Bushman god want people to fear him? If the gods were not seen as punitive parents or moral policemen, which the Ju/wa gods were not, fear might seem unnecessary. But perhaps the god was setting an example after all. Lions and other predators, those good observers with their intelligence and ability to plan, did well to respect the Ju/wasi. Don't come too near us and we won't hit you with burning branches, was the people's message to the lions. Perhaps the god offered the people a similar message. Fear god and don't bother him, and he'll more or less leave you alone, the Ju/wa bible said.

The eastern god had many names, one of which was Ba, or Father. But mostly he was called ≠Gao N!a, which was simply an ordinary man's name with the respectful adjective that would apply to an old person. In the 1950s, we knew at least seven people named ≠Gao, which gave the god a common touch that at first I found surprising. To replicate this in our culture, we would call God Rick or Jim. But we as a culture admire the powerful and grant them extra importance, which the Ju/wasi did not, hence we give our gods important, lofty names, unlike the Ju/wasi. The entire Ju/wa culture was aimed at leveling its members—an extremely useful practice in a hunter-gatherer society, and timeworn, too, if thirty-five thousand years mean anything—and the gods are not exceptions.

Nevertheless, despite his common name, ≠Gao N!a is the Creator. In one of the Ju/wa creation myths, ≠Gao N!a first created himself. Then he created the other god, whose name is //Gauwa. Then he created a wife for himself, Mother of Bees, and then a wife for //Gauwa. Then he created the earth in which he made waterholes, then he created water to fill the holes, then he created the sky with sun, moon, and stars, also rain, wind, and lightning, then he created the plants and animals, giving them their names and their coloring. Finally, he created the people.[2]

Such is his divinity. Yet among the Ju/wasi whom we visited, many stories told about ≠Gao N!a portray him as a fool. In the stories, the god in question is the exact opposite of the familiar trickster figure found in many cultures—the small, intelligent hare or fox who outwits powerful bullies—because the bullying figure who is outwitted in the Ju/wa stories is ≠Gao N!a himself. Again and again, his relatives (often his in-laws) play terrible practical jokes on him, so that he is robbed, burned, lied to, and tricked into eating forbidden or disgusting things. In one story he unwittingly eats pieces of his wives' genitals, which the wives have cut off for that purpose and which they tell him is meat from an animal. In another story, he is tricked so that he jumps into a hidden pit filled with feces—also the work of his wives. Again and again, he is battered and humiliated, but he never catches on. Every time his wives or his kinsmen tell him some whopper, he believes them, to his sorrow. (Look, a baby eland, can you see him? *No, I can't.* He's under those leaves, so jump right there and you'll catch him. *Really?* Yes, but hurry, he's escaping!) Soon the great god is dragging himself, befouled, from the pit full of feces, while in the distance, bitterly, he hears the laughter of his wives. If the god of these stories was a product of our culture, he'd walk around in a T-shirt saying, "Hi, I'm Stupid," unaware that a sign saying "Kick Me" was pinned to his sagging pants.

At first, the tenor of these stories seemed to me excessive. I found it hard to understand why a god would be seen in such a negative light. Compounding the puzzle, I thought, was that the Ju/wasi found the stories so funny, whereas in real life, a practical joke would never be seen as funny. Yet perhaps this is because a practical joke, according to our definition, is played by one person on another. An ordinary mishap, on the other hand, could certainly be seen as funny—a joke played on a person by Fate. Among the Ju/wasi, no one would ever trip or push the lame man, !Kham, for example, yet if he fell down, which he sometimes did, people laughed and didn't help him. Thus if only one human being—the victim—is involved, then a god might be the prankster. No one, for instance, would burn someone else for a joke, but the gods could and did, and the innocent bystanders could laugh as some of us might laugh at someone's pratfall or similar misfortune. (We don't condone such laughter, but we laugh just the same.) A mishap to an animal could seem equally funny. I will always remember a springbok who, when gut shot by a member of our expedition, kicked upward at the bullet hole as if she thought that something was biting her. The young Ju/wa men thought that her mistake was hilarious and imitated the suffering creature. Readers of this book will probably not see the humor, and neither did I, but then, we aren't hunter-gatherers.

So perhaps the ≠Gao N!a stories are something like the trickster stories after all, but trickster stories in reverse, with the protagonist as the loser, not the winner. Satisfyingly, a powerful figure is brought low, and if the figure is none other than a god, well, he is only getting back some of the bad luck he sends randomly to people who don't need it, who want only to survive, who are trying as hard as they can. Yet his real-life victims do not retaliate. How could they? No, it is the god's own wives or his relatives who humiliate him, and, well, if they do, who can keep from laughing?

The other god, //Gauwa, was a different kind of being entirely. No derogatory stories were told about this god by the people we knew, at least not at /Gautscha. Interestingly, many years later in Botswana, the anthropologist Megan Biesele found many stories in which this god is the humiliated protagonist.[3] These Botswana Ju/wasi evidently saw things somewhat differently from the people of Nyae Nyae. But that, of course, is the very nature of folklore, with fluid as well as fixed aspects.

As for Nyae Nyae, it cannot be stated too strongly that the god of the west whom the Ju/wasi called //Gauwa was no figure of fun. Yes, he was supposedly the lesser god, but he was strongly associated with death. He had no other name than //Gauwa. On the contrary, he didn't even have the exclusive use of that name, as *//gauwa* is also the word for the spirit of a dead person. The word is more often heard in the plural, *//gauwasi*, the spirits of the dead. Did they bear his name, or did he bear theirs? No one knows—this is lost in the mists of time.

However, it has been suggested that //Gauwa is a much older figure than ≠Gao N!a. //Gauwa is known widely and is named among many distinct groups of Bushmen and also among the Khoikhoi, suggesting that, like eland music, he was already in place before the groups diverged. If this is true, //Gauwa might be the oldest recognized god in the world and his role or his character or both, if not necessarily his name, might even be that of the first god.

One of his main roles is to receive the dead after ≠Gao N!a has accepted them. When a person dies, according to the Ju/wasi of Nyae Nyae, the spirit travels east to ≠Gao N!a, who gives it everlasting life and then sends it west to the other god, //Gauwa, who cures it in a special smoke until it becomes a *//gauwa*. What happens next says, I think, something important about the Ju/wa concept of a life span, because a *//gauwa* continues to grow old, just as he or she would do if living, and is rejuvenated by ≠Gao N!a after reaching old age. In contrast, the spirits of children remain children and do not grow up. But how could they? They would not have hunted successfully or reached the menarche, and would not have advanced to the next state.

Interestingly, after death, the spirits lose their short, curly hair and grow long, straight hair. ("Long," in this case, would be about five or six inches, long only by comparison.) The concept has no ready explanation and in this respect could be something like our concept of ghosts as amorphous clouds. If there is a reason for the cloudlike quality of ghosts, we don't remember it. I'd be tempted to think of the longish, straight hair as a passed-on recollection of our rain forest hair, but this is a bit of a stretch, even though, by my reasoning, those who became spirits in rain forest times would indeed have had longish, straight hair all over their bodies. But the concept of a spirit life among Pleistocene chimpanzees has yet to be established, and even in the unlikely event that the concept arose so long ago, it would be hard to communicate without language. So, no matter how entrancing I find this hypothesis, I must admit that the image is likely to be more recent.

But this is not to say that long, straight hair has no meaning. I believe it does. On the savannah, the only other straight, dark, six-inch hair to be found on anyone's head is in the manes of dark-maned lions. And in many ways, the *//gauwasi* are deeply entwined with real-life lions. Perhaps this is why their hair is similar.

After //Gauwa has developed the spirit by smoking it in a special fire, it becomes a messenger for the gods. Occasionally a male spirit will notice a beautiful woman among the living and will cause her death so that he can have her, but mostly the spirits don't act on their own. Instead, they bring good or bad luck to people as the gods direct. To do this, they travel over the savannah on invisible threadlike trails that float in the air like spiderwebs. Now and then, under special circumstances to be discussed later, someone would see a *//gauwa*, and judging from where the person's eyes were directed when the sighting took place, these trails seemed to be about fifteen feet off the ground.

The spirits were not particularly happy, and they were not particularly sad. And the afterlife was neither a punishment nor a paradise. It was merely continued existence but in a different form.

As has been said, the Ju/wa gods did not try to bend people to their will. No deity laid out a moral code, or sanctioned any foods or behaviors. Even so, some foods and behaviors were prohibited by rules that had been handed down through the generations. People knew of these rules because the old people told them, and kept them because to break them would bring illness or sometimes death. The gods did not promote the rules as, say, the Judeo-Christian God promoted the Commandments, so the reason that people kept the rules had less to do with the gods' displeasure and more to do with practical consequences. Young people didn't eat ostrich eggs, for instance, not because it was thought that the gods would disapprove, but because it was thought that ostrich eggs would make them sick. In all likelihood, no medical reason or personal experience is behind this prohibition—it is simply a food taboo with origins lost in antiquity. Yet it was the fear of bad results, not the anger of gods, that made people respect these prohibitions.

As the gods did not try to force human behavior, so people did not try to force the natural world. They did not, for instance, try to make rain, or make animals fertile, or make plants grow. With the exception of burning dry grass now and then in order to encourage green grass, they did not try to make things happen. The concept of trying to control nature belongs to the agricultural peoples, but not necessarily to those of the Old Way.

An excellent example of the people's noncontrolling, noninterventional attitude could be seen in the quality called *n!ow*. As has been said, only people, giraffes, and large antelopes (and perhaps also duikers) had *n!ow*, showing the unity, the oneness, of the Ju/wasi and their primary prey. *N!ow* was a quality that the Ju/wasi could readily envision but that Westerners can scarcely comprehend.

My mother made an extensive study of *n!ow* and found that among the Ju/wasi of Nyae Nyae it occupies no special spot in the body and is invisible, just as thoughts are invisible. Interestingly, however, Megan Biesele, working in Botswana in 1971, found that some people feel that *n!ow* stays at the nape of the neck.[4] Biesele's informants pointed out that this is where your skin prickles if, say, the wrong person sits behind you. (It is also, perhaps, your most vulnerable spot, where your hackles would rise if you were scared and where a feline predator would grab you.) The name of that spot (spelled //*nao* or //*now*) differs only slightly from the *n!ow* it contains.

N!ow is more like energy, in that its effects are visible even if the quality itself is not. *N!ow* could be cold and wet or hot and dry, and it manifests itself by changing the weather. This happens when the *n!ow* of one *n!ow*-holding creature interacts with that of another, as, for instance, when a woman gives birth and her birth water falls on the ground, at which time her *n!ow* interacts with the *n!ow* of her baby and, depending on the two types of *n!ow*, may result in a change in weather. A similar interaction could take place when a man kills an antelope. When the blood of the antelope falls on the ground, the hunter's *n!ow* interacts with the *n!ow* of the antelope, and can also bring about a change in the weather. *N!ow* has further effect when a man urinates on a fire, whereupon his *n!ow* interacts directly with the fire to change weather. A person with a cold, wet *n!ow* could urinate on a fire to bring cold, wet weather, for instance. That, very briefly, is how *n!ow* works.

What is *n!ow* for? It isn't *for* anything. The Ju/wasi we knew did not try to use the energy of *n!ow* to alter the weather. People would merely note the changes that occur when *n!ow* became activated. This was how you learned what kind of *n!ow* you had, the hot, dry kind or the cold, wet kind. Theoretically, a man could deliberately urinate in a fire to change the weather, or so said the Ju/wasi, but as the years went by, we never saw or heard of anyone actually doing it. Nevertheless, people were very firm about the effect of *n!ow* as something to notice, something that just happens, like a rainbow after rain.

An outsider such as myself has much difficulty understanding *n!ow*, finding it hard to imagine having a quality that could alter the environment without trying to use it for that purpose. Over the years I have been twisting the concept, trying to make sense of it. And the best I have been able to do is to visualize *n!ow* almost as a force of nature.

Thus it would seem to me that *n!ow* shows one of the very important differences between the Ju/wasi and ourselves. During the Neolithic, when people realized that they could, in fact, alter their environments slightly by planting crops and domesticating animals, they obviously developed grandiose ideas of their power over their surroundings (and they attributed similar power to their gods). The savannah hunter-gatherers had no such illusions and did not feel as we do, enclosed as we are in our cities and houses and farms. We are outside the natural world, which we think of as something far away, something out in the country, something to be suppressed or managed. Not so the Ju/wasi. Natural phenomena happened all around them and happened within them. And *n!ow* is part of that.

So perhaps the best way to visualize *n!ow* is to think of it as a feature that appears in those who matter the most, those who best enable human survival and who have been joined together ever since large antelopes became our preferred prey. It could be said that people, giraffes, and savannah antelopes are joined together as plants are joined to rain. Plants don't make rain. They interact with it. When it comes, they put out their flowers and berries. To see *n!ow* in that light makes plenty of sense.

That *n!ow* was not deliberately used in weather management did not mean that the Ju/wasi never tried to interact with the forces of nature. They did, and when they did, it was in the most profound manner. Sometimes when the moon was full, they held magnificent trance dances. During these events, these ordinarily quiet people filled the landscape with loud, breathtakingly beautiful music, danced to exhaustion, fell into moaning, trembling trances, washed themselves with burning coals and fire, and raced madly into the night to confront and curse the death givers—the lions and the spirits of the dead.

The songs the people sang were special songs, given by the gods to people in dreams and used only at such dances, and these songs contained great power. But unlike agricultural and industrial peoples who want to influence the natural world, the hunter-gatherers wanted to join with it and use its powers. This, too, is one of the most profound differences between these hunter-gatherers and the rest of us. During a drought, we might visit a place of worship to pray earnestly for rain, trying to persuade our deity to alter the environment and make it rain. Not the Ju/wasi. They would feel the change in the air, notice the behavior of the clouds that built in the western sky, know that rain was coming, and make themselves ready to join with the oncoming storm and participate in its power. There was a rain song, for instance, and with it, a rain dance. But the dance was not meant to bring rain or make rain. No, it was used to gather the power of the oncoming rain and use that power to help people.

At /Gautscha, where the days and nights are almost of equal length year-round, the full moon would rise as the sun was setting. For a few moments, these two great, round bodies, one deep red, one pale pink, would balance each other on the grassy rim of the earth. The evening wind would lift. Around the faraway edges of /Gautscha pan, the flocks of guinea fowl would fly to their roosts in the trees with calls and whirring wings. Then the men who had been wanting to have a dance would begin urging the women to start one. As the sun was disappearing under the horizon and daylight in the zenith was fading, some women would stand up from their fires and, choosing a place about fifty feet from the encampment, they would bring wood and coals from their own fires, and they would start another fire, bigger than their family fires—perhaps three or four large sticks producing a foot-high flame. Then they would smooth the hems of their leather capes behind their knees and fold their legs to sit down on their heels, facing the fire in a partial circle, leaving a downwind space for the smoke. As the last of the sunset was going and the stars were coming out, one or two of the women would begin to sing and clap in a businesslike manner. Others would join in. Still other women, also bringing wood, would come from the camp to join the singers, who made room for them in the ring. In high, almost piercing voices they sang songs of heart-stopping beauty—very intricate, complex, contrapuntal songs without words, which they accompanied by contrapuntal clapping done with the hands stiff and slightly cupped, producing a sound as loud and sharp as the ring of a loud wooden gong. The clapping held several different rhythms all at once and did not sound like applause, and neophytes couldn't do it. The technique had to be carefully learned and then practiced.

Presently, some of the men would begin to dance, circling behind the women. Some of the men would be wearing dance rattles wound around their legs. The rattles looked something like narrow belts—long strings of dried cocoons lined up side by side and tied together, filled with bits of ostrich eggshell that, when shaken, made the sound. One or two men might begin the dancing, progressing by short, strong steps, almost little jumps, their heels stamping, each step enhanced by the rattles. The first dancers would soon be joined by others and the sound of the rattles and the pounding heels would grow louder, producing a third element of the music, again in counterpoint. It was, as my mother put it, a symphony of bodies.

After a time, one of the men would fall into a trance. Staggering, he might approach the fire, wash himself with the flames or with the coals, and put coals on his head. His hair might burn. He would be heating the power in his body, moaning as he did, and then might stumble over to one of the women in the circle and, putting a trembling hand on her chest, the other hand on her back, he would draw in his breath with a moaning sound again and again, until suddenly he would stand straight up and scream at the sky. What was he doing? He was drawing sickness out of the woman and screaming it into the air. He was giving it back to the spirits of the dead. They are drawn to such dances, and they hang in the night air somewhere near the dance circle, or they lurk in the shadows beyond the firelight, perhaps with lions. The trancing man would move on to the next person, then to the next and the next. By this time another man would also be in trance, then another and another.

What was the sickness that the trancing men took out of their people's bodies? Not a common illness, although if people were physically sick, trance dances might be held to cure them. But usually, the sickness that the trancers removed was called "star sickness," which was not what we would call a disease but was the force that pervades a group of people and causes dissent and jealousy, anger and quarrels and failures of gift giving—the evils that drive people apart and damage the unity that is life itself on the savannah. Physical illnesses are bad, but star sickness is worse, and it was this that the trancing men flung back to the surrounding spirits, they who were waiting just beyond the firelight.

Sometimes a trancing man would fall full length on the ground, where others in trance would moan and scream and place their trembling hands on him. Sometimes a man would fall in the fire. The other men would pull him out. When a fallen man stood up again, others would help him circle the dance fire, supporting him as he drew sickness out of the people, or would run behind him, holding his wrists, if he suddenly dashed out of the firelight into the dark to confront the spirits or the lions who might be there. He would scream out the sickness at the spirits, hurling profanities at them, commanding them to take all the bad things they brought with them and leave. Or perhaps he would scream his curses at the lions, they who were jealousy, danger, and death.

The song would change. The dance would continue. The song would change again. The dancers would circle the fire. All through the night the singing and dancing would continue, not all men in trance but few emerging from it. People would get tired, but they would not stop, because it was important to keep going until sunrise. Sometimes the younger people could endure no longer and might leave the dance circle, but the older people never faltered, and when the first light of dawn showed on the eastern horizon, they seemed to gather extra energy. Then the singing would become louder and the dance faster. As the sun rose, the dance would reach its final, most powerful intensity, and suddenly, it would stop.

That was it. Some of the men might still be deep in trance, some might be lying on the ground, but other men would be tending to them, slowly massaging their arms and legs. The tired women would stand up stiffly, having been sitting on their heels for almost twelve hours, strenuously singing and clapping without rest. They would talk, laugh, stretch, and look around for leftover firewood. Each woman, of course, would know exactly which sticks she had brought, and taking those sticks and no others, she would make her way back

*Sometimes when the moon was full, the !Kung held magnificent
trance-dances that lasted until dawn. During these events, these ordinarily
quiet people filled the landscape with loud, breathtakingly beautiful music,
danced to exhaustion, fell into moaning, trembling trances, washed
themselves with burning coals and fire, and raced madly into the night to
confront and curse the death-givers—the lions and spirits of the dead.*

to her *tshu* and her fire, ready to relax and take a nap. A few at a time, the tired men would also leave the dance circle, perhaps after having a drink of water from an ostrich eggshell that someone would be passing, and return to the encampment to join their families.

The full moon would set and the sun would rise, the moon pale pink, the sun pale yellow on the grassy rim of the horizon. The dance fire would have burned to embers, birds would begin to fly overhead, the dawn wind would lift, and nothing would be left but the bed of the dance fire with a deep double track in the dust around it, made by the dancers' feet. The spirits and the lions would have been driven away, and the tired people would be relaxed and happy. The healing that came to people from the dance would last for a long time and accrued to everyone, from little babies to the oldest people. Who would not want that kind of healing? Even the spirits seemed to want it. Sometimes on nights of the full moon, the spirits held their own trance dances. The moon was their dance fire, which they circled, and the hazy ring that would form around it was the dust rising under their feet.

How old is this dancing? Could it be as old as eland music? As old as the name of the older god? Could it be older still, this art form? Later in life I learned that at sunrise and sunset, when the warm air of day slides over the cold air of night, sound carries better than at other times. It has to do with the different density of the two kinds of air, and with the fact that sound travels farther in dense, cold air. This, I learned, is why birds sing at dawn and dusk. They want their songs to carry as far as possible, so that the greatest possible number of their rivals will know that their territories are occupied. I also learned that animals who gather in groups to vocalize do so because they want their distant rivals to know that they are many. It must be daunting to lions, for instance, or wolves, or howler monkeys to hear large groups of their own kind vocalizing in the distance. We won't go there, they tell themselves.

I then wondered if the Ju/wa trance dances once had a similar function. Very few things made loud noises in the Kalahari, where even the wind is quiet. Not counting overhead thunder, lions were the loudest, and ostriches roared almost as loudly as lions, so the sound of a trance dance was probably the third loudest noise to be heard. The sharp sound of women clapping seemed to carry almost as far as the sound of the large West African gonglike talking drums, and the singing was pitched at about the same frequency as a scream—a sound intended for long-distance travel—so, in the dry, cool air and utter silence of the African veld at night, a group of people holding a trance dance could be heard for many miles. If a lion can be heard at twenty miles, the sound of a trance dance might travel almost that distance. So it is not completely impossible that at one time, such cooperative sound making served the same purpose as that of other creatures, a notice to others far away that a large group was present in a certain place—present, vigorous, and very much united.

So to me, it seems significant that the people would continue a trance dance until dawn, when the sound would travel farthest. Of course, there were better reasons to continue a dance through the entire night. A dance was seen as a single process that should begin at sunset and continue until sunrise, and only at sunrise could the dancers avail themselves of the sun's power. But if in earlier times a distant group of people, different people, would hear on the early morning wind the faint sound of this forceful, coordinated music, they would know that a big group was over there, perhaps a bigger group than one would want to encounter. Perhaps there was a time when such things were important. If so, it would have been natural. It would have belonged very firmly to the Old Way.

I remember the first dance that took place after we came, and how I sat in the ring of women at their invitation, not knowing the wordless song, which was very difficult and complex and had nothing in common with music I knew, and I remember how I was able to keep time by clapping one line of the rhythm, trying to copy the woman next to me. I still remember how it felt when one of the trancing men, with a touch as light as a bird's wing, put his trembling hands on my chest and shoulder, and with his head beside mine pulled in his breath with long, slow groans, then suddenly leaped back and shrieked at the sky, then, almost staggering, moved on to the next woman. He had taken something out of me and thrown it into the night. At the time, such trance dancing was not known to the Western world, and I had no idea what he was doing or what I should do. So I did what the women on either side of me were doing, and continued clapping. By then, other trancing men were leaning over other women in the circle, over the children squeezed in beside their mothers, over the little babies in their mothers' capes, pulling something out of us, screaming it up to the sky.

In time, I came to understand what had been happening, what most of it meant, and I would later sit in the circle of women at many other dances, but I will never forget that first one—the dancers between the fire and the moon, the voice of the healer in my ear, the heat of his face against mine with strange, loud singing all around us. To have been part of that, that's something to remember now that I am among the last of those people to be left alive, after everything has changed.

PART TWO

....

18

Tsumkwe

Since the 1950s, change has been rapid. The San [Bushmen] are no longer allowed to hunt the animals they once did and they have inevitably been caught up in the political changes that have taken place in Namibia and Botswana. They now have access to schools and hospitals, but poverty is their overwhelming lot. They manage to earn some money by making curios for tourists and by performing the medicine dance, [but] for the most part they live around small villages such as Tsumkwe. Tin shanties have started to take the place of traditional dwellings, and firearms are greatly coveted.

The Marshall family, however, has not abandoned them. John Marshall still works with the San, helping them with boreholes and limited cattle ranching. Other organizations, too, continue to assist the San, but life in the Kalahari will never return to the sort of existence that the Marshalls found.

—David Lewis-Williams and David Pearce, *San Spirituality*, 2004

In 1998, in the huge, packed auditorium of the American Museum of Natural History during the Margaret Mead Ethnographic Film Festival, my brother's film, *A Kalahari Family*, was featured. During the question period that followed, a member of the audience asked my brother if he did not feel guilty for having opened the way to the Kalahari interior, bringing the Western world to the Bushmen and beginning the process of change.

. . . .

How dare this man criticize my brother? I leaped to my feet and demanded to know how anyone could possibly imagine that any place on earth might still be pristine today. Even Antarctica was swarming with tourists! It was the best thing possible that John Marshall had visited the Bushmen, I said, because at least he offered them some help.

I had seized the high ground. The audience applauded. The critic had been stamped upon, was cowed, and sat down apologetically. I sat down, too. "That was my sister," explained John, and he proceeded to answer the question.

I didn't hear what he said because I was still fuming, but in fact, we were partly responsible for starting the change, and not just with our truck tracks. Our presence certainly alerted the Ju/wasi (those who had never been slaves on farms) to the life beyond the Kalahari, and our presence in Nyae Nyae certainly reminded the white settlers and the Bantu pastoralists of the great, untouched grasslands that lay beyond the farms. In the intervening years, the globe has shrunk so significantly that today the once pristine bushland of the Kalahari interior is now famous for, of all things, its thermal updrafts, which bear aloft extreme adventurers in paragliders—rich young foreigners who come to surf the air.

Some groups of Brazilian Indians have managed to stave off a few incursions from the outside world, partly because of their alleged ferocity and partly because the people who would exploit them cannot easily get through the jungle. But the Kalahari is not the Mato Grosso. In the Kalahari, truck travel is generally possible, and anything on the ground can be seen from the air. Short of building a great wall around the Kalahari to protect it forever from the rest of the world, the Old Way could hardly have lasted. Actually, a fence was built, but for a more malignant reason, not to protect the Kalahari interior but to keep the wild game from entering the farmlands. The fence put an end to animal migrations, which was its purpose, and resulted in a miserable slaughter. The animals died trying to continue their journeys, and their bodies lay rotting by the thousands, pressed up against the fence.

The question, then, was not whether change could be prevented, but what form it would take when it came. In the 1950s, my father had taken a guess at the future. He had seen the profound changes that would affect the Bushmen. He also had known what the Bushmen could not have known, that their future was uncertain, that they were already wanted as laborers, and that other people wanted their land and were only too ready to take it from them because, in the eyes of the white farmers and Bantu pastoralists, the Bushmen "did nothing" with it. They "didn't use it," and the whites and pastoralists would. My father also knew something about the governments of the countries that shared the Kalahari and understood how ready they were to assist their constituents in land acquisition. Perhaps no one could have predicted the year that the Old Way would end, but obviously it wasn't going to last forever.

In 1954, the Department of Bantu Administration in South West Africa had expanded to include a Bushman Affairs Commission, headed by a man named Claude McIntyre. Although all this took place far away in Windhoek, McIntyre was the government official who had accompanied our first trip. Contrary to a pervasive image, the government of South West Africa was not, in those days, composed entirely of ultraconservative, apartheid-driven Boers; it also contained an important element that was considerably more progressive. Fortunately, Claude McIntyre was one of these people. Because he had come with us to /Gautscha and knew something of the interior, he was chosen to establish a government post to keep back the cattle of the pastoralists so that they wouldn't intrude on the farmlands, to prevent the white farmers from raiding for slaves, and to secure the area as much as possible against independent diamond prospectors, as diamonds had been found at the edges of the Kalahari, right on the surface, and the owners of the South African diamond mines were eager to preserve their monopoly.

The post was established in 1959 at a place called Tsumkwe,[1] once a semipermanent waterhole near a black baobab tree that stood alone against the sky about thirty miles northeast of /Gautscha, the *n!ore* of a small group of people. But when Tsumkwe was under consideration as a government post, my father, being a civil engineer, considered the size and age of the baobab and felt that more water might be present underneath it. With a shovel, he dug a hole near the baobab, and soon enough the hole filled partway with water. Much later, farm-style boreholes drilled by drilling rigs and powered with windmills or gasoline-driven pumps supplied Tsumkwe with water. (In about 1996, the baobab tree died, collapsing into itself, some say because of disease, but more likely because too much water was pumped out from under its roots.)

Interestingly, another person who foresaw the coming change was ≠Toma. He was perhaps in his early fifties at the time and was greatly respected, not only by his own people but also by McIntyre. Not for nothing was he called ≠Toma Word. He had, after all, been captured by a farmer and knew something of the world beyond Nyae Nyae, and could guess what lay in store for some of his people if measures were not taken. He agreed to take McIntyre's message to his people, to learn if some would agree to move to Tsumkwe and help to establish the government post. By this time, the negative image of white people formerly held by the Bushmen had been somewhat mitigated by my mother and perhaps by the rest of us as well, and although the Bushmen certainly did not expect to find others like my parents and my brother, or to form great friendships with the whites, the image of white people had been revised enough so that many people of Nyae Nyae could imagine themselves in a cooperative relationship such as McIntyre was offering. McIntyre retained his formal, authoritarian stance among the Bushmen and was careful to keep the rules of apartheid, but, like an army officer who does not fraternize with the enlisted men, he was decent enough, and certainly did not abuse anyone, and the people saw that. He was, in short, unlike most of the white farmers, and in those days that was an advancement.

In 1960, McIntyre moved his family to Tsumkwe—a progressive gesture that other officials were not to imitate for many years to come. He established a clinic and introduced primitive farming along the lines of ordinary European-type farming, which was at the time the only paradigm, beginning with a herd of goats and an experimental planting of corn and millet. His intentions, of course, were good, and goats were chosen instead of cattle because, although both provide milk, the owner of a goat might kill it for food but would be unwilling to kill a cow because, according to McIntyre, he would have to share it. (In fact, the Ju/wasi would have shared either animal.) Goats, corn, and millet damage the ecosystem, but back then, environmental matters were poorly understood and largely ignored, especially by those who set government policy. Because the same mind-set is almost universal, especially at government levels, McIntyre can hardly be blamed for the fact that goats fall easy prey to leopards and hyenas, also to cheetahs, caracal, and jackals, none of which can kill cattle, and, unlike cattle, goats eat the landscape down to the sand, consuming not only all the grass but also every leaf and twig and the bark of every tree within range, even climbing the trees to reach the upper branches. Corn and millet were also bad choices, providing limited nutrition, leaching the already fragile earth, and requiring plenty of water. Nyae Nyae was no ordinary farmland, and the experiment collapsed, to everyone's disappointment.

Yet the development of Tsumkwe did not stop. Bushman laborers, using shovels and baskets to carry dirt, cleared an airstrip and began work on a ninety-mile road connecting Tsumkwe to the nearest farm settlements at Grootfontein, at which point one could turn right and follow a cart track that ran north in the general direction of Angola, or turn left and go south to Windhoek, four hundred miles away, mostly along a roadlike path scraped by a grader that, when in action, lumbered slowly and noisily across the veld. The grader, however, was a municipal vehicle working at taxpayers' expense and couldn't be expected to go as far as Tsumkwe, so from there to Grootfontein, the Bushmen did its work.

In 1970, the government of South West Africa officially established a homeland for the Bushmen, which not only the original inhabitants but also all Bushmen from all language groups and cultural backgrounds would be encouraged to inhabit. The motive for this sprang from apartheid policy, whereby each group of people—whether Herero, Tswana, Kavango, or Ambo—was assigned a tract of land and expected to stay there unless provided with work permits or passes from white people. Because of the pristine state of Bushmanland, and because at first so few Bushmen lived there (only 3 percent of all Bushmen in the country), the area became administered by the Department of Nature Conservation. In keeping with the policies promoted at Etosha National Park, which the department also administered, Bushmen were prevented from hunting their traditional game. These developments sent many Bushmen to Tsumkwe, and by 1975, most of the hunter-gatherers of Nyae Nyae were concentrated there.

. . . .

Claude McIntyre had since retired for reasons of declining health and was replaced by others who did not share his motives. The new representatives of the Department of Native Affairs had little interest in the Bushmen, did not think that they could better themselves, and offered them no help. On the contrary, while preventing the Bushmen from hunting, government officials armed with high-powered rifles began to hunt in the Tsumkwe area themselves. They also did this in the Etosha wildlife preserve as late as the 1980s, and perhaps beyond. It wasn't policy, it wasn't even legal, but the distances were so great and the enormous veld so undeveloped that they believed that they could get away with it. And they were right. They got away with it. For one thing, they almost certainly belonged to Broderbond, a secret society formed to preserve Afrikaner culture and so pervasive that one had to be a member to get any meaningful job. Even the bishop of the Dutch Reformed church belonged to Broderbond. Broderbond members wouldn't snitch on one another for something as trivial as poaching—far otherwise. Commercial hunters were also allowed to hunt to supply the biltong factories that were developing around the edges of the Kalahari (biltong is dry, flavored meat, a kind of jerky). It would seem that the factory owners, too, were Broderbond.

Soon enough, scarcely an animal could be found in most of Nyae Nyae. The officials also forbade the Bushmen from setting wildfires (as was true in Etosha Park), thus retarding the natural mechanism that caused much of the Kalahari to reseed itself. Without fire to control it, thornbush flourished, bringing about an environmental change not only in the plants but also in what remained of the fauna. The life of the Old Way became almost impossible, certainly in the vicinity of Tsumkwe. Among the new developments at Tsumkwe were a police station and a jail, where any Bushman caught hunting or setting a brushfire was imprisoned.

Meanwhile, along the newly constructed road, a burgeoning bureaucracy of other government personnel was arriving to build suburban-style bungalows and develop jobs for themselves by regulating the Bushmen. The Bushmen were required to live in a distant, government-built "village," a cluster of tiny concrete huts the size and shape of closets among which a broken tap dripped water dismally and flies bred maggots in an overworked latrine. All South

African and South West African towns and cities had similar arrangements for the nonwhite populations—these areas were called "locations." Tsumkwe had become a South West African town, so it, too, needed to have a "location." The sedentary, unsanitary, overcrowded conditions of course brought disease, and the people began to get all manner of sicknesses to which they had no immunities, including TB, malaria, bilharzia, venereal diseases, and later, of course, AIDS. Fortunately, the traditions of early marriage and marital fidelity have significantly curbed the spread of AIDS in the Ju/wa population.

Also along the road came all manner of ideologues, seeing the supposedly virgin minds of the Bushmen as newly discovered blank slates ready to receive a variety of dogmas, ranging from fundamentalist Christian creationism to radical Marxist feminism propounded by two white women. None of the ideologues spoke !Kung, nor did they respect Ju/wa culture. These failures were to their disadvantage, as most of their teachings missed the mark. Nowhere was this seen more clearly than in some of the Bible stories, such as, for instance, the story about the woman in the well (John 4:1–32).[2] The woman should have avoided Jesus, according to the Bushmen. Obviously, she was alone and, as the story makes clear, when Jesus asked her where her husband was, he already knew she didn't have one. And why did he tell her to bring him water? He was perfectly capable of getting it himself. Instead, he just sat there, painting himself in glowing colors, telling her how important he was, even admitting that he was supernatural. He might as well have come right out and said, "I'm a sorcerer." A man such as that might *jum* and turn into a lion. What kind of people were the missionaries, to see this as positive?

The missionaries didn't seem to know what had happened to their stories, and the Marxist feminists did no better. The Ju/wa women didn't want to rise up against their men. With the loss of the Old Way, most of the food they had was provided by the men. And were their children to have no fathers? And why would anyone want to cut herself off from her husband's people? To whom could she turn in her hour of need? Who could find merit in the harangue of these two adamant white women?

The ideologues of Tsumkwe must have seemed to be a knot of powerful but unpleasant whites who quarreled and undermined one another. For instance, missionaries from one Protestant denomination directed their energies to reconverting a group of Bushmen who earlier had converted to a rival denomination.[3]

The only philosophy that could be said to have taken hold well was that of Western capitalism and the introduction of a money economy. The people were literally starving, and with the bush foods diminishing, they needed money and jobs. At first, roadwork and other menial labor provided most of the jobs, but all this changed in 1978 when the South African Defense Force established a post in Tsumkwe and began to recruit Bushmen as soldiers to combat the guerrilla army of the South West Africa People's Organization, or SWAPO, which then was in Angola but was raiding white settlements across the border. One of the first South African organizations to mitigate racial discrimination, the South African Defense Force paid all soldiers equally regardless of race and, tempted by the high wages (R.600 per month, or about $690),[4] many young Ju/wa men enlisted. Others heard of the money their soldier relatives were earning. The population of Tsumkwe increased to one thousand, and without an adequate supply of wild foods, virtually everyone became dependent on the wages and food rations supplied to the working men.

The anthropologist and filmmaker Claire Ritchie, who participated in extensive studies of the transition from the Old Way to the new, points out that with all these developments, the economic aspect of the culture reversed itself. Formerly, all the adults had produced food for the community, sharing with one another, supporting the young and the old. In the past, women had provided about 80 percent of the food. But by 1980 at Tsumkwe, only the few men who had jobs were able to acquire food, either because they were paid in food or because they bought it. Their unemployed relatives depended on them, but there wasn't enough for all. Claire Ritchie and my brother made a survey of the diet of the people of Tsumkwe and found that on many days, many people ate nothing, meanwhile suspecting that somewhere, some of their equally desperate relatives were eating but not sharing. Jealousy and anger, those destructive emotions that once the people had suppressed with such dedication, flamed into life and infected everybody.

Still, there was money to be made in Tsumkwe, either via the

army or via the government. With help from the latter, an Ambo en-
trepreneur set up a store that sold hard liquor in addition to some of
the other items that the government people needed, such as canned
food and gasoline. Ritchie found that after one army payday in October 1982, the storekeeper in just half an hour took in R.715 ($822)
from the sale of liquor, most of it bought by Bushman soldiers. After
every payday, terrible fights broke out, men against men, men against
women, resulting in many tragic deaths. Short /Kwi was killed at this
time, knifed in the stomach by his intoxicated son-in-law. Di!ai's two
sons were also killed. Ritchie tells of a dead-drunk woman who
rolled over on her baby and suffocated it, for which the baby's father,
also drunk, blamed the baby's grandmother, beat her to the ground,
and stomped on her head with his heavy boots, breaking her skull
and injuring her brain. She was taken to a hospital in a coma, from
which she never awoke. She died six months later.

Especially on paydays, attendance at the clinic was swelled by
the injured, including those with self-inflicted poison arrow wounds,
the would-be suicides. The survey of the population made by Ritchie
and Marshall found that the death rate was rapidly exceeding the
birth rate. Di!ai's daughter, N!ai, composed a song about Tsumkwe.

> *Now people mock me and I cry.*
> *My people abuse me.*
> *The white people scorn me.*
> *Death dances with me.*

Death was indeed dancing with these people. Ritchie wrote: "If
the sounds that characterized life with the Ju/wasi in the 1950s were
the clapping and chanting of the great curing dances, or the gentle,
almost inaudible music of the mouth bow, today they are angry
shouts and blows, and a woman wailing endlessly in the bush."

19

Return

Throughout the 1960s, my parents continued their work in Nyae Nyae, returning home between visits, until the end of the decade, at which time my father was eighty and my mother seventy. I did not continue with them after 1955 because I was married and off on other projects. However, my brother, John, became a considerable presence in that country. He belonged among the Ju/wasi of Nyae Nyae, particularly among the people of /Gautscha, and he spoke !Kung fluently if with an American accent. His mentor and best friend was ≠Toma, who had given him his name, so that he was also ≠Toma, nicknamed ≠Toma Longface. When he was in his early twenties, he fell in love with and married a Ju/wa woman. Although they both married other people later, they remained friends for life, and although they had no children together, their relationship placed him forever in the social fabric, giving him obligations that he willingly accepted. In ways, he was less like an expatriate who had come to help the Ju/wasi and more like one of the people themselves, albeit with a vehicle, with English and Afrikaans in addition to the language of the Ju/wasi, and with the knowledge one needs to move through the Western world with all its politics and complications.

In later years, he was accused by officials of the new, independent government of Namibia, and by expatriates and other non-Bushmen who wanted to help the Bushmen, of favoring the people of Nyae Nyae beyond all others and of creating "Fortress Nyae Nyae," wanting to help people there rather than helping all equally needy people. All I can say about this accusation, which in some ways is true, is that he was tied to those people in a way that other non-Bushmen were not, and he could not imagine not helping them.

Early on, his blatant disregard for the apartheid government earned him such notoriety that the police became concerned. Perhaps they heard that he was involved with a nonwhite woman (which was then against the law), or perhaps they got wind of the fact that together with ≠Toma he was trying to persuade people to leave the hellhole of Tsumkwe and return to their *n!oresi*. Mainly, however, he was trying to implement a plan to help Ju/wa families start new lives as subsistence farmers, not with goats this time but with cattle, and not with large herds like those of the Bantu pastoralists that would overgraze the fragile countryside but with small herds to provide meat, clabbered milk, and some money from the sale of meat and hides. (Clabbered milk, also called thick milk, is curdled and considered more digestible than fresh milk. It is used by people unaccustomed to dairy products who might have milk intolerance.) John also was making films about the current situation of the Nyae Nyae Ju/wasi, as he had done when they lived in the Old Way. Some of the film he took at that time later became part of *A Kalahari Family*, featured at the Margaret Mead Film Festival.

None of this was particularly pleasing to officials of the former apartheid government. Probably what caused them most concern, however, was that his color-blind, anti-apartheid stance was so conspicuous. One evening, for example, he and some Ju/wa men had been driving from Windhoek back to Tsumkwe, and at the end of the day when all were hungry, he invited the men to be his guests at a bar-restaurant in a small town. Apartheid protocol prevailed in the Boer population of the countryside, holding that the white man should eat in the restaurant and send the Bushmen to the alley behind the kitchen for a bowl of cornmeal porridge.

But John had a way of ignoring views he didn't share. Together with the Ju/wa men, who were not fully aware of the impending problems, he went into the restaurant and sat down. The owner of the establishment, a white man, didn't quite know what to make of his Bushman guests, who possibly were the first nonwhite people ever to sit down at one of his tables. Even so, he was preparing to serve them when two husky Boer farmers who were drinking at the bar made loud, aggressive remarks. One of them got up and went out to get his horse, which he brought into the restaurant, saying that if Bushmen could eat there, so could his horse.

Matters quickly degenerated into a brawl between John and the owner of the horse, from which John—a big, strong guy and no stranger to this kind of barroom difficulty—emerged a clear winner. The proprietor persuaded the other farmer to remove his defeated companion and the horse, and then served dinner to John and his party. John compensated the proprietor for damage resulting from the fighting, and he and the Ju/wa men, who had sat transfixed through the brawl and were much impressed by all of this, departed into the night.

Given instances such as this and others like it, the government decided to deport John. At first the police couldn't find him. They put Wanted posters with his picture on them in the post office and on trees. This yielded nothing, so they eventually traveled four hundred miles to look for him in Nyae Nyae. There they found him and told him that his visa was invalid. He was deported, and not allowed back for many years. A legend arose about his return. It is said that upon arriving at the Windhoek airport, John was asked by the immigration official for his visa. He pulled out a Wanted poster and put it on the desk. "This is my visa," he told the official. Legend or not, by then he was himself a legend. According to the story, the official looked at the poster, looked at John, realized who he was, and welcomed him into Namibia without asking to see his passport.

After his return, he and a group of Ju/wa men formed the Ju/wa Farmers' Union, a self-help organization composed mainly of Bushmen from Nyae Nyae, with the aim of assisting all those who wanted to keep small herds of cattle (usually fewer than twenty head, thus small enough not to cause overgrazing) and to plant gardens, not only for the purpose of laying claim to their own lands but also to feed themselves and their families. Some members of these families would tend the livestock and the gardens, while others would get jobs, if possible, to provide income. For as long as the wild foods remained available, the people could gather these, too. The farming villages would be more or less permanent, with water obtained from boreholes with windmills or gas-powered pumps. In many ways, the farming communities resembled the communities of old, with traditional owners living at their *n!oresi*, respecting their traditional values of equality and sharing, but with a new method of food production.

John paid for much of this with his own money, and with a starter fund of $30,000 established by our parents to which I later contributed $10,000. Over time, the Ju/wa Farmers' Union received more substantial grants from international charities. The money was used to buy cattle, drill wells, and set up windmills to pump water.

Opinions about my brother were divided, often along racial lines. Some people didn't like him. Others did. I learned how people felt when I returned to Namibia, which I had not been able to do until 1986. My reason for going had to do with a zoological research project in Etosha that I had been privileged to join, but when the project ended, I took a side trip to visit the Ju/wasi. I had no reason to discuss my plans, so hardly anyone knew where I was going. Yet somehow, word of my journey spread like wildfire. At a restaurant where I stopped for a meal, for instance, the entire kitchen staff dropped everything and came into the dining room to greet and applaud me. I didn't know any of them and don't know how they knew who I was. At all kinds of villages along the way, large multiethnic crowds would gather to welcome me with smiles and cheers and even singing. I had done nothing to merit such attention except to be John Marshall's sister, so the experience was something like that of a queen who has never done anything especially useful and owes her eminence to an accident of birth.

When he died in 2005, he was in the process of editing *A Kalahari Family* for presentation on PBS so that its message could be distributed more widely. With the last of his strength he was trying to help his adopted people, as he had done for the fifty-five years that he had known them. No wonder that he was loved and respected.

My journey brought me to the outskirts of Tsumkwe. I was alone in a pickup truck, which I had been driving nonstop for many hours, and when I came to the section of road near the towering black baobab tree, I wondered if perhaps I had been the person who pioneered the road. On the day we first went to Tsumkwe from /Gautscha, I had been driving the lead vehicle.

I then remembered an episode that had occurred many years earlier, when I had witnessed the creation of a path. An encampment of people was on the move, traveling west through dry grass. No path lay ahead for them to follow, but because they were walking in single file, a path was appearing behind them. Almost everything likes a path, and later, large and small animals began to use this one. Soon enough, the path became established, and when the people returned a few months later, they also used it. That happens with vehicle tracks, too, of course, as it is much easier to follow a track than to crash through bushes. Why would someone make another track when he or she could follow my track? I felt sure I had pioneered this section of the road.

Under the tree was a large bungalow—the home, I later learned, of the top-ranking official of the area, the commissioner. Nearby was an outdoor tap that took its water from the well that had been hand-dug by my father. Because I was very thirsty, when I saw the tap I stopped and got my tin cup to get a drink.

But I was immediately chased away by a German houseguest of the commissioner, who came bustling out the front door to tell me to stay back, that the tap was private. Surprised, I said I only wanted a cupful and asked if he really meant I couldn't have it. That was indeed what he meant, he said, as the water belonged to the commissioner. I didn't tell him that I had probably laid down the track that now seemed to be the commissioner's driveway, or that I was the daughter of the man who had dug the commissioner's well. I decided to be thirsty.

Beyond the baobab tree, I passed rows of suburban-type bungalows surrounded by lawns and shrubbery. These were the quarters of the police and government officials, the missionaries, the medical people, and the business owners who had settled at Tsumkwe in the intervening years. Near these rows of houses was the small store with its gas pump. My truck needed gas, but the store (possibly with a cold can of diet soda for sale in its refrigerator) was closed, as were all offices and buildings during the lengthy siesta period. I parked beside the gas pump and sat down to wait on the shady side of my truck.

. . . .

There I waited, and I waited. From time to time, small groups of Ju/wasi would walk by. Most were barefoot, but the men wore shorts or trousers and most of the women wore tattered knee-length dresses. Even so, the women also wore tattered shawls or leather capes in which rode their babies—a residue of the Old Way. I didn't know any of these people, but each of them looked carefully into my face to see who I was, and even though they didn't recognize me, they smiled warmly anyway, greeting me kindly. Then came two young white women. They noticed my truck. In this small community, everybody would have known everybody else and also every vehicle, and my truck wasn't familiar to them. Then suddenly they noticed me. They almost startled. *Whoa! What have we here?* They didn't speak but watched me suspiciously out of the corners of their eyes as they circled the truck, keeping some distance from the white stranger with gray hair, all alone, wearing bush clothes and covered with the dust of several hundred miles of backcountry travel. After the two young women had passed, they glanced back over their shoulders. I was still looking in their direction. One of them gave a perfunctory nod. They kept going, showing none of the innate courtesy of the Ju/wasi.

At long last, the Ambo storekeeper returned from his siesta and opened the store. I bought a bottle of Fanta, drank it, and returned the bottle. The storekeeper politely invited me to fill my canteen with water from the tap in his sink, then went outside to fill my gas tank. I wanted to fill my spare gas can, too, and when I brought it around to the sunny side of the truck, I saw more of the white quarters of Tsumkwe with their gardens and green lawns and sprinklers. Bushman labor explained the landscaping, of course. Far away in the distance, past several properties, a Ju/wa man was raking a lawn. He happened to glance up, and he noticed me.

Then he stopped raking and seemed to look at me more closely. I wondered why. He dropped the rake and started toward me, not as I might have done, by following the driveway to the street and following the street around the corner, but by coming straight at me, cutting across the lawns and gardens of the houses in between us. These features of Western culture meant less to him, evidently, than they did to the white residents of Tsumkwe.

Soon he was standing in front of me. Smiling broadly, he looked me straight in the eyes and said, "You're Di!ai."

. . . .

My god. I *was* Di!ai. No one had called me by that name for more than thirty years, and I must have stared at him, astonished. "Yes," I said. But who was he? He saw that I didn't recognize him and he told me his name, /Gai. But many people are named /Gai, and I still couldn't place him. Apologetically, I asked the names of his mother and father, and the name of the place where they had lived, his *n!ore*. He told me.

So that's who he was! And finally the full force of this moment struck me, because the last time /Gai and I saw each other, he was a baby. How could he remember me? How could he possibly recognize me, thirty years older, thirty years later, covered with dust, and at such a distance? /Gai had seen my brother more recently, of course, and I have been told that I look like my brother, but actually we merely shared a family resemblance, and no Western person would ever have made the connection, certainly not from so far away. Many people would not have recognized us as siblings even if we were standing together. But that's the Ju/wasi for you, with their formidable powers of observation and memory.

I laughed. I cried. I laughed and cried. /Gai gently asked where I was going. I said I was going to /Gautscha. He said he'd go with me. I was delighted and offered to wait for him to finish his work or get the rake. No need, he said. He was ready. So I paid the kind store-keeper, who had been watching all this, smiling, and we got in the truck and drove away, and traveled together to /Gautscha, where cattle had eaten most of the grass and people had cut down the trees for firewood. The people were living in huts made of tin, scraps of wood, and sheets of cardboard, with a thornbush enclosure as a pen for their cattle, five or six skeletal dogs, and a wind-powered pump to provide them with water.

On that trip I found ≠Toma, by then an old man, also his wife, !U, and her sister, Di!ai, for whom I was named. I found Tsamko and /Guyshe, ≠Toma's sons, also his daughter, Norna, named for my mother, also their younger son, born after I left during the 1950s but well-known to my parents and brother, also Lame ≠Gao, by then married with children, also N!ai and /Gunda, also //Kushe and Lazy /Kwi, the people who brought us from /Gam to /Gautscha. Their boy had been killed in a drunken fight. They had no living children.

Many other people were also gone, including my father, who had died in 1980. So for a while we spoke about those who were no longer living, but although this saddened us all, we nevertheless rejoiced to see one another. !U took my face between her hands and smiled forcefully right at me so that I wouldn't miss her meaning. She also gave me the bead necklace mentioned earlier, the necklace that I will give to my granddaughter. I had brought gifts for everyone. To receive the necklace and to give the gifts made me think of the Old Way, and of the gifts that joined the people, as if I, too, were joined in some measure.

20

The Present

If you happen to see a contemporary film or photo showing Bushmen dressed in skins, perhaps beside a small grass shelter or following a line of antelope footprints or handling a bow and arrow, you are seeing a reenactment. Today, nobody lives in the Old Way. All Bushmen, unless they put on skins for a photographer, wear the clothing of the dominant cultures—invariably Western dress for men, and Western or African dress for women—and none live by hunting and gathering, although with these activities they sometimes supplement their meager diet, which today is often cornmeal provided by the Namibian government as a welfare ration. They have jobs if they can get them, although many cannot; they listen to popular music on the radio, dance the popular dances, are influenced to some degree by Christianity, and are aware of the larger world and national politics.

The great interior of the Kalahari that we visited in the 1950s has been subdivided. Twenty-five thousand square miles of the former Bushmanland was reallocated, some made into a game park and the rest assigned to Bantu pastoralists. The resident Bushmen were removed from the game parks and have no rights of tenure in the Bantu lands, from which they can be evicted at the Bantu people's pleasure. /Gam, the waterhole where we first found Lazy /Kwi and //Kushe, along with hundreds of square miles of surrounding land, was given to the Herero people on the basis that two Hereros lived there. Numerous Bushmen lived there, too, of course, but their presence was not counted. Perhaps one of the Herero people was Kavesitjue, that kindly, sensitive, pioneering woman whom we met when we first came to /Gam. Perhaps the other was her son. Today, /Gam is a substantial community with a sizable Herero population.

Only the small area squeezed between the nineteenth and twentieth parallels remains to the Ju/wasi we knew. Of the fourteen waterholes of the former Nyae Nyae, only five are within the area, which is now known as the Nyae Nyae Conservancy. But, thanks largely to my brother, the Ju/wa residents of the conservancy are the only group of Bushmen in Namibia who have any land at all. The rest live on white people's farms as farmworkers or on the outskirts of pastoralist villages without rights of tenure. In Namibia, as in all southern African countries, the Bushmen are the poorest ethnic group by far, with the greatest unemployment. The Namibian government does what its apartheid predecessor did not do—under circumstances based on rainfall in certain parts of the country, it feeds its poor with welfare rations of cornmeal, fish, and oil. However, many Bushmen live in remote areas where the welfare delivery comes at three-month intervals, or does not come at all.

Many of the Ju/wasi live at Tsumkwe, where several ministries of the Namibian government are represented—the Ministries of Water, Rural Development, and Agriculture, for example—and where there are churches, a police post, a clinic, and a school. A number of Ju/wasi have jobs in Tsumkwe—some people I know have government jobs as policemen, drivers, and health workers, for example—and some of these people live in bungalows built for government workers. But there are not enough jobs for everyone by any means, so many other people live in a sprawling shantytown that has sprung up around the outskirts. Most of these people are the unemployed relatives of the people with the jobs or of the elderly people with pensions. The government of Namibia allocates about $80 per month to each of its elderly citizens, and because the Ju/wasi share their slim resources, this is a very important source of income for many Ju/wa families.

The anthropologist Polly Wiessner, who has been conducting studies in Nyae Nyae and its surroundings since the 1970s, writes this of Tsumkwe: "While Conservancy land is restricted to Ju/'hoan [Ju/wa] occupation, land within a five kilometer radius of Tjum!kui [Tsumkwe] is open to all Namibians. Drawn by a good school, government services, and the substantial cash flow into Ju/'hoan population, numerous entrepreneurs from other parts of Namibia move to Tjum!kui. There they open small businesses, mostly drinking establishments, to attract Ju/'hoan customers. On paydays, Tjum!kui becomes a throbbing disco converting cash that has not been spent on food or goods to alcohol. Ju/'hoansi drink for a variety of reasons: for entertainment, out of boredom or frustration over unemployment, to relieve social tension, or to get some pleasure from their work before unrelenting relatives relieve them of the rest of their income. Up to a third of Ju/'hoan income is spent on alcohol."[1]

Most of the Ju/wasi who do not live around Tsumkwe live in communities throughout the conservancy, many on the sites of the old encampments, but now no longer in the small grass shelters. People build with whatever materials they can get, such as pieces of wood, sheets of corrugated metal, plywood, or cardboard, and even cloth. People also make dwellings of poles with grass thatches such as are found in traditional Bantu villages. The communities are more or less permanent, and most of them are or were farms.

This has not been easy for the Ju/wasi. Farming in Nyae Nyae has many problems, not the least of which is the low, seasonal rainfall, about fifteen inches a year. However, the Ju/wa farms are modest in concept, with small herds of livestock, mostly cattle, and small gardens, and originally were intended to provide part of the subsistence of a family community, with some of its members tending the farm, others producing craft objects for sale to tourists or to stores in Windhoek, others getting jobs if possible, still others continuing to hunt or gather wild plants, and the children attending school to acquire the education that would help the family in the future. When I visited in the 1980s, the South African Defense Force was still at Tsumkwe and would send an army truck around to the communities to pick up the schoolchildren and deliver them to a boarding school. On Fridays, the truck would bring them home for the weekend. Not all children went to school, and many dropped out after the first few grades, but a few finished high school and then, as adults, were able to get jobs.

Over time, however, problems began to arise. Hunting and gathering, the fallback of the farmers, became increasingly difficult. A sedentary life is not compatible with gathering, as any area produces only a certain amount of wild foods, and under continued pressure these get used up. The small animals that were slow game were under the same pressures as the plant communities, and big-game hunting, while still possible in theory, had in the past produced only about 20 percent of the food. There were other problems with big-game hunting. On their own conservancy, the Ju/wa men were permitted to hunt only with bow and arrow. But the men with the skills to bow hunt were aging, and many of the younger men did not want to be bound by Stone Age technology. They hunted with rifles if they had them, or on horseback with spears and dogs if they didn't. The latter method was only too easy—the antelopes were afraid of people on foot but were not afraid of horses. A man on horseback could ride right up to an antelope and jab it with a spear. The method was illegal but, because many people did not know this, it was practiced anyway, and combined with the commercial biltong hunting, mentioned earlier, had taken a serious toll of the antelope population.

By the 1990s, the supplemental ways of getting food were seriously diminished, and jobs and farming were increasingly important. Some of the men of the farming families sought other sources of income and walked the eighty or ninety miles to the farms of the whites to look for work. Others worked in a Namibian mine at the edge of the Kalahari. Meanwhile, the people at the farms struggled on. The biggest problem of the farmers was, of course, water.

When the farms were established, a number of donor organizations had contributed money to drill boreholes and equip these with pumps or windmills. Even the farms at permanent waterholes such as /Gaustsha needed pumps and boreholes. To keep these maintained was a constant problem that was exacerbated hugely by refugee elephants who, during the last twenty years or so, have gathered in Nyae Nyae, driven from their original homes by poaching, culling, and loss of habitat resulting in an overcrowded population. Today, perhaps one thousand elephants live in Nyae Nyae where none had lived before. All but the infants are immigrants, and all are a terrible problem to the people. The elephants need plenty of food,

. . . .

so they raid the farmers' gardens and visit the few remaining mangetti and marula groves, vacuuming up the nuts that once sustained the Ju/wasi. But even more important, they destroy the farmers' sources of water. An adult elephant needs about forty gallons of water a day, meaning that every day, the one thousand elephants of Nyae Nyae need forty thousand gallons. Surely none of the natural waterholes of Nyae Nyae produce that amount of water. In their thirst, the elephants smell the water in the farmers' boreholes and, trying to reach it, push down the windmills and pull out the pumps and all their wiring. The farmers try to build barriers against the elephants, but with one exception that I know of, when a group of three or four men hand-dug a moat forty feet wide, ten or twelve feet deep, and perhaps two hundred feet in diameter around their well—a moat that in the end did not successfully keep out the elephants—a barrier must be made of rocks that could require a crane to lift and a vehicle to carry. Or a barrier can be made of large concrete slabs.

But all this costs money, and the Ju/wa farmers had none. Help from the government departments of agriculture or rural development came slowly and in small quantities, as Namibia is not a wealthy nation, and help from the donor agencies was rapidly diminishing.

When a farmer lost his source of water, his people might be able to lower a tin can through the pipe in the narrow borehole (at least one community managed to do this, tying a long string to a can, putting a stone in it, and lowering it slowly down a pipe for more than fifty feet), but they couldn't water their garden or their cattle by this method. Without the pump or windmill, the garden would wither and the cattle would die. The community would have little choice but to sell their cattle for what they could get and resort to the inadequate supply of wild foods, or try to obtain a welfare ration. Some members of some of these communities had faraway jobs and, thanks to the Ju/wa system of sharing, would contribute store-bought foods when they could bring them. But too often the community went hungry. Polly Wiessner spoke with an old man who told her, "In the past, we could always pick up and move when there was no food or water. Today we just sit and go hungry."[2]

He was speaking of the long-ago days when a group would leave its encampment and go to relatives or *xaro* partners who lived at a distance and would share the food supply of the area. In fact, the people of the farming communities that lost their water to elephant damage often did pick up and move, but they went to Tsumkwe, where almost everyone had relatives, where violence and alcohol were everywhere, where they could be robbed or killed by human marauders, where their daughters exposed themselves to AIDS by whoring for Bantu men to get money for alcohol. But the families had no choice. They had to go where they had relatives who would help them and where they could find welfare food and water.

How did this happen? Where were the organizations that in the past had invested so much money into the development of the farms, drilling wells, equipping them with windmills and even with solar pumps, buying cattle, securing veterinary services?

My brother called the problem "death by myth." "Death by Myth" is the title of the final section of his film *A Kalahari Family*. The myth is that the Bushmen are hunter-gatherers, not farmers, even after thirty years of transition, even after the establishment of permanent farming communities, even after the traditional options for survival have disappeared. The myth is that they can resume their former life. If the myth were fact, the best choice—some would say the only choice—of the Ju/wa people would be to return to their former lifestyle. The failure of the farms was cited as proving the point.

My brother's film suggests that the myth is inherent in our thinking about Bushmen and has shaped the plans of the nongovernment organizations that became involved with the Bushmen. Only by embracing the myth could these organizations have reached their damaging conclusions. Polly Wiessner, who has studied the food supply over time and in detail, has copious data that refutes the myth. She documents the loss of important wild foods and shows the factors that rendered the people unable to travel to new sources of supply, the lifeline of the Old Way. In 1996, she found in the Xamsa community, for instance, that people were getting more than 70 percent of their food from stores or government welfare rations,[3] the reason for this being that they could obtain very few calories per hour of gathering. By spending calories on gathering forays, the gatherers were losing more energy than they gained. In the Old Way, this means starvation. Of course people ate store-bought food if they could get it and government rations when available. This is very far from anything resembling hunting and gathering.

My brother's film begins with footage he shot in the 1950s showing the Ju/wasi hunting and gathering. It goes on to show the development of Tsumkwe, the arrival of the South African Defense Force, the development of farming, and the many conferences held by the Ju/wasi among themselves and with potential donors to determine their future. The film shows the Namibian Independence celebrations and the Ju/wa involvement with the new government. Throughout these sections, the film chronicles the continued progress of the farms. Finally, it shows the beginnings of the conservancy and what appears to be a takeover by nongovernment organizations.

John made the film to alert the world to the desperate situation of the people he knew so well, the people who had taken him in as one of them, the people who over a lifetime had helped him, and who looked to him to help them. His film is devastating, and for this it will continue to be criticized. But its object was not to show all points of view or to present all aspects of a situation. The film has its own bitter story.

As its final section, "Death by Myth," begins, my brother interviews a nice Italian tourist who has come to the Kalahari to see Bushmen. He asks her what she thinks the Bushmen need. Gesturing toward a clump of bushes, she says they need food. My brother prods her a bit, and she adds that they also need water. Her gesture and words exemplify the myth. The Bushmen take their living from the savannah.

Meanwhile, the establishment of the conservancy is in process. Two groups provide the leadership, the Ju/wa Farmers' Cooperative, better known as the Farmers' Co-op, and the Nyae Nyae Development Foundation of Namibia, better known as the Foundation. The former has derived from the self-help organization formed by the Ju/wasi when the farms were getting started. The latter has derived from a fund-raising organization consisting mainly of expatriates and other non-Bushmen that was formed to partner with the farmers. As most Ju/wasi lacked the education to deal effectively with the outside world, the conservancy has hired an expatriate manager. In concept, the conservancy will provide for all Ju/wasi who are its registered members. They will receive shares of the income that the conservancy will generate. Income is expected from tourism, from trophy hunting, from filmmakers who will use the landscape as a location, and from the sale of plant products such as mangetti and marula nuts as well as devil's claw, an herbal palliative for arthritis. The people can gather and sell these plant products themselves, or they can, via the management, lease the gathering rights to commercial enterprises.

We learn that a contract has been signed by World Wildlife, LIFE (Living in a Finite Environment) in connection with USAID, and the government of Namibia. We learn that USAID has allocated sixteen million Namibian dollars for various Namibian projects, one of which is to be the conservancy. We learn that the conservancy will become a wildlife preserve or a wildlife management area. This will not be very compatible with farming. LIFE had substantially helped the Ju/wa farmers in the past, but in the new scenario, according to the film, no further money will be allocated for farming.

The film shows a report for 1992–93 supplied to the conservancy stating that 80 percent of the Bushman diet consists of bush foods obtained by gathering. In the film, my brother interviews a Ju/wa farmer who calls the report a lie. "No Ju/wa person tells lies like this," says the farmer. He had a point. Bush foods were 80 percent of the diet in the distant past, as was determined in the 1970s by anthropologists, but not in 1992–93. Polly Wiessner's research of 1996 suggests that the food situation would have been just the opposite, that only 27 percent of the Ju/wa diet was obtained by gathering *and* hunting, which means that even less than this was obtained by gathering alone. In Xamsa village in 1996, she found, "19% of subsistence income in calories was obtained from hunting, 9% from gathering, 1% from gardening, 34% from store bought foods . . . and 37% from government rations."[4] This, of course, is far from the traditional lifestyle.

We see the conservancy headquarters at a place called Baraka. We see new buildings, a fleet of sparkling new white vehicles, and the expatriate German manager of the conservancy whom one of the Ju/wa farmers calls "the big chief." The film captures him telling the farmers in English via an interpreter that the land is not actually theirs, and their *n!oresi* do not matter, because the land belongs to the government. He seems impatient. He tells the farmers, "You are always holding up your noses and talking about your 'nores.' This is communal land. It is not your land." He is partly right, of course, as the government retains control over it. He then describes the life that the Ju/wasi are to live on their communal land, saying that they will be watching over the wildlife. They will be "taking game out, selling the game, even letting tourists come to pay to see the game." He says that the Ju/wasi might get money from America to buy more game and drill boreholes for wild animals. But unless the land becomes a wildlife area, he says, the people will not be able to exclude the pastoralists.

My brother disagrees. The film cuts to an interview with Namibia's president, Samuel Nujoma, who says that in most of Namibia, people can live wherever they like, but in certain areas, namely the conservancies, outsiders can come in only with permission from the owners. My brother, who narrates some of the film, says this means that, contrary to what the manager has said, the Bushmen can exclude the pastoralists. In the past, the police had often driven Herero cattle out of Nyae Nyae. My brother asks, rhetorically, that if the Bushmen did not have the right to exclude Herero cattle, why did the police help them do it?

In the film, the manager praises hunting and gathering. "If we want to maintain the culture," he says, "we must get the young people to learn it again." He suggests that experienced hunters be brought in to teach their stalking and tracking skills to the Ju/wa schoolchildren. He would not be saying this, of course, if the old lifestyle still existed. But it has gone, and it will be up to the children to renew or re-create it. The contract between the donor organizations and the Namibian government determined that Nyae Nyae is a wildlife management area. Because wildlife management is antithetical to farming, the Ju/wa boys should know how to hunt in the traditional manner, as this will be their future.

A meeting is held at conservancy headquarters and is attended by a young expatriate representing World Wildlife. He praises Nyae Nyae, saying that he likes what he finds there because, he says, the Ju/wasi live "in harmony with nature." Whatever that means, it can apply only to the past, because, as the young man adds, during his visit he has seen no wild animals. He is right. In the forty-odd years that have passed since the Ju/wasi lived in their traditional manner, the animal population has been in decline except for elephants—yet another reason that the Ju/wasi want support for their farming.

The film shows a safari lodge near the border of Nyae Nyae. The safari company holds a concession for which it pays the conservancy. The film shows a few overweight white tourists with tote bags trudging away from the camera. They have come to see wildlife and also "traditional" Bushmen. Ju/wasi are employed to perform trance dances and take people on nature walks or demonstrate tracking, but to do this, they may be required to wear skins in order to appear authentic. Some Ju/wa men are willing to wear skins, although most would rather not. Most women won't wear skins, as traditional attire leaves their breasts bare. But the tourists would not be present if not for the wildlife and perhaps also the famous Bushmen.

The film shows scenes of a South African film company at work making *The Gods Must Be Crazy*. Ju/wa actors dressed in skins repeat the same scene over and over as the cameras whirr. *The Gods Must Be Crazy* was shot in Nyae Nyae long before the formation of the conservancy. Its producers paid some of the Ju/wa actors but did not pay to use the location, as they would have been required to do later (when, as Megan Biesele put it, "the film-makers learned that the 'harmless people' were no longer going to work *gratis*"). In this case, a film that made a fortune for the producers by trading on the myth of the hunter-gatherer did not benefit the Ju/wasi but strongly intensified the myth in the eyes of the international public.

A plan is made to restore the wildlife. A report shows that two million dollars have been allocated for the purpose of importing wildlife. The conservancy imports one thousand assorted antelopes and also new lions. The film doesn't show this, but the imported antelopes have ear tags to mark them as off-limits to Bushman hunters. Any Bushman caught hunting them can go to jail. The imported animals include roan antelopes and a herd of specially bred, disease-free African buffalo, although these water-dependent animals have not been indigenous to Nyae Nyae, or not for a very long time. They will not find enough water without plenty of help, so new water points are established to supply them. The film shows a white schoolteacher showing Bushman children a picture of a buffalo and asking if they have ever seen one. The children don't respond.

The film shows many elephants near the windmill of a Ju/wa farm. They have come to push down the windmill, which they will do after dark. The film shows pumps that have been pulled out of the wells by elephants who have bent the pipes and torn the wiring. The film shows a bleeding, dying elephant about thirty years old who is lying on her side in the torn-up bush. A white trophy hunter stands beside her.

The film shows an assembly of people at Baraka, where a representative of LIFE will ask ten or fifteen Ju/wasi to decide which sources of income the conservancy should encourage. The LIFE representative lays on the floor a large sheet of paper with drawings of a camera (for filmmaking), a tourist (for tourism), an animal (for trophy hunting), and a building (for conservancy headquarters). There is no drawing of a farm. The Ju/wasi are supposed to put beans on the pictures of the items they favor. They cannot, of course, fully grasp the choices—they have no idea, for instance, of the vagaries of international tourism—but they squat on the floor and put beans on the pictures anyway. Most of the beans fall on the picture of the animal because trophy hunting is earning the most money. Others fall on the picture of the building, because the conservancy employs about five full-time and twenty part-time Ju/wasi.

The film shows a Ju/wa woman being handed a few coins and bills. The money is her share of the earnings from trophy hunting over a two-year period. It is about $10, less than she expected, and she looks down at it grimly. There is little that she can do about it, however. She must rely on higher-ups and outsiders to provide her with a dole. The film shows a Ju/wa man saying, "We want to keep our farms, our cattle, the things we own ourselves. But we are no longer working for ourselves. We are working for the donors."

The film shows my brother talking with a representative of LIFE. He asks her why no help is given to the farmers. She says that the farms are not viable. However, earlier sections of the film have made clear that a number of the Nyae Nyae farms had once been functional, proving that it could be done, and also that the Ju/wasi were learning. At that very moment, a number of farms just outside of Nyae Nyae were fully functional under identical conditions. In addition, one Nyae Nyae farm did splendidly, becoming a model farm with an enviable garden and a healthy herd of cattle. Other

Nyae Nyae farms did almost as well. At /Gautscha in the 1980s and thereafter for a while, the cattle had been in good condition, giving milk and wearing ear tags to show they had been vaccinated. Some of the men who once had been indifferent farmers had become better farmers and were ardent supporters of farming. My brother points all this out to the LIFE representative, saying that earlier, the farms were working. She says she has just recently started her job and doesn't know about the past so cannot comment on it.

The film shows a Ju/wa man saying that the Farmers' Co-op and the Foundation are a waste. "So much money has been spent," he says, "and there is still so much suffering." With donor help, agronomists from dry countries such as Israel and Egypt could be hired to advise the farmers. Instead, biologists have been hired to study bush foods and predators. The film shows a group of wildlife biologists with earphones and an antenna trying to locate a radio-collared leopard. The film shows a Ju/wa farmer commenting on these biologists as they surround a tranquilized leopard. The farmer says that the plan had been to sell the problem predators, but this has not been done. Instead, he says, the predators have been encouraged. This seems to be true. The film shows a lioness who has killed a cow. The lioness hears the photographer and turns her head, eyes round, lips pressed, to stare at the camera.

The film shows a young white cultural expert asking a Ju/wa man through an interpreter how much hunting he expects to do in the future. The Ju/wa man says quietly that he will be watering his garden. The film shows two Ju/wa women picking berries. Very few berries are left on the bush, and those that remain are rotten. The women taste a few and throw the rest on the ground. By this time the viewer has gathered that no Ju/wa person who appears in the film has the slightest interest in the old life.

The film shows the family of a Ju/wa man who works for the conservancy. He is washing his car outside his bungalow, his teenage children are dancing in the driveway to music from a radio, and inside the house his wife is playing solitaire on a computer. This family will not abandon their home and live in a grass shelter. This man is not going to wear skins and go bow hunting. His wife is not going to take a sharp stick and dig for roots. And these parents will not take their children out of school and teach them botany and track-

ing. This family is living as most Namibians live. Other Ju/wasi
would like to do the same. As Polly Wiessner would later write of
A Kalahari Family, "The [film] footage of how people lived for the
past 30 years in and of itself debunks the myth that most Ju/'hoansi
can, or will, resurrect their old ways of life to support them in the future. In my experience, the voices of Ju/'hoan leaders resonate with the
desire to join the mainstream of Namibian rural society."[5]

The film shows a young white woman in the conference room at
Baraka where the white people, donors and others, are having a
meeting. She is idealistic. She hopes that wildlife will be there for the
grandchildren and great-grandchildren of the present generation.
She is expressing the hope of many Western liberals, because wildlife
preservation and cultural preservation are significant elements of
our ideology. No one mentions that it is our idealogy, not that of the
Ju/wasi, that the Ju/wasi will be forced to uphold.

The scene shifts to the Waterberg Nature Reserve in 1994. The reserve
is three hundred miles from Nyae Nyae. There, the management of the
conservancy will meet with the donors. People from LIFE, World
Wildlife, and the government's Department of Nature and Tourism are
present. Many Ju/wa farmers wanted very much to attend the meeting,
too, but they are not present. The film cuts to a group of them back in
Nyae Nyae, worrying about decisions that could be made without their
input. They say they had wanted to attend the meeting but were prevented from taking conservancy vehicles to Waterberg, even though, as
registered residents of the conservancy, they owned the vehicles. Then,
when they asked for rides from the white people, the white people said
that their vehicles were full. Only three Ju/wasi were invited. Outside
the building, one of them tells the camera, "The whites don't want
us here. That's why they came here alone." He adds, "There are only
three Ju/wasi, and very many whites."

My brother, who is on the board of the conservancy Foundation,
is also barred from the meeting. He has "forgotten" to turn off his
camera, which he holds at his side like a briefcase as it captures the
conservancy manager and the people from LIFE telling him he cannot
attend. He points out that he and many of the Ju/wasi have known
one another for a lifetime, and that the meeting might benefit from

his counsel. The whites are unmoved. One of the conservancy higher-ups angrily starts toward him. They want him out. They want him gone. They know, of course, that he will argue for the farmers.

So he goes back outside the building where one of the invited Ju/wa men tells him he fears that the whites will make a game reserve out of Nyae Nyae. Perhaps the whites at the meeting will present the Ju/wasi as hunter-gatherers who want to live on bush foods. No wonder they don't want Ju/wasi present, or my brother. But one young white man, a land-use consultant, is not at all sure that this is what the Ju/wasi want. He has also come outside the building, where he folds his arms, looks at the camera, and says frankly that the Ju/wasi who claim to want bush foods have probably been primed by members of the Foundation.

The film includes several scenes showing that after the meeting at Waterberg, pressure from the farmers becomes so great that, in the face of a near mutiny, the manager of the conservancy leaves his job. We see him turn his back and walk away as a crowd of Ju/wa men watch him. A Zambian is hired to replace him. The Zambian seems even less favorable than the former manager to farming. The Zambian tells the camera that it takes centuries for people to become agriculturalists. Perhaps he is speaking of his own people, whoever they may be, or perhaps he shares a widespread prejudice about the alleged incompetence of Bushmen. But he's right about the centuries—many will pass before there is agriculture in Nyae Nyae unless the farmers get some help. They don't, and the farms continue to disintegrate.

Donor money subsides to a trickle. This is not mentioned in the film, but at the time, there were rumors of mismanagement and corruption. Baraka disintegrates. The film shows that some of the buildings are crowded with people who are probably the extended families of the Ju/wasi who work for the Foundation. These would be family members, in-laws, and perhaps even *xaro* partners who have nothing but know that their relative or partner has a job and therefore money. They have come so that he can help them.

The once-new vehicles no longer sparkle. The highest-ranking Ju/wa employee of the Foundation spends his time assigning vehicles to visiting foreigners. The film shows him pushing a broken-down truck. Hunger remains a serious problem in many villages of Nyae

Nyae, and by the year 2000, fifty years after our first visit, only six people still live at /Gautscha.

In 1992, thirty-five Ju/wa communities were farming. In 1998, the conservancy was established with its focus on hunting and gathering. In 2004, Polly Wiessner conducted a month of demographic studies in the village of Xamsa in Nyae Nyae. "During the period of hunger in 2002," she writes, "Xamsa men went hunting once or twice a week. They awoke in the morning, drank numerous cups of tea thick with sugar, and set out. When unsuccessful, the hunters returned to the village and collapsed. In one case, the men hunted for hours, stalked an animal and cornered it, but when they saw the ear tag, they retreated for fear of arrest."[6]

When she finished her studies and was preparing to leave the village, the people asked her what they would eat when she was gone. She tried to find an answer for them. "I spent the better part of the night," she writes, "pondering over veld foods that yielded a mere 230 kcals per hour, the failed hunting expeditions, the poor market for crafts, few tourists, and no employment opportunities. I could not come up with a single suggestion—there simply was no way for people to help themselves before the rains came."[7]

The death toll of the Ju/wasi has not been measured, nor could it be. How would the number be assessed? Would it include only the people who did not survive an illness because of malnutrition after their farms had disintegrated, after they could not hunt, after there were no bush foods? Or would it also include the people who were forced to move to Tsumkwe and were killed by violence? Lame ≠Gao, the k'xao n!a of /Gautscha and the brother of !U and Di!ai, was killed just recently at Tsumkwe as he was leaving a shebeen or little homemade barroom, where liquor was made and sold. Another man, very drunk, just walked up to him and stabbed him. Lame ≠Gao had moved to Tsumkwe because life at /Gautscha was not possible. Would his death be counted? My brother might have said that myth killed these people.

His film omits a number of things. The Namibian government, for instance, supplies some help to the farmers, although Namibia, of course, has other ethnic groups to consider as well as the Bushmen. The film does not show all the various government and non-government agencies that were and are working in Nyae Nyae and may underplay the job and management training that today are said to be in progress. At the time the film was being made, not much training was going on. Nor does the film consider the conservancy's projection that by 2015, with wildlife management the annual meat allocation from hunting elephants and other game will be forty-one kilograms per capita, and the annual earnings will be four thousand Namibian dollars per registered adult member. Perhaps this projection will come true, but perhaps not. If it does, in the eyes of the donors it will contribute to "cultural survival," which will be good because the Ju/wasi are "proud of their culture." And so they should be. But what constitutes this culture? Is it hunting and gathering? If so, the Ju/wasi should be proud of their ancestors, as they probably are. But can any group be "natural" wildlife managers? It would certainly seem that most Ju/wasi would prefer to be something else, but who can blame the donor organizations for seeing them as "naturals"? These organizations are supported by people such as myself who contribute much of our earnings to wildlife or to the betterment of indigenous populations. Such organizations have no choice but to carry out their missions. No wonder that they wish to save traditional Nyae Nyae, a place where an indigenous population occupied an ecosystem for thirty-five thousand years without ruining it. Who would not want the survival of a lifestyle that could accomplish that?

The myth was that the Ju/wasi wanted it.

We should consider our cultural view of the Ju/wasi. We call them Bushmen because the bush is where we first encountered them. We call them hunter-gatherers because that is how they got their food. We tried to elevate matters a bit by renaming them San, but even though that name was coined by the Khoikhoi, not by Western people, it nevertheless involves the Bushmen's poverty and our desire for rectitude, so this name, too, reflects our culture.

These same people, however, do not define themselves by the shrubbery or how they once ate or by their poverty. Instead, they define themselves by their sense of community. They call themselves the Clear People, the Worthwhile People, the People Who Have Left

Their Weapons Somewhere Else, the Harmless People. *Ju*, as has been said, means "person" and */wa* (also */'hoan*) however hard to interpret, obviously does not refer to landscape, food gathering, or poverty. Instead, it reflects the way the people live together and relate to one another. And that is what really defines the Ju/wasi, not Western notions about the bush, or poverty, or our own moral rectitude, or food production.

Polly Wiessner tells the following story. She had spent a day listening to "rhetoric about cultural preservation," probably among expatriates and other white people at the conservancy headquarters at Baraka. That night in the Ju/wa community where she stays while in Nyae Nyae, while she was sitting with Ju/wa people by one of their little fires, she asked them what they thought was the essence of their culture. They told her "that it was not myth, trance, or hunting with poisoned arrows, but the nature of relationships between people."[8]

Of *A Kalahari Family*, she has this to say: "The camera provides a powerful counterpoint to rosy development projections by documenting the shift from a time when all individuals were 'owners of the future' through their capacity to feed their families to a time when many Ju/'hoansi have become 'owners of asking' for handouts. Figures on subsistence income, social ties, and demographic conditions support Marshall's portrayal of decreasing self-sufficiency, though in comparison to film, these figures are but a pale means of exposition."[9]

Polly owned land in Vermont, which she sold to raise money for wells, water pumps, and elephant barriers, so that people who had lost their farms could return to their communities and resume their self-sufficiency through their continued farming. This way, they would not be the clients of their own conservancy, they would not depend upon the vagaries of international tourism or on the arrival of filmmakers, or on the popularity of trophy hunting. With farming, they would not be on the dole. Polly came to visit my brother as he was dying, and he asked her to continue his work with the farmers. She said she would. Her gift was made in his memory. I, too, hope to contribute to the effort of farming and will give proceeds from this book to two funds, to the Kalahari People's Fund, which is managed by Megan Biesele, and to the Tradition and Transition Fund, which Polly has established.

I learned recently that the family of the people we knew so well, the people of /Gautscha, decided to leave Tsumkwe where they had been living and find a new home. They looked around until they found an empty area, a kind of no-man's-land, within walking distance of Tsumkwe so that those with jobs could walk to work, but far enough away to be free of the problems. They made a small settlement there.

To me, this is a story of cultural survival. It looks very much like a story of the Old Way but without some of the trappings. None of these people hunted or gathered anything to speak of, except perhaps to set a snare for guinea fowl, or keep an eye out for a vine with melons, but their social and family ties remained strong and in keeping with their culture. Over the years they had been spread out over distance, some working for the government, some working for white farmers, some at /Gautscha, some at Baraka, some in Tsumkwe, but they did not forget one another and they did not consider their less fortunate relatives expendable. The Ju/wasi are sometimes criticized for this—no individual can get ahead, it is said, because his hungry, unemployed relatives will swarm all over him and take away his earnings or eat the produce of his garden. But our species would not still be on this planet if we had not taught ourselves to help our own. By working together in many different ways, the family had coped with the blows that fortune dealt them. One or two family members who evidently had problems with alcohol and might have been discarded by a Western family found that their Ju/wa family, the people from /Gautscha, continued to value and protect them—it was said that the move away from Tsumkwe and its alcohol was in part for their benefit. Even the move itself was characteristic of Ju/wa culture—when things become impossible in one location, the best thing to do is to settle in a new place where you can improve your situation. As in the past these people would have moved away from intergroup dissent or inadequate food or difficult lions, so today they move away from crime and alcohol.

Ah, but the new place belonged to someone after all. It belonged to World Wildlife, in that it was in a Bushman-free zone established by that organization for wildlife and tourism. A large, luxurious safari lodge was to be built nearby. My guess is that the tourists, who might be glad to see the ever-popular hunter-gatherers dressed in skins, would not want to see poor people dressed in Western clothes and living in shanties. The family was told to leave. But they did not want to leave. They had nowhere to go.

At the time of this writing, these people have not moved. Could the hotel compromise and employ some of them? It could, but it may not. Ju/wasi are seldom employed as hotel workers because the hotel managers fear that they will beg from the guests and come to work irregularly. There is some truth to this perception. So probably these people will be evicted eventually—evicted from land that had belonged to them and their ancestors since the Upper Paleolithic and now seems controlled by World Wildlife and tourism. When the tourists arrive, they can view from their windows the land that the First People have lost, but now with an unusual array of wildlife that bears little resemblance to the original fauna. With elephants, roan antelope, and African buffalo in the picture, this land will be a kind of Kruger Park West with a big hotel, a paradise for tourists who, if they want to see hunter-gatherers, will have to hire actors. My brother would call the place a hunter-gatherer museum. As for that particular family of First People, unless something better can be worked out for them, they will probably be back in Tsumkwe.

No culture today obtains its livelihood in its traditional manner. But most cultures keep some of their ancestral features. Our languages, our family patterns, many of our values, and perhaps our religious beliefs are often those of our ancestors. But most of us are lucky enough to belong to cultural communities so strong and widespread that others can't easily destroy them. Will the Ju/wasi be so lucky? Not all of them, surely. Yet perhaps some pockets of their culture can remain. Perhaps the real culture, the social culture, can be preserved by the First People.

To do this, the farms are important, at least for now. On these lonely little farms, so small that one can see the entire outlay from halfway up the windmill, people carry water for their gardens in jerry cans and cut thornbushes to protect their small herds from lions. But on these farms, the people are together, they are independent, and they are in their *n!oresi*, from which they can eventually reach, on foot if necessary, their kin and partners on other *n!oresi*, in similar communities. They can supply themselves with food, as they did in the past, and they can support themselves and one another by their own efforts, also as they did in the past, if with a different set of plants, animals, and implements. They will be isolated from the fluctuations of tourism and trophy hunting, as they were in the past. All this should seem traditional enough, even for the most ardent preservationists.

Even in Tsumkwe, old traditions are still observed, despite the dire condition of the Tsumkwe people. In fact, the need of the people increases some of the old habits. Many an elderly woman, living in the dust in the squalid Bushman quarters of Tsumkwe with drinking, robbery, and prostitution all around her, supports others with her pension. Why? Because the people with whom she shares are hungry. Because they are her people. Because if she has something and they have nothing, then she and they are not equal. So she helps her people as her mother helped her in the hand-holding chain that goes back through time, a chain that depends upon community. If in the future her grandchildren help others as she does today, it will be because their group has held together in a community large enough and strong enough to keep going.

Who knows the antiquity of these cultural features? Did they serve our ancestors in rain forest times? Were they developed on the savannah? Whenever they started, they served our species well and many of us still admire them, but mainly it's the Ju/wasi who continue to uphold them. Thus the many individuals involved with Nyae Nyae—those in the Namibian government, those associated with the conservancy and its donors, and those who farm or who support the farmers—will do humanity an enormous service if they help to preserve the social treasure that is the Ju/wa people.

Notes

1. The research was done by Alison Brooks and John Yellen.

2. The image of the hand-holding mother comes from Richard Dawkins in *New Scientist*, 5 June 1993, and has at the time of this writing a Web site of its own called "Meet My Cousin, the Chimpanzee." The numbers for this image include a time line of five million years. The Web site does not give full details so I am imagining fourteen years per generation, giving us about 360,000 hand-holders, who would form a line about three hundred miles long.

3. Jane Goodall describes the nest building of chimpanzees as follows: "I found that every individual, except for infants who slept with their mothers, made his own nest each night. Generally this took about three minutes: the chimp chose a firm foundation such as an upright fork or crotch, or two horizontal branches. Then he reached out and bent over smaller branches onto this foundation, keeping each one in place with his feet. Finally he tucked in the small leafy twigs growing around the rim of his nest and lay down. Quite often a chimp sat up after a few minutes and picked a handful of leafy twigs, which he put under his head or some other part of his body before settling down again for the night. I found that there was quite complicated interweaving of the branches in some [of the nests]" (*In the Shadow of Man*, pp. 29–30).

Dian Fossey describes the nest building of gorillas: "Gorillas are diurnal and build their nests in different locations each evening. Adult night nests are sturdy, compact structures, sometimes resembling oval, leafy bathtubs made from bulky plants such as *Lobelia (Lobelia giberroa)* and *Senecio (Senecio erici-rosenii)*. Construction is concentrated on the rim of the nest, which is composed of multiple bent stalks, the leafy ends of which are tucked around and under the animal's body for a more 'cushiony' central bottom. Nests can be built in trees as well as on the ground, but because of adult gorilla's great weight nests are more commonly found on the ground" (*Gorillas in the Mist*, p. 47).

Lorna Marshall describes a woman building a *tshu* or grass shelter: "First she digs a row of from twelve to twenty holes, four or five inches deep, loosening the sandy soil with her digging stick, scooping it out with her hand. The holes form a crescent. She then gathers some slender, flexible branches, pulling them from the bushes. The branches are five or six feet long and an inch or so in diameter. She stands a branch in each hole and tamps it down. When the branches are firmly in place she bends their tops together and weaves them into each other, thus making the frame of the shelter. Next she brings armloads of any nearby tall grass, which she lays on the frame, grass-heads down. She simply pats the grass into place unless the winds are high, in which case she might bind the grass onto the frame with two or three long strands of sansevieria fibers (*Sansevieria scabrifolia* Dinter) or strips of bark, drawn horizontally around the shelter. The usual finished shelter is a half-hemisphere in shape, four or five feet high at its peak, about five feet wide on its open side, about three or four feet deep in the middle" (*The !Kung of Nyae Nyae*, pp. 87–88).

4. The probable weights of our ancestors is based on Nowak, *Walker's Mammals of the World*, who says that the most complete specimen, Lucy, who was an *Australopithecus afarensis*, was "thought to have been about 1 meter in height and 30 kg. in weight. The males of her species may have been up to 1.5 meters tall and 68 kg. in weight." Nowak reports the general agreement (not unchallenged) that the split between ourselves and chimpanzees took place about four to five million years ago (p. 511).

5. In this account, a foraging range is determined by the distance from a source of water. Five or six miles is a rough estimate of the distance a forager can travel in a day and still get back by night for a drink of water. Hence the radius of a hypothetical range is 5.5 miles. This account assumes that a day's supply of water would lengthen the radius by 2.5 miles.

CHAPTER 3: MEAT AND FIRE

1. Heinrich, *Why We Run*.
2. Estes, *The Behavior Guide to African Mammals*, p. 192.
3. Lewis-Williams, *Images of Mystery*, pp. 16, 42, 56.
4. England, *Music Among the Zhu/'twasi*.
5. Personal communication from Richard Estes.

6. Biesele, *Women Like Meat,* pp. 124–38.
7. Wrangham et al., "The Raw and the Stolen," pp. 567–90.

CHAPTER 4: THE KALAHARI

1. Tswana people—a branch of the Sotho—were the first settlers, arriving with their cattle to occupy what is now eastern and central Botswana in the early 1700s, and making serfs of the local hunter-gatherers. This would have introduced metal to the Bushmen—bits of steel to make blades for knives and spears, also wire to make arrowheads.

2. We believe that during the previous seventy-five years, about forty Europeans had penetrated the interior, most of whom were together as a party of voortrekkers who in 1905 crossed the Kalahari in ox wagons on their way to Angola. Other non-Bushmen also penetrated, some of them carving their names or initials on baobab trees. The earliest of these were N L and Rees (with the *s* backward) in 1878, at which time only 137 Europeans lived in South West Africa. Who were N L and Rees? Probably hunters, looking for ivory or ostrich feathers. Two Germans later visited the interior, escaping imprisonment during World War I. Later still came a party of local daredevils looking for diamonds, also a few farmers looking for slaves, also police officers looking for Bushman fugitives, and, in the late 1940s, two men from the Protectorate Administration attempting to find and vaccinate as many hunter-gatherers as possible in an effort to eradicate smallpox.

The Boers went by ox wagon, the German fugitives went on foot, the police officers rode camels, and the farmers, the prospectors, and the smallpox officials went in vehicles, but none of these people stayed for any length of time and few penetrated deeply except the voortrekkers, who went straight across, leaving thousands of square miles on either side of their track unvisited. One of our visits is commemorated on a baobab tree in /Gautscha. We simply wrote "1951."

3. Gordon, *The Bushman Myth,* p. 6.

4. In contrast, others who ventured into the Kalahari in later years had all sorts of mishaps, largely because of bad planning. One or two people died of heatstroke after their vehicles broke down, stranding them in the burning sun without water. One author tells how he tied a barrel of gasoline to the front of his jeep, then tried to bushwhack back to his camp, with disastrous results when the barrel fell off and his jeep ran over it. Others more recently have died of heatstroke or sunstroke when their vehicles became disabled at great distances from help. When these unfortunate people ran out of water, they started walking and didn't make it.

5. Over the years, among the people who came with us on trips that I also accompanied were Theunis Berger, Daniel Blitz, J. O. Brew, William Cass, Bill

Donnellan, Robert H. Dyson, Brian Enslin (or perhaps Enslen), /Gani, Philip
Hameva, Charles Handley, Charles Koch, Heinrich Kreitchmar, Kernel Ledimo,
Carey McIntosh, Claude McIntyre, Fritz Metzger, and Robert Story. Only one
woman, the wife of one of the interpreters, came very briefly. The deep bush
wasn't a place for women, or so it was said by those who somehow missed the
fact that women had lived in the deep bush since women began.

6. Alan Barnard, review of Lorna Marshall's *The !Kung of Nyae Nyae*, in
Africa: Journal of the International African Institute 48, no. 4 (1978): 411.

CHAPTER 5: THE SEARCH

1. Many publications address the antiquity of !Kung in the context of the
origin of language. The question of genetic separation and linguistic similarity
is referenced in Elizabeth Pennisi, "Evolution of Language," *Science* 303, no. 27
(February 2004): 1319.

2. Ritchie, "From Foragers to Farmers," p. 311.

3. Marshall, *The !Kung of Nyae Nyae*, p. 3.

CHAPTER 6: PLACE

1. Wiessner, "Style and Social Information."

2. Wrangham and Peterson, *Demonic Males*, p. 166.

3. Personal communication from Sarah Hrdy.

4. Marshall, *The !Kung of Nyae Nyae*, p. 187.

CHAPTER 7: HUNTING

1. Wrangham and Peterson, *Demonic Males*, p. 216.

2. The figures given here are average weights for females and males, from
Estes, *Behavior Guide to African Mammals*. References can be found under the
names of the antelopes. It should be noted that if large, water-dependent antelopes had lived in Nyae Nyae, the Ju/wasi would have hunted them, too, of
course, and surely would have included them among the beings who have *n!ow*.
Biesele, *Women Like Meat*, includes roan antelope and tsessebe among the rit-
ually important antelopes, as she learned from Bushmen in Botswana. But roan
antelope and tsessebe were not found in Nyae Nyae. Both these antelope are
water dependent, although according to Estes the tssessebe is less so, as a

tsessebe can live without water as long as it can eat green, fresh grass. Without fresh grass, the tsessebe drinks water daily.

3. This and the next two quotations are from Marshall, *The !Kung of Nyae Nyae*, pp. 130–31.

4. The click sounds of the Khoisan languages have been suggested as the sounds with which prehumans originated language, perhaps eight hundred thousand years ago. An early relationship between the Hadza and Khoisan peoples with respect to their languages and their genetic relationship as demonstrated by the Y chromosome is discussed by the linguist Bonny E. Sands, "Linguistic Relationship Between Hadza and Khoisan," pp. 265–83.

5. Marshall, *The !Kung of Nyae Nyae*, p. 178.

6. Ibid., p. 299.

7. Ibid., p. 177.

CHAPTER 8: GATHERING

1. The term *root* is generic here and includes tubers, corms, bulbs, etc. The term *nut* includes a nut or bean called *tsi* that grows on a vine on the ground. A complete list of the foods eaten by the Ju/wasi can be found in Marshall, *The !Kung of Nyae Nyae*.

2. Our lineage emerged from the early primate stem in the Eocene, before which our ancestors, the early true primates, were probably more like modern-day tarsiers than anything else. The three modern species of tarsiers occur separately, and the family crosses a boundary known as Wallace's Line, which divides Eurasia from Australasia, the implication being that before the original landmass came apart, the tarsiers were a single species and simply rode the continents to their present locations, or to put it differently, this family could be forty million years old.

CHAPTER 9: POISON

1. Koch, "Preliminary Notes," pp. 49–54. Dr. Koch accompanied us on several expeditions to Nyae Nyae, where he studied the beetles of the area, identifying those used for poison as *Diamphidia nigro-ornata* Stäl with its parasite *Lebistina subcruciata* Fairmaire; *D. vittatipennis* Baly with its parasite *L. holubi* Peringuey; and *Polyclada flexuosa* Baly with its parasite *L. peringuey* Liebke. The host plant of *D. nigro-ornata* and parasite is *Commiphora angloensis*. The host plant of *D. vittatipensis* and parasite is *C. africana*. The host plant of *P. flexuosa* and parasite is *Sclerocarya caffra*.

. . . .

2. Recently, I learned of a few would-be suicides who were rescued by others who immediately slapped aside the arrow and sucked the wound. The people got sick but didn't die. Because these tragic events took place during the 1980s after the Old Way had all but vanished, after the life of the Ju/wasi had changed profoundly, the men rarely hunted and the poison was probably "cold," as the Ju/wasi would say, meaning that it had been on the arrow for a long time and had lost much of its potency.

3. According to *The Columbia Encyclopedia*, sixth edition, 2001, the first archaeological evidence for the bow and arrow is from Mousterian sites in Europe, dated at approximately 40,000 B.P.

4. The people we knew obtained metal wire in trade from Bantu ranchers at the edge of Nyae Nyae, and cold-hammered the wire into arrowheads that resembled and replaced bone or wood arrowheads but did not represent a change in design or technology. Metal and bone arrowheads were both in use when we arrived, and we even saw one or two wooden arrowheads.

5. Yellen, "Settlement Patterns of the !Kung San," pp. 47–72.

6. Some ancient wooden objects did, of course, become preserved, to be found by archaeologists. A bow made of elm wood nine thousand years old, just for example, is reported by F. Alrune in the *Journal of the Society of Archer-Antiquaries* 35 (1992): 47–50.

7. Kilham, *Among the Bears.*

CHAPTER 10: DANGEROUS ANIMALS

1. To the best of my knowledge this survey, while incorporated into the research of several people, has not yet been published as such. The data was recorded on thousands of file cards, and I was able to see most but not all of them. I was also able to discuss certain findings of this study with John Marshall and Claire Ritchie. For years, John kept the file cards in his barn and eventually gave them to the anthropologist Polly Wiessner.

2. Marshall, *Nyae Nyae !Kung Beliefs and Rites*, p. 183.

3. Marshall, "Medicine Dance," p. 374. I render a phrase in the sixth sentence as, "They took their children in their arms . . ." In the article, the phrase is, "They took their screaming children in their arms . . ." I omitted the word *screaming* because, without further explanation, it didn't seem possible. Ju/wa children didn't scream, and in my experience, when faced with lions, the children made no sound at all. To scream could have substantially increased the danger, and probably if they had screamed their parents would have tried to shush them. The wording came by way of an interpreter, and also was rephrased by Lorna Marshall, and is clearly not intended to be exactly that of the Ju/wasi. Perhaps the children screamed, perhaps they didn't, but I think if they had, the

storyteller would have pointed it out, not just glossed over it. The purpose of the article was to discuss trancing, not behavior in the face of lions, and therefor the problem may have been overlooked.

CHAPTER 11: LIONS

1. Montgomery, *Spell of the Tiger*, provides a full discussion of the hunting habits of Sundarbans tigers.
2. The area that is now Etosha National Park was designated as early as 1907 but was not developed with roads and tourist facilities until much later.
3. Estes, *The Behavior Guide to African Mammals*, p. 435.
4. Personal communication from Megan Biesele.
5. Biesele points out that one of the avoidance words for lion is "calf muscle," suggesting the tension in the body of a stalking lion. The tension in the arm of someone making the hand sign indicates the tension in the lion.
6. This quote and the next are from Marshall, *Nyae Nyae !Kung Beliefs and Rites*, p. 238.

CHAPTER 12: MEN AND WOMEN

1. Kimura, "Sex Differences in the Brain," p. 34.
2. Marshall, *The !Kung of Nyae Nyae*, p. 266. The quoted material has been altered slightly to omit personal names that have not appeared earlier in the text and will not be familiar to the reader.
3. Ibid., p. 266.
4. Ibid., p. 279.
5. Ibid., p. 286.

CHAPTER 13: THE LIFE CYCLE

1. The material on fertility and infant mortality in this chapter largely derives from Howell, *Demography of the Dobe !Kung*.
2. Biesele, *Women Like Meat*, p. 93.
3. A member of the Harvard Group, Marjorie Shostak, in ≠*Nisa: The Life and Words of a !Kung Woman* (Cambridge, MA: Harvard University Press, 1981), presents a somewhat different picture of Ju/wa childhood. It is important to recognize that Shostak did her work in a community in Botswana that was already under outside pressure. The lives of the people were not the same as

those of the people we knew almost twenty years earlier in Namibia. In addition, I've been told that after Shostak's book was published, ≠Nisa herself admitted to some exaggeration.

4. Marshall, *The !Kung of Nyae Nyae*, pp. 317–18.
5. Lee, "!Kung Kin Terms," pp. 77–102.
6. This and the following quotations are from Biesele, *Women Like Meat*, pp. 9–20.

CHAPTER 14: THE SOCIAL FABRIC

1. Marshall, *The !Kung of Nyae Nyae*, p. 287.
2. Ibid., p. 293.
3. Ibid., p. 293.
4. Ibid., p. 291.
5. Wiessner, "Hxaro: A Regional System of Reciprocity for Reducing Risk among the !Kung San."

CHAPTER 15: PEACEKEEPING

1. Lee and DeVore, *Kalahari Hunter-Gatherers*.
2. Marshall, *The !Kung of Nyae Nyae*, p. 53.

CHAPTER 17: RELIGION

1. Marshall, *Nyae Nyae !Kung Beliefs and Rites*, p. 265.
2. Ibid., pp. 18–19.
3. Biesele, *Women Like Meat*, finds that among the Ju/wasi in Botswana, the god most often mentioned, whether in ridicule or respect, was the god designated herein as the western god. In my work his name is //Gauwa. In her work his name is G//aoan. (My spelling is geared to a lay audience, hers to a scholarly audience, as explained in the preface of this book.). Another of his names is Kaoxa.
4. Biesele, *Women Like Meat*, p. 109.

CHAPTER 18: TSUMKWE

1. This name is also spelled Tjum!ui, Tshumkwe, and Tchumkwe, and probably has other spellings, too. Today the formal spelling used by the Namibian government is Tsumkwe. Evidently the name means "Crotch Hair."

2. Claire Ritchie (personal communication) described this misunderstanding.

3. Suzman, *Assessment of the Status of the San*, p. 44.

4. For the rest of this chapter, information concerning Tsumkwe is from Ritchie, "From Foragers to Farmers," pp. 312–23.

CHAPTER 20: THE PRESENT

1. Wiessner, *Visual Anthropology Review*, p. 152.
2. Ibid., p. 152.
3. Ibid., p. 152.
4. Ibid., p. 158.
5. Ibid., p. 149.
6. Ibid., p. 152.
7. Ibid., p. 152.
8. Ibid., p. 158.
9. Ibid., p. 158.

Bibliography

Berger, Dhyani J., with Kxao Moses ≠Oma, Hosabe /Honeb, and Wendy Viall. "The Making of a Conservancy: The Evolution of Nyae Nyae Conservancy: Restoring Human Dignity with Wildlife Wealth, 1997–2002." Windhoek, Namibia: WWF/LIFE Programme, 2003.

Biesele, Megan. *Women Like Meat: The Folklore and Foraging Technology of the Kalahari Ju/'hoan.* Bloomington: Indiana University Press, 1993.

England, Nicholas. *Music Among the Zhu'/'wasi and Related Peoples of Namibia, Botswana, and Angola.* New York: Garland Publishing, 1995.

Estes, Richard D. *The Behavior Guide to African Mammals.* Berkeley: University of California Press, 1991.

Felton, Silke, and Heike Becker. *A Gender Perspective on the Status of the San in Southern Africa.* Windhoek, Namibia: Legal Assistance Centre, 2001.

FitzSimons, Vivian F. M. *Snakes of Southern Africa.* London: Macdonald, 1962.

Fossey, Dian. *Gorillas in the Mist.* Boston: Houghton Mifflin, 1983.

Goodall, Jane. *The Chimpanzees of Gombe: Patterns of Behavior.* Cambridge, MA: Harvard University Press, 1986.

———. *In the Shadow of Man.* Boston: Houghton Mifflin, 1971.

Gordon, Robert J. *The Bushman Myth: The Making of a Namibian Underclass.* Boulder: Westview Press, 1992.

Heinrich, Bernd. *Why We Run: A Natural History.* New York: Ecco, 2002.

Hitchcock, Robert. "Decentralization and Development Among the Ju/wasi, Namibia." *Cultural Survival Quarterly* 12, no. 3 (September 30, 1988).

———. "Sharing the Land: Kalahari San Property Rights and Resource Management." In *Property and Equality: Encapsulation, Commercialization, Discrimination,* edited by Thomas Widlok and Wolde Gassa Tadesse. New York: Berghahn Books, 2005.

————. "We Are the First People: Land, Natural Resources and Identity in the Central Kalahari, Botswana." *Journal of Southern African Studies* 28, no. 4 (December 2002): 797–824.

Howell, Nancy. *The Demography of the Dobe !Kung.* New York: Academic Press, 1979.

Hrdy, Sarah Blaffer. *Mother Nature: A History of Mothers, Infants, and Natural Selection.* New York: Pantheon, 1999.

Kilham, Benjamin. *Among the Bears: Raising Orphan Cubs in the Wild.* New York: Henry Holt, 2002.

Kimura, Doreen. "Sex Differences in the Brain." *Scientific American* 12 (May 13, 2002): 32–37.

Koch, Charles. "Preliminary Notes on the Coleopterological Aspect of the Arrow Poison of the Bushmen." Pamphlet No. 20, South African Biological Society, 1958.

Lee, Richard B. "!Kung Kin Terms: The Name Relationship and the Process of Discovery." In *The Past and Future of !Kung Ethnography: Critical Reflections and Symbolic Perspectives: Essays in Honour of Lorna Marshall,* edited by Megan Biesele, Robert Gordon, and Richard Lee. Hamburg: Helmut Buske Verlag, 1986.

————. *The !Kung San: Men, Women, and Work in a Foraging Society.* New York: Cambridge University Press, 1979.

————, and Irven DeVore, eds., *Kalahari Hunter-Gatherers: Studies of the !Kung San and Their Neighbors.* Cambridge, MA: Harvard University Press, 1976.

Lewis-Williams, David. *Images of Mystery: Rock Art of the Drakensberg.* Cape Town: Double Storey Books, 2003.

————. *The Mind in the Cave: Consciousness and the Origins of Art.* New York: Thames & Hudson, 2002.

————, and David Pearce. *San Spirituality: Roots, Expressions, and Social Consequences.* Walnut Creek, CA: AltaMira Press, 2004.

Macdonald, David, ed. *The Encyclopedia of Mammals.* New York: Facts on File, 1984.

Marshall, John. *A Kalahari Family.* Five-part documentary film distributed by Documentary Educational Resources, 101 Morse Street, Watertown, MA 02472.

————, and Claire Ritchie. "Where Are the Ju/hoansi of Nyae Nyae? Changes in a Bushman Society, 1950–1981." Cape Town: Centre for African Studies, University of Cape Town, 1984.

————, and Orasiu Shonganyi. "Report on 21 Villages in Nyae Nyae: August, 2004." Unpublished report.

Marshall, Lorna. *The !Kung of Nyae Nyae.* Cambridge, MA: Harvard University Press, 1976.

———. "The Medicine Dance of the !Kung Bushmen." *Africa* 39, no. 4 (1969): 347–81.

———. *Nyae Nyae !Kung Beliefs and Rites.* Cambridge, MA: Peabody Museum Monographs, Harvard University, 1999.

Montgomery, Sy. *Spell of the Tiger: The Man-Eaters of Sundarbans.* Boston: Houghton Mifflin, 1995.

Nowak, Ronald M., ed. *Walker's Mammals of the World.* 5th ed. Baltimore: Johns Hopkins University Press, 1991.

Ritchie, Claire. "From Foragers to Farmers." In Biesele et al., *The Past and Future of !Kung Ethnography.*

Sands, Bonnie E. "The Linguistic Relationship Between Hadza and Khoisan." In *Langauge, Identity, and Conceptualization Among the Khoisan,* edited by Mathias Schladt. Köln: Rudiger Köppe, 1998.

Speeter-Blaudszun, Sonja. *Die Expeditionen der Families Marshall: Eine Untersuchung zur ethnographischen Erforschung der Nyae Nyae !Kung.* Munster: Lit Verlag, 2004.

Suzman, James. *An Assessment of the Status of the San in Namibia.* Windhoek, Namibia: Legal Assistance Centre, 2001.

Thomas, Elizabeth Marshall. *The Harmless People.* New York: Knopf, 1959.

———. *The Tribe of Tiger.* New York: Simon and Schuster, 1994.

———. "The Old Way." *The New Yorker,* October 15, 1990.

———. *Warrior Herdsmen.* New York: Knopf, 1965.

Turner, Alan. *The Big Cats and Their Fossil Relatives: An Illustrated Guide to Their Evolution and Natural History.* New York: Columbia University Press, 1997.

Wiessner, Polly. "Hxaro: A Regional System of Reciprocity for Reducing Risk among the !Kung San." Photo dissertation, Department of Anthropology, University of Michigan, Ann Arbor (1977).

———. "Owners of the Future? Calories, Cash, Causalities and Self-Sufficiency in the Nyae Nyae Area Between 1998 and 2003." *Visual Anthropology Review* 9 (2004): 49–159.

———. "Style and Social Information in Kalahari Projectile Points." *American Antiquity* 48, no. 2 (1983): 253–76.

Wrangham, W. R., J. H. Jones, G. Laden, D. Pillbeam, and N. Conklin-Brittain. "The Raw and the Stolen: Cooking and the Ecology of Human Origins." *Current Anthropology* 40, no. 5 (December 1999): 567–94.

———, and Dale Peterson. *Demonic Males: Apes and the Origins of Human Violence.* Boston: Houghton Mifflin, 1996.

Yellen, John E. "Settlement Patterns of the !Kung San and Their Neighbors." In Lee and DeVore, *Kalahari Hunter-Gatherers.*

Acknowledgments

In preparing this book, I am greatly indebted to Megan Biesele, Naomi Chase, Nancie Gonzalez, Sarah Hrdy, John Marshall, Sy Montgomery, Peter Schweitzer, and Richard Wrangham for reading the manuscript in various stages of its progress, detecting errors, and offering invaluable advice and information. Despite their efforts, however, the book may still contain errors. I hope not, but if so, they of course are mine.

For generously sharing information concerning the present condition of the Bushmen and for providing me with many published and unpublished papers and manuscripts, I am deeply indebted to Claire Ritchie, Polly Wiessner, Robert Hitchcock, and again in this context to Megan Biesele, who also generously shared important information about Bushman language and mythology. I am also very grateful to Sarah Hrdy for sharing publications that pertain to this book, to David Lewis-Williams for his advice concerning the early rock paintings made by Bushmen, and for sharing photographs of these paintings.

I am equally grateful to the members of our expeditions, especially Daniel Blitz, who took many of the photographs that appear in these pages, and to the late Charles Handley for educating me about the wildlife of Nyae Nyae. I also offer special thanks to Patricia Kervick, associate archivist at Harvard's Peabody Museum, for her help in locating photographs for this book. The help and generosity of all these people have been immeasurable.

My greatest debt, however, is to the Ju/wasi of Nyae Nyae, especially the people of /Gautscha, the people who taught us with such endless patience. I must especially mention !U, /Kwi, //Kushe, Tsamko, ≠Gao, N!ai, and /Gunda, some of whom were very young when I first met them and now are leaders in their community. Many of the people who offered the most help are no longer living. First among these people were ≠Toma Word, Gao, Di!ai, and Short /Kwi, also Kernel Ledimo and /Gani.

The published and unpublished work of my mother, Lorna Marshall, has been a primary source of information, as was the published and unpublished work of my brother, John Marshall, and, most important, his landmark film *A Kalahari Family.* The entire enterprise took place because of the efforts and the abilities of my father, Laurence Marshall. To him and to all my family, my gratitude is endless.

Throughout this book I have tried to identify every thought or fact that did not originate with me unless it was general knowledge. This can be a problem. For instance, in a peer-reviewed paper for an anthropological publication, I mentioned that the adult female lions of a pride are related to one another but not to the adult males in their midst. A reviewer complained that the statement was not cited. What to do? Lions had been studied in depth thirty years earlier by George Schaller, and by now their social arrangements appear in field guides everywhere and are familiar not only to field biologists but also to many people with an interest in animals. The reviewer of course was an expert in his or her field but may have been unfamiliar with the world of lions. Similar problems may appear in this book, as most of us today are specialized in our interests. Thus the reader should assume that if a similar piece of information has not been cited, this may be because it has been around for a while, seems to be generally accepted, and most likely is known to laypersons with an interest in its subject.

Index

Page numbers in *italics* refer to illustrations.

flu virus, 214

food, 6, 11–12, 19, 25–42, 52–53, 76; gathering, 106–22, 138, 175, 211, 215; gods and, 264; hunting, 25–42, 86–105; loss of wild foods, 284, 295, 297, 299, 301, 305, 37, 308; meat, 39, 40, 86–105; new sources of, 289, 297, 299–300, 301; plant, 12, 13, 25, 86, 106–22; preparation, 41–42; protein, 87, 90, 130; sharing, 107–108, 215–17, 280, 284, 298–99, 313; taboos, 264; welfare rations, 294, 295, 299, 300

Fossey, Dian, 315n3

Foundation, 300–301, 305, 306, 307

fruits, 25, 26, 110

!Gai, 97–98, 135–36, 292

/Gaishay !Khoa, 169–70, 228

/Gam, 58–61, 64, 157, 294–95

gangrene, 239

/Gani, 49

Gao Beard, 96

Gao Feet, 68, 71, 96, 133–34, 180–82, 189, 220, 239, 258

≠Gao N!a, 260–62

gathering, 87, 106–22, 123, 138, 175, 202, 211, 215, 251; modern difficulty of, 297, 301; roots, 109, 110, 117–22; trips, 63, 110, 111–22

/Gautscha, 64 and n, 65–70, 71–85, 96; author's return to, 286, 289–93; gathering trips, 111–22; lions at, 148–54, 155–73; men and women, 174–91; peacekeeping,

225–43; religion, 253–73; social fabric, 210–24; waterhole, 27, 74

//Gauwa, 260, 262–63

gazelle, 32

gemsboks, 24, 86–87, 92, 97, 259

gender, 36–38, 174–91; beauty and desirability, 38; children, 174–75; equality, 46–47, 103, 108, 175, 179, 196; *k'xua* role, 71–79; marriage and, 179–91; names and, 46–47; ownership and, 71–85; societal roles, 46–47, 76–85, 174–91; *see also* females; males

gifts, 190, 220–24, 293; exchanges, 221–23, 239–43; jealousy and, 239–42; *xaro*, 220–24

giraffes, 86, 92, 233, 264, 266

glaciers, 8, 18, 19

goats, 280–81

gods, 168, 171, 253, 257, 258–64, 267, 322n3; death and, 263–64; food and, 264

Gods Must Be Crazy, The (film), 244, 245, 303

Goodall, Jane, 315n3

Gordon, Robert, 47, 227

gorillas, 10, 315–16n3

government policy on Bushmen, 279–85, 287, 294–97, 300, 308–309

grasses, 11, 31, 86; fires, 39–40, 41, 282; green, 39, 41

graves and burials, 7, 129, 130, 144, 145, 196, 209, 213, 220, 240

Green Leaf Horn, 254

Grootfontein, 281

group behavior, 43, 44, 45, 84, 138–39, 210–24, 309–10

grubs, 11; arrow poison from, 123, 126, 130–37, 246
Gumtsa, 180–81
/Gunda, 181, 182, 184–85, 186, 189, 192, 220, 292
//gwashi, 247
/Gwi, 48

Hadza, 65
hair, 263; ornaments, 61, 69, 190, 221
Handley, Charles, 246, 248
Harmless People, The (Thomas), 50, 51
hartebeests, 87, 92, 97
Harvard Kalahari Research Group, 46, 249
Harvard University, 10, 51
healer-shamans, 168; who became lions, 168–72
height, 80
Heinrich, Bernd, 30
Herero people, 295
hind-leg runners, 29–31
Homo erectus, 17, 33, 41
Homo habilis, 17, 33
Homo sapiens, 7, 17
homosexuality, 188
honey, 259
honey badger, 167
honeyguides, 167
Hottentots, 46
housing, *see* shelter
Howell, Nancy, 196
hunger, 38, 76, 93, 195, 217, 230, 248, 284, 307–308
hunter-gatherers, 3, 6, 16, 20, 26–42, 59, 60–61, 75, 83, 102,

108, 249, 260, 267; loss of Old Way, 277–85, 294–313; myth of regaining old lifestyle, 299–310; *see also* Bushmen; gathering; hunting; Ju/wasi; Old Way
hunting, 26–42, 77–78, 86–105, 123–37, 149, 175, 176, 202, 233; adolescent lessons in, 95–96; bow and arrow, 29, 35, 92–100, 123–37; chase-and-grab, 28–29, 31, 33; commercial, 282; distribution of meat, 101–102; government restrictions on, 281, 282, 297, 303, 308; hand signs, 97; lengthy hunts, 94–95; methods, 26–42, 92, 93–96, 123–28, 149, 297; parties, 96–101; running and, 29–31, 33–34, 35–36, 92, 94; stolen meat, 87–90; territorial infringement, 96; tracking, 98–100; water and, 95; *see also specific animals*
hyenas, 98–99, 141–48, 160, 168, 217; as predators, 141–48

ice age, 8, 18, 19
incest taboos, 186
infant diarrhea, 193, 195
infanticide, 196, 198
infant mortality, 193–95
infibulation, 36, 38
Islam, 60
Iziko Museum, Cape Town, 134

jealousy, 169–70, 218, 228, 231, 269, 284; gifts and, 239–42
jewelry, 61, 62, 103, 222, 243, 293

Elizabeth Marshall Thomas was nineteen when she began her sojourns in the pristine, pre-contact Kalahari, and thus she is one of very few people still alive who saw something of the Old Way as our ancestors lived it. The experience permeates all her work, both fiction and nonfiction, and was the subject of her first book, *The Harmless People*, published in 1959.

DATE DUE

FEB 01 07			
GAYLORD			PRINTED IN U.S.A.